4JC Complete Review for SAT* Math

2011 Edition

By Willa Kosasih, M.Sc.

Editorial

Eva Nosal, PhD, B.Ed , Editor in Chief

Linda Fung, M.Sc, Editor

Eileen Kosasih, M.M, Editor

Thirza Odishaw-Dyck, B.Ed, Editor

Production Service

Ram Sapkota, M.Sc

Ashley Eugene, B.Comm (intern)

Technical Support

Scott Steven, BS.Eng (intern)

Brian Jenkins, BS.Eng

Copyright © 2011 by 4JC Tutoring

Published by 4JC Tutoring

www.4jc-tutoring.com

ISBN: 978-0-9868743-0-7

*SAT is a trademark registered and owned by the College Board, which was not involved in the production of, and does not endorse, this product.

"This book applies fresh concepts about learning SAT math. Through the use of modeling, it teaches how to solve challenging problems and develops a deeper understanding of logical reasoning. It integrates basic skills, concept development, application and problem solving for a complete and thorough SAT math review.

Its comprehensiveness and easy-to-use quality make it an excellent resource for students and teachers in preparation for the exam."

- John R. Pierce, M.S., CAGS, Education Consultant, MA

"This book is a mind-opening way of learning:
     understanding through examples.

It is a strong foundation to success:
     strengthening math skills through practice."

- Dr. T. Fung , Senior Mathematical Consultant, Univ. of Calgary, AB

About the Author

Willa Kosasih is the manager of 4JC Learning (www.4jc-tutoring.com) in Calgary, Alberta. She teaches numerous students preparing for standardized tests each year. Prior to 4JC Learning, Willa was a faculty member at Westborough High School, MA, and taught tutorials at University of Windsor, Ontario. Willa also worked over ten years as a software engineer for Nortel, Ontario. However, teaching and writing teaching materials are her greatest passions, diagnosing students' difficulties, and creating teaching tools. From years of priceless teaching experience she created this book. She wants students to realize that SAT Math can be learned in a clear and understandable way and wishes to help them succeed on the exam.

Willa holds a B.Sc. from York University, Toronto, Ontario and a M.Sc. from University of Windsor, Windsor, Ontario.

Special Thanks

I thank Dr. Eva Nosal, who walked through the creation of this book with me. Her dedication to superior quality and valuable mathematical input helped strengthen the book in every step.

I thank Linda Fung for her outstandingly accurate work that helped refine the book.

I thank Eileen Kosasih for the professionalism of her work.

I thank Scott Steven, Thirza Odishaw-Dyck, Ram Sapkota, Ashley Eugene, and Brian Jenkins for their important contributions.

I thank all my students throughout the years; they taught me how to write this book.

I thank my friends Sylvia, Martha, and Carol for their precious supportive prayers.

I thank my family for their loving support and encouragement.

Most of all, I thank God, who gave me strength and inspiration each day for writing and completing this book.

Without your help, this book would not be possible.

> "Happy is the man who finds wisdom, the man who gains understanding."
>
> Proverbs 3:13

About the book

- ## Objective

  As an avid teacher, I am constantly identifying student training needs for the SAT exam, evaluating effectiveness of resources, and developing strategies and tools for the students. I believe that having a good book is the first step toward success! This is an excellent ready-to-use book for students to do a self-study or for teachers to run an SAT math class.

  The unique strengths of this book:

  1. During math review, no student wants to be overloaded with too much text reading. Rather, he or she wants to learn how to solve problems as quickly as possible, with clear directions. Therefore, I base my book on **Teaching through Examples**, which is a quick and clear way of learning.
  2. Instead of focusing too much on strategies that teach guessing and eliminating and only lightly touch upon problem-solving skills, I focus on teaching important and foundational math skills that give students confidence in solving problems and answering correctly.
  3. "Practice makes perfect," is crucial to math review, hence the well thought-out structure and exhaustive practices and solutions in every chapter. The best strategies to solve problems are also taught and demonstrated in the lessons and practice solutions.

  A wise proverb says, "I see, I remember; I do, I understand." The objective of this book is to see through examples and remember, do through practice and understand.

- ## Content

  This book is a complete, in-depth, yet concise math review for the SAT. It divides step-by-step reviews into four main sections: Basic Math, Algebra, Data Analysis and Geometry. Each section contains various chapters that teach problem-solving skills, and each chapter includes practices and solutions. The book includes five practice tests to familiarize students with the SAT testing format. Very little text reading is required, as the relevant examples work as the fundamental teaching tool. The practice drills with solutions and sample tests make the learning internalized and complete.

About the SAT Test

The SAT test is made up of three main sections: Writing, Math and Critical Reading. The score of each section can range from 200 to 800, and the final score will be the total of all three sections, ranging from 600 to 2400.

The Math section is made up of three subsections, including:
  - one 25-minute section with 20 multiple choice questions,
  - one 25-minute section with 8 multiple choice and 10 *student-generated* response questions (grid-in),
  - one 20-minute section with 16 multiple choice questions.

One 25-minute additional section is either in Writing, Math, or Critical Reading (ref 1).

Table of Contents

Basic Math

1. Numbers

Prime Numbers: Numbers that have no other factor besides 1 and themselves: 2, 3, 5, 7...

Odd Numbers: ... , $-3, -1, 1, 3, 5, 7, ...$ **Even Numbers**: ..., $-4, -2, 0, 2, 4, 6, 8, ...$

Integers: ... $-4, -3, -2, -1, 0, 1, 2, 3, 4, ...$

Consecutive numbers: Numbers which follow each other in order, such as 12, 13, 14 are three consecutive numbers.

Symbol: the " $\therefore$ " symbol means " Therefore".

Even and Odd Integers:

					Easy way to remember:	Examples
Odd	+/−	Odd	=	Even	One add one is two. (even)	1+1=2 or 7 − 3 = 4
Odd	+/−	Even	=	Odd	One add two is three. (odd)	1+2=3 or 6 − 5 = 1
Odd	*	Odd	=	Odd	One time one is one. (odd)	1*1=1 or 3 * 3 = 9
Odd	*	Even	=	Even	One time two is two. (even)	1*2=2 or 3 * 2 = 6

ex.1. If $x + 2y$ equals an odd integer, which of the following must be true?

    a) both x and y are even

    b) both x and y are odd

    c) either x or y is odd

    d) x is odd

    e) y is odd

Solution: Since $2y$ is always even regardless if y is even or odd,

    in order for $x + 2y$ to be an odd integer, x must be an odd integer.

    (Testing with numbers is not a proof, but it can be used

    to find the correct answer for "Even/Odd " problems.)

    y can be either even or odd, but x must always be odd.

      Try with $x = 1$, $y = 2$, $\therefore$ $1 + 2(2) = 5 \longleftarrow$ odd

      Try with $x = 2$, $y = 3$, $\therefore$ $2 + 2(3) = 8 \longleftarrow$ even

    Answer is (d).

ex.2. If x is an odd integer, and y is an even integer, which of the following results in an even integer?

    a) $x + y$ b) $x - 2y$ c) $3x + y$ d) $3(x + y)$ e) $4x + y$

Solution: Since x is odd and y is even, (a), (b), (c) and (d) are always odd.

    In (e): $4x$ results in an even number, and y is even, therefore

    $4x + y$ is even.

    Alternatively, test with two numbers, try: $x = 1 \; and \; y = 2$

    and test on each. Only (e) gives an even result.   Answer is (e).

1.1 Practice and Solutions

1. All of the following are true EXCEPT
   - (A) Odd + Odd = Odd
   - (B) Even + Odd = Odd
   - (C) Odd * Odd = Odd
   - (D) Odd * Even = Even
   - (E) Even * Even = Even

2. If $5x + 22$ is even, which of the following is true?
   - (A) $x > 0$
   - (B) $x < 0$
   - (C) x must be even
   - (D) x must be odd
   - (E) x can be either even or odd

3. If m is odd and $(n - 1)$ is even, which of the following must always be true?
   - (A) $m + n$ is prime
   - (B) $m + n$ is odd
   - (C) $m - n$ is odd
   - (D) mn is odd
   - (E) mn is even

4. Suppose $b = 6 * (a + 3) * 7$, which of the following is always true?
   - (A) b is always greater than a
   - (B) b is always smaller than a
   - (C) b is odd only if a is odd
   - (D) b is always odd
   - (E) b is always even

5. If $(x - 2)(y - 3)$ is odd, for $x > 2$ and $y > 3$, which of the following must always be true?
   - I. $x + y$ is odd
   - II. $x + y$ is even
   - III. xy is even
   - (A) I only
   - (B) II only
   - (C) III only
   - (D) I and III only
   - (E) II and III only

Solutions to 1.1 Practice: 1(A), 2(C), 3(D), 4(E),5(D)

1. All of the following are true EXCEPT
    - (A) Odd + Odd = Odd
    - (B) Even + Odd = Odd
    - (C) Odd * Odd = Odd
    - (D) Odd * Even = Even
    - (E) Even * Even = Even

    $odd + odd = even$
    $Ex: 3 + 5 = 8$

2. If $5x + 22$ is even, which of the following is true?
    - (A) $x > 0$
    - (B) $x < 0$
    - (C) x must be even
    - (D) x must be odd
    - (E) x can be either even or odd

    $5x + 22 = even$
    $5x = even - 22$
    $= even - even = even$
    x must be even since 5 is odd

3. If m is odd and $(n - 1)$ is even, which of the following must always be true?
    - (A) $m + n$ is prime
    - (B) $m + n$ is odd
    - (C) $m - n$ is odd
    - (D) mn is odd
    - (E) mn is even

    $n - 1$ is even $\therefore$ n is odd
    $m * n = odd * odd = odd$
    Ex: $m = 3, n = 5$
    $\therefore (A), (B), (C), and (E)$ are not true

4. Suppose $b = 6 * (a + 3) * 7$, which of the following is always true?
    - (A) b is always greater than a
    - (B) b is always smaller than a
    - (C) b is odd only if a is odd
    - (D) b is always odd
    - (E) b is always even

    b is always Even since
    it is a multiple of $6, \therefore (E)$ is true.
    (A) and (B) are not always true.

5. If $(x - 2)(y - 3)$ is odd, for $x > 2$ and $y > 3$, which of the following must always be true?
    - I. $x + y$ is odd
    - II. $x + y$ is even
    - III. xy is even
    - (A) I only
    - (B) II only
    - (C) III only
    - (D) I and III only
    - (E) II and III only

    Since $(x - 2)(y - 3)$ is odd, so
    both $x - 2$ and $y - 3$ must be odd.
    This means that:
    $\{ x$ is odd & y is even, as $x = 5$, $y = 4 \}$
    Then $x + y$ is odd and xy is even.
    $x + y = 5 + 4 = 9$ is odd , (I) is true
    $xy = 5 * 4 = 20$ is even, (III) is true

2. Place Value

Name	Sample Value	
Hundred millions	700,000,000	$7 * 10^8$
Ten millions	20,000,000	$2 * 10^7$
Millions	3,000,000	$3 * 10^6$
Hundred thousands	500,000	$5 * 10^5$
Ten thousands	30,000	$3 * 10^4$
Thousands	6,000	$6 * 10^3$
Hundreds	700	$7 * 10^2$
Tens	40	$4 * 10^1$
Ones	5	$5 * 10^0$
Decimal	.	.
Tenths	0.2	$2 * 10^{-1}$
Hundredths	0.08	$8 * 10^{-2}$
Thousandths	0.005	$5 * 10^{-3}$

The sum of all the numbers above will be: 723,536,745.285

ex.1 Which of the following represents four millions, two hundred thousands, five hundreds and twenty eight?

a) 40,200,528   b) 4,200,528   c) 4,225,028   d) 4,250,028   e) 4,205,028

Solution:

4 millions , 2 hundred thousands , five hundreds , twenty eight

4,000,000 +   200,000   +   500   + 28

= 4,200,528

The correct answer is (b).

ex.2 What is the value of $(2 * 10^7) + (4 * 10^5) + (3 * 10^3) + (2 * 10^1) + 4$?

a) 200,403,024   b) 20,4400,324   c) 20,400,324   d) 20,403,024   e) 20,043,024

Solution: $2 * 10^7$, $4 * 10^5$, $3 * 10^3$, $2 * 10^1$,   4

20,000,000 +   400,000   + 3,000   + 20   +   4

= 20,403,024

The correct answer is (d).

2.1 Practice and Solutions

1. What is the value of $(4 * 10^5) + (3 * 10)^4 + (2 * 10)^2$?
   (A) 4,030,200
   (B) 4,30,200
   (C) 432,000
   (D) 430,200
   (E) 43,200

2. What is seventy five thousands adding two millions, one hundred thousands, three hundreds and three?
   (A) 20,175,303
   (B) 2,175,303
   (C) 2,085,303
   (D) 2,017,803
   (E) 285,303

3. Which of the following represents fifty millions, eight hundred thousands, twenty thousands, forty five and two hundredths?
   (A) 500,820,045.02
   (B) 58,020,045.2
   (C) 50,820,045.02
   (D) 50,808,45.02
   (E) 582,045.2

4. If $a = 2,903.4435$ and $b = 44.2351$, what is the value of $a - b$ rounded to the nearest hundredth?
   (A) 28590.208
   (B) 2859.21
   (C) 2859.208
   (D) 2859.2
   (E) 285.92

5. What is the value of $(2 * 10^5) + (4 * 10^3) + (3 * 10^{-1}) + (2 * 10^{-3})$?
   (A) 204,000.302
   (B) 204,000.32
   (C) 24,000.302
   (D) 24,000.32
   (E) 24,003.2

Solutions to 2.1 Practice: 1(D), 2(B), 3(C), 4(B), 5(A)

1. What is the value of $(4 * 10^5) + (3 * 10)^4 + (2 * 10)^2$?

   (A) 4,030,200
   (B) 4,30,200
   (C) 432,000
   (D) 430,200
   (E) 43,200

   > $4 * 10^5 = 400,000$
   > $3 * 10^4 = 30,000$
   > $2 * 10^2 = 200$
   > $sum = 430,200$

2. What is seventy five thousands adding two millions, one hundred thousands, three hundreds and three?

   (A) 20,175,303
   (B) 2,175,303
   (C) 2,085,303
   (D) 2,017,803
   (E) 285,303

   > $75,000$
   > $2,000,000$
   > $100,000$
   > $+303$
   > $sum = 2,175,303$

3. Which of the following represents fifty millions, eight hundred thousands, twenty thousands, forty five and two hundredths?

   (A) 500,820,045.02
   (B) 58,020,045.2
   (C) 50,820,045.02
   (D) 50,808,45.02
   (E) 582,045.2

   > $50,000,000$
   > $800,000$
   > $20,000$
   > 45
   > $+0.02$
   > $sum = 50,820,045.02$

4. If $a = 2,903.4435$ and $b = 44.2351$, what is the value of $a - b$ rounded to the nearest hundredth?

   (A) 28590.208
   (B) 2859.21
   (C) 2859.208
   (D) 2859.2
   (E) 285.92

   > $2,903.4435$
   > -44.2351
   > 2859.2084
   > ≈ 2859.21

5. What is the value of $(2 * 10^5) + (4 * 10^3) + (3 * 10^{-1}) + (2 * 10^{-3})$?

   (A) 204,000.302
   (B) 204,000.32
   (C) 24,000.302
   (D) 24,000.32
   (E) 24,003.2

   > $200,000$
   > $4,000$
   > 0.3
   > $+0.002$
   > $204,000.302$

3. Order of Operations

3.1 Order of Operations:

1. Parentheses,
2. Exponents,
3. Multiplication/Division,
4. Addition/Subtraction

ex.1   What is the value of $4 + 2 * 5$?   30 is wrong, and 14 is correct.
Solution: $4 + 2 * 5 = 4 + 10 = 14$

ex.2 $22 + (18 - 3 * 5) * 6 + [(34 - 3^3) * (4^2 \div 2^2)]$
$= 22 + (18 - 15) * 6 + [(34 - 27) * (16 \div 4)]$
$= 22 + 3 * 6 + [7 * 4]$
$= 22 + 3 * 6 + 28$
$= 22 + 18 + 28$
$= 40 + 28 = 68$

3.2 Operations with Signed Numbers:

Addition and Subtraction

Same sign:	ex.1	$8 + 3 = 11$	
	ex.2	$-7 - 21 = -28$	
Different sign:	ex.3	$15 - 7 = 8$	
	ex.4	$6 - 17 = -11$	
	ex.5	$-8 + 2 = -6$	

> **Rules:**
> Same sign:
> Add them, and keep the sign.
> Different sign:
> Subtract them, and keep the
> sign of the larger number.

Multiplication and Division

positive * positive   = positive
negative * negative = positive
positive * negative   = negative

Same rules for division

ex.1 $8 * 2 = 16$, $-11 * 3 = -33$, $12 * (-2) = -24$, $-5 * (-7) = 35$

ex.2 $12 \div 3 = 4$, $-36 \div 3 = -12$, $72 \div (-8) = -9$, $\frac{-48}{-4} = 12$,

Note: $(-1)^2 = (-1) * (-1) = 1$ and $(-1)^3 = (-1) * (-1) * (-1) = -1$
$\therefore$ $\boxed{(-1)^{even\ power} = 1 \quad \text{and} \quad (-1)^{odd\ power} = -1}$

$(-3)^2 \neq -3^2$, since $(-3)^2 = 9$, and $-3^2 = -(3^2) = -9$
$\therefore$ $\boxed{-x^n = -(x^n)}$

3.3 Practice and Solutions

1. All of the following are true EXCEPT
   (A) $-4^2 = 16$
   (B) $(-5)^2 = 25$
   (C) $(-3 + 9)^2 = 36$
   (D) $(9 - 3)^2 = 36$
   (E) $(-9 - 3)^2 = 144$

2. If $x = 12 - 3 * (3 - 4)$, what is the value of x?
   (A) -9
   (B) 9
   (C) 15
   (D) 33
   (E) 63

3. If $x = 8 - 4 * (12 \div 2^2)$ and $y = -2^2 * (2 - 5)$, what is the value of xy ?
   (A) -48
   (B) -28
   (C) 12
   (D) 48
   (E) 68

4. What is the value of $(2 - 3 * 4) \div (1 + 3^2)$?

   (A) -1
   (B) 0.4
   (C) 1
   (D) 1.6
   (E) 4

5. Which of the following represents the correct order of evaluating
   $(17 + 3) - 4 * 5^2$?
   I. *addition*
   II. *subtraction*
   III. *multiplication*
   IV. *exponent*
   (A) I, II, III, IV
   (B) I, II, IV, III
   (C) I, IV, II, III
   (D) I, IV, III, II
   (E) I, III, IV, II

Solutions to 3.3 Practice: 1(A), 2(C), 3(A), 4(A), 5(D)

1. All of the following are true EXCEPT

   (A) $-4^2 = 16$

   $$\boxed{-4^2 = -(4^2) = -16}$$

   (B) $(-5)^2 = 25$

   (C) $(-3 + 9)^2 = 36$

   (D) $(9 - 3)^2 = 36$

   (E) $(-9 - 3)^2 = 144$

2. If $x = 12 - 3 * (3 - 4)$, what is the value of x?

   (A) -9

   (B) 9

   (C) 15

   (D) 33

   (E) 63

   $$\boxed{\begin{aligned} x &= 12 - 3 * (3 - 4) \\ &= 12 - 3 * (-1) \\ &= 12 + 3 \\ &= 15 \end{aligned}}$$

3. If $x = 8 - 4 * (12 \div 2^2)$ and $y = -2^2 * (2 - 5)$, what is the value of xy ?

   (A) -48

   (B) -28

   (C) 12

   (D) 48

   (E) 68

   $$\boxed{\begin{aligned} x &= 8 - 4 * (12 \div 2^2), \qquad y = -2^2 * (2 - 5) \\ &= 8 - 4 * (12 \div 4) \qquad\quad = -4 * (-3) \\ &= 8 - 4 * 3 \qquad\qquad\quad = 12 \\ &= -4 \\ xy &= (-4) * 12 = -48 \end{aligned}}$$

4. What is the value of $(2 - 3 * 4) \div (1 + 3^2)$?

   (A) -1

   (B) 0.4

   (C) 1

   (D) 1.6

   (E) 4

   $$\boxed{\begin{aligned} &(2 - 3 * 4) \div (1 + 3^2) \\ &= (2 - 12) \div (1 + 9) \\ &= -10 \div 10 = -1 \end{aligned}}$$

5. Which of the following represents the correct order of evaluating $(17 + 3) - 4 * 5^2$?

   I. *addition*

   II. *subtraction*

   III. *multiplication*

   IV. *exponent*

   (A)   I, II, III, IV

   (B)   I, II, IV, III

   (C)   I, IV, II, III

   (D)   I, IV, III, II

   (E)   I, III, IV, II

   $$\boxed{\begin{aligned} &(17 + 3) - 4 * 5^2 \\ &= 20 - 4 * 5^2 \\ &= 20 - 4 * 25 \\ &= 20 - 100 \\ &= -80 \end{aligned}}$$

4. Factors and Multiples

Factors: x is a factor of y if y is divisible by x.

ex.1 the Factors of 16 are 1, 2, 4, 8, 16 and
       the Factors of 12 are   1, 2, 3, 4, 6, 12
       the Common Factors of 12 &16 are   1, 2, 4
       ∴ the **Greatest Common Factor** (GCF) of 12 & 16 is 4

ex.2   The GCF of 12 & 18 is 6

ex.3   Find the GCF of 28 & 42
          since the factors of 28 are 1, 2, 4, 7, **14**, 28
           and the factors of 42 are 1, 2, 3, 6, 7, **14**, 21, 42
           ∴   the GCF of 28 and 42 is 14

Multiple:

ex.1 the Multiples of 3 are 3, 6, 9, 12, 15, 18, 21, 24, 27, 30, 33, 36, …
       the Multiples of 4 are 4, 8, 12, 16, 20, 24, 28, 32, 36, …
       the Common Multiples of 3 and 4 are 12, 24, 36, …
       ∴ the **Lowest Common Multiple** (LCM) of 3 and 4 is 12

ex.2 Find the LCM of 12 & 15
          since the multiples of 12 are 12, 24, 36, 48, **60**, 72, …
          and the multiples of 15 are 15, 30, 45, **60**, 75, …
          ∴   the LCM of 12 and 15 is 60

4.1 Practice and Solutions

1. List some multiples of 5.

2. List all factors of 24.

3. Find the Greatest Common Factor of 36 and 56.

4. Find the Lowest Common Multiple of 7, 8, and 10.

5. Which of the following is the Greatest Common Factor of 98 and 126?
   (A) 2
   (B) 7
   (C) 14
   (D) 28
   (E) 42

6. Which of the following is the Lowest Common Multiple of 6, 9, and 11?
   (A) 36
   (B) 54
   (C) 99
   (D) 198
   (E) 594

7. If x is a multiple of 7 and y is a multiple of 6, which of the following could be the value of $x*y$?
   (A) 36
   (B) 49
   (C) 56
   (D) 64
   (E) 84

8. If a is a factor of b, which of the following is always true?
   (A) $\frac{a}{2}$ is a factor of b
   (B) $2a$ is a factor of b
   (C) a^2 is a factor of b
   (D) $a - 2$ is a factor of $b - 2$
   (E) $2a$ is a factor of $2b$

9. If x is the Lowest Common Multiple of a, b and c, which of the following is always true?
   I. a is a factor of x
   II. ab is a factor of x
   III. ac is a factor of x
   (A) I only
   (B) II only
   (C) III only
   (D) I and II only
   (E) I, II and III

Solutions to 4.1 Practice: 1 (5,10,15...), 2 (1,2,3,4,6,8,12,24), 3 (4), 4 (280), 5(C), 6(D), 7(E), 8(E), 9(A)

5. Which of the following is the Greatest Common Factor of 98 and 126?

   (A) 2
   (B) 7
   (C) 14
   (D) 28
   (E) 42

   > *can't be (D)or (E): 28 and 42 are not factors of 98.*
   > *14 is a factor of both 98 and 126.*
   > $98 = 7 * 14, \qquad 126 = 9 * 14$

6. Which of the following is the Lowest Common Multiple of 6, 9, and 11?

   (A) 36
   (B) 54
   (C) 99
   (D) 198
   (E) 594

   > *36 and 54 are not the multiples of 11,*
   > *99 is not the multiple 6,*
   > *198 is the multiples of all 6, 9 and 11.*

7. If x is a multiple of 7 and y is a multiple of 6, which of the following could be the value of $x*y$?

   (A) 36
   (B) 49
   (C) 56
   (D) 64
   (E) 84

   > $x * y$ *must be a multiple of both*
   > *6 and 7. (A)to (D)are not a*
   > *multiple of both, but (E)is.*
   > $84 \div 7 = 12,$ *and* $84 \div 6 = 14,$
   > *so x could be 14, and y coulb be 6.*

8. If a is a factor of b, which of the following is always true?

   (A) $\frac{a}{2}$ is a factor of b
   (B) $2a$ is a factor of b
   (C) a^2 is a factor of b
   (D) $a - 2$ is a factor of $b - 2$
   (E) $2a$ is a factor of $2b$

   > *It's very easy to prove that*
   > *(A) to (D)are false by testing with*
   > *simple numbers, say* $a = 7, b = 21$
   > *(E) is always true, since*
   > *if* $ak = b,$ *then* $(2a) * k = 2(ak) = 2b$

9. If x is the Lowest Common Multiple of a, b and c, which of the following is always true?

      I. a is a factor of x
      II. ab is a factor of x
      III. ac is a factor of x

   (A) I only
   (B) II only
   (C) III only
   (D) I and II only
   (E) I, II and III

   > *Only* I. *is to be always true.*
   > II. *and* III. *do not have to be true.*
   > *For example, choose* $a = 4, b = 8,$ *and* $c = 16.$
   > *LCM is 16, but* $ab = 32$ *is not a factor of 16*
   > *and neither is* $ac = 64.$

5. Remainders

A remainder is the amount that is left over after division.

ex. $15 \div 6$ equals 2 with the remainder of 3, $\quad 15 = 2*6 + 3$

$$\begin{array}{r} 2 \leftarrow \text{Quotient} \\ 6\,\overline{\smash{)}\,1\,5} \leftarrow \text{Dividend} \\ \underline{1\,2} \\ 3 \end{array}$$

Divisor

Remainder $\longrightarrow$ 3

$$\boxed{\begin{array}{c} \text{For } m \div n = a \text{ with a remainder of } r, \\ m = an + r \quad \text{(where } r < n \text{)} \end{array}}$$

<u>A typical SAT remainder problem:</u>

ex.1 If 5 is the remainder when a number x is divided by 8, what is the remainder when $3x$ is divided by 8?

    a) 2   b) 3   c) 5   d) 6   e) 7

Many SAT books teach this:

1. Pick a number that produces a remainder of 5 when it is divided by 8, say $x=13$,
2. Find: $3x$, $3*13 = 39$
3. 39 divided by 8, produces a remainder of 7. $\quad \therefore$ (e) is the correct answer.

Here is a faster way:

1. Multiply the remainder 5 by the 3, (from $3x$): $\quad 3*5 = 15$
2. 15 divided by 8, produces a remainder of 7.

$\therefore$ The correct answer is (d).

Mathematical proof of the above (skip the proof if not interested):

$$\frac{x}{8} = a + \frac{5}{8}, \text{ where } a \text{ is the whole number,}$$

Now multiply the equation by 3, and we have

$$\frac{3x}{8} = 3a + \frac{3*5}{8},$$
$$= 3a + \frac{15}{8},$$

$\therefore$ The remainder should be the remainder of $15 \div 8$ which is 7.

ex. 2. When n is divided by 8 the remainder is 7, and when n is divided by 5, the remainder is 3. What is the smallest possible integer n could be?

    a) 15   b) 18   c) 23   d) 28   e) 31

    Solution: The multiples of 5 are: 5, 10, 15, 20, 25, 30, ...

        Add 3 to each of the above: 8, 13, 18, **23**, 28, 33, ...

        The multiples of 8 are: 8, 16, 24, 32, ...

        Add 7 to each of the above: 15, **23**, 31, ...

        $\therefore$ 23 is the number.

The correct answer is (c).

5.1 Practice and Solutions

1. Which of the following produces a remainder of 1 when divided by 3, 4, 6 and 8?
   - (A) 91
   - (B) 96
   - (C) 109
   - (D) 181
   - (E) 193

2. If 7 is the remainder when a number x is divided by 9, what is the remainder when $3x$ is divided by 9?
   - (A) 7
   - (B) 4
   - (C) 3
   - (D) 1
   - (E) 0

3. When n is divided by 7 the remainder is 4, and when n is divided by 6, the remainder is 3. What is the smallest possible integer n could be?
   - (A) 28
   - (B) 39
   - (C) 46
   - (D) 48
   - (E) 57

4. When $a + b + c$ is divided by x it equals to y with a remainder of z., which of the following is true?
   - (A) $a + b + c = x + y + z$
   - (B) $a + b + c = xy$
   - (C) $a + b + c = yz + x$
   - (D) $a + b + c = xy + z$
   - (E) $a + b + c = xz + y$

5. When $k + 2$ is divided by 7, the remainder is 1. When k is divided by 6, the remainder is 2. What is the value of $2k$?
   - (A) 40
   - (B) 36
   - (C) 27
   - (D) 28
   - (E) 20

Solutions to 5.1 Practice: 1(E), 2(C), 3(B), 4(D), 5(A)

1. Which of the following produces a remainder of 1 when divided by 3, 4, 6 and 8?

    (A) 91

    (B) 96

    (C) 109

    (D) 181

    (E) 193

    > *Subtracting* 1 *from each number we get*
    > 90, 95, 108, 180, *and* 192. *We need one that*
    > *is divisible by* 3, 4, 6, *and* 8. *Only* 192 *works.*

2. If 7 is the remainder when a number x is divided by 9, what is the remainder when $3x$ is divided by 9?

    (A) 7

    (B) 4

    (C) 3

    (D) 1

    (E) 0

    > *when* $\dfrac{x}{9}$ *has a remainder* 7,
    > $3 * 7 = 21$
    > $\dfrac{21}{9} = 2$ *with a remainder of* 3.

3. When n is divided by 7 the remainder is 4, and when n is divided by 6, the remainder is 3. What is the smallest possible integer n could be?

    (A) 28

    (B) 39

    (C) 46

    (D) 48

    (E) 57

    > *Add* 4 *to each multiples of* 7:
    > 11, 18, 25, 32, 39, 46, 53, ...
    > *and add* 3 *to each multiples of* 6:
    > 9, 15, 21, 27, 33, 39, 45, ...   ∴ *only* 39 *works.*

4. If $a + b + c$ is divided by x it equals to y with a remainder of z, which of the following is true?

    (A) $a + b + c = x + y + z$

    (B) $a + b + c = xy$

    (C) $a + b + c = yz + x$

    (D) $a + b + c = xy + z$

    (E) $a + b + c = xz + y$

    > $\dfrac{a + b + c}{x} = y + \dfrac{z}{x}$ *Multiply by* x:
    > $a + b + c = xy + z$

5. When $k + 2$ is divided by 7, the remainder is 1. When k is divided by 6, the remainder is 2. What is the value of $2k$?

    (A) 40

    (B) 36

    (C) 27

    (D) 28

    (E) 20

    > *Check each answer from* (A) *to* (E): *In* (A):
    > $2k = 40,$ $k = 20,$ $k + 2 = 22 = 3 * 7 + 1$
    > $k + 2$ *has a remainder of* 1 *when divided by* 7
    > *and* k *has a remainder of* 2 *when divided by* 6.

6. Fractions

$$\text{Fraction} = \frac{Numerator \longrightarrow \frac{2}{}}{Demorminator \longrightarrow 3}$$

6.1 Addition and Subtraction

ex.1 What is the value of $\frac{2}{3} + \frac{1}{2}$

Find the common denominator when adding/subtracting fractions. Use the LCM method (see section 4 above) to find a common denominator:

for 3 and 2, the LCM is 6

$$\therefore \frac{2}{3} + \frac{1}{2} = \frac{2*2}{3*2} + \frac{1*3}{2*3} = \frac{4}{6} + \frac{3}{6} = \frac{7}{6}$$

ex.2 What is the value of $\frac{6}{7} - \frac{5}{8}$?

$$\frac{6}{7} - \frac{5}{8} = \frac{6*8}{7*8} - \frac{5*7}{8*7} = \frac{48}{56} - \frac{35}{56} = \frac{13}{56}$$

6.2 Multiplication

No common denominator is needed; simply multiply the two numerators and the two denominators:

ex.1 $\frac{3}{5} * \frac{1}{2} = \frac{3*1}{5*2} = \frac{3}{10}$, ex.2 $3 * \frac{2}{7} = \frac{3*2}{7} = \frac{6}{7}$

ex.3 $42 * \frac{15}{6} = \frac{42*15}{6} = 7*15 = 105$

6.3 Division

No common denominator is needed. When dividing a fraction A by fraction B, simply multiply A by the **reciprocal** (flipping) of B.

ex.1 $\frac{5}{6} \div \frac{2}{7} = \frac{5}{6} * \frac{7}{2} = \frac{35}{12}$

ex.2 $\frac{\frac{3}{4}}{\frac{7}{8}} = \frac{3}{4} * \frac{8}{7} = \frac{3*8}{4*7} = \frac{24}{28} = \frac{6}{7}$

6.4 Reduced Fractions

ex.1 $\frac{10}{25}$ both 10 & 25 have factor of 5

$\therefore \quad \frac{10}{25} = \frac{10 \div 5}{25 \div 5} = \frac{2}{5}$

ex.2 $\frac{4}{12} = \frac{1}{3}$

6.5 Improper fractions and mixed numbers

Improper fraction:

Fractions with numerator greater than the denominator:

ex.1 $\frac{21}{6}$,   ex.2 $\frac{9}{2}$

Mixed fraction:

Fraction with a whole number and a fraction combined:

ex.1 $3\frac{2}{7}$,   ex.2 $4\frac{2}{5}$

Converting from Improper Fraction to Mixed Fraction

ex.1 $\frac{21}{8}$, $21 \div 8 = 2$ with a remainder of 5,

$\therefore \quad \frac{21}{8} = 2\frac{5}{8}$ 2 is the whole number & 5 is the remainder

ex.2 $\frac{9}{2}$, $9 \div 2 = 4$ with a remainder of 1,

$\therefore \quad \frac{9}{2} = 4\frac{1}{2}$ 4 is the whole number & 1 is the remainder

Converting Mixed Fraction to Improper Fraction

ex.1 $4\frac{1}{2}$,

1. Use the whole number part to multiply the denominator,
   i.e. $4 \times 2 = 8$
2. Add the numerator of the fraction to the product above,
   $1 + 8 = 9$, the sum is the new numerator.

$\therefore \quad 4\frac{1}{2} = \frac{9}{2}$

In general, $\boxed{a\frac{b}{c} = \frac{ac+b}{c}}$ ex.2 $7\frac{3}{8} = \frac{7*8+3}{8} = \frac{59}{8}$

6.6 Practice and Solutions

1. If $a = \frac{3}{5}$, $= \frac{2}{3}$, and $c = \frac{3}{4}$, what is the value of $2a + b * c$?

   (A) $\frac{57}{60}$

   (B) $\frac{27}{10}$

   (C) $\frac{11}{10}$

   (D) $\frac{17}{10}$

   (E) $\frac{7}{5}$

2. $\frac{3}{4}$ of the 264 grade ten students in a high school took the Algebra I course, but $\frac{1}{9}$ of them failed. How many students passed the course?

   (A) 198

   (B) 176

   (C) 165

   (D) 162

   (E) 159

3. Jade had completed $\frac{7}{8}$ of the total of 168 math practice problems, while Kim had finished $\frac{6}{7}$ of them. Who had done more and by how many?

   (A) Jade had done 3 more than Kim

   (B) Jade had done 7 more than Kim

   (C) Kim had done 2 more than Jade

   (D) Kim had done 5 more than Jade

   (E) Jade and Kim have done the same number

4. Which of the following is the correct value of $5\frac{7}{9} - 6\frac{2}{3} + 4\frac{5}{7}$?

   (A) $2\frac{62}{63}$

   (B) $3\frac{22}{63}$

   (C) $3\frac{44}{63}$

   (D) $3\frac{52}{63}$

   (E) $4\frac{11}{63}$

5. Amy has 60 coins, $\frac{1}{4}$ of them are nickels, $\frac{3}{5}$ are dimes, and $\frac{3}{20}$ are quarters. How much are these coins worth in total?

   (A) $11.25

   (B) $9.80

   (C) $8.75

   (D) $7.20

   (E) $6.60

Solutions to 6.6 Practice: 1(D), 2(B), 3(A), 4(D), 5(E)

1. If $a = \frac{3}{5}$, $b = \frac{2}{3}$, and $c = \frac{3}{4}$, what is the value of $2a + b * c$?

   (A) $\frac{57}{60}$

   (B) $\frac{27}{10}$

   (C) $\frac{11}{10}$

   (D) $\frac{17}{10}$

   (E) $\frac{7}{5}$

   $$2a + b * c = 2 * \frac{3}{5} + \frac{2}{\cancel{3}} * \frac{\cancel{3}}{4}$$
   $$= \frac{6}{5} + \frac{2}{4}$$
   $$= \frac{6}{5} + \frac{1}{2}$$
   $$= \frac{12}{10} + \frac{5}{10} = \frac{17}{10}$$

2. $\frac{3}{4}$ of the 264 grade ten students in a high school took the Algebra I course, but $\frac{1}{9}$ of them failed. How many students passed the course?

   (A) 198

   (B) 176

   (C) 165

   (D) 162

   (E) 159

   The number of students who took the course is
   $\frac{3}{4} * 264 = \frac{3 * 264}{4} = 3*66= 198$
   $\frac{8}{9}$ *of* 198 *students* $= 8 * 22 = 176$. 176 *passed.*

3. Jade had completed $\frac{7}{8}$ of the total of 168 math practice problems, while Kim had finished $\frac{6}{7}$ of them. Who had done more and by how many?

   (A) Jade did 3 more than Kim

   (B) Jade did 7 more than Kim

   (C) Kim did 2 more than Jade

   (D) Kim did 5 more than Jade

   (E) Jade and Kim did the same.

   Jade completed $\frac{7}{8} * 168 = 7 * 21$
   $= 147$ *problems.*
   Kim finished $\frac{6}{7} * 168 = 6 * 24 = 144$

4. Which of the following is the correct value of $5\frac{7}{9} - 6\frac{2}{3} + 4\frac{5}{7}$?

   (A) $2\frac{62}{63}$

   (B) $3\frac{22}{63}$

   (C) $3\frac{44}{63}$

   (D) $3\frac{52}{63}$

   (E) $4\frac{11}{63}$

   $$5\frac{7}{9} - 6\frac{2}{3} + 4\frac{5}{7} = (5 - 6 + 4) + \frac{7}{9} - \frac{2}{3} + \frac{5}{7}$$
   $$= 3 + \frac{49}{63} - \frac{42}{63} + \frac{45}{63}$$
   $$= 3 + \frac{52}{63} = 3\frac{52}{63}$$

5. Amy has 60 coins, $\frac{1}{4}$ of them are nickels, $\frac{3}{5}$ are dimes, and $\frac{3}{20}$ are quarters. How much are these coins worth in total?

   (A) $11.25

   (B) $9.80

   (C) $8.75

   (D) $7.20

   (E) $6.60

   Total amount
   $$= \left(\frac{1}{4} * 60\right) * 0.05 + \left(\frac{3}{5} * 60\right) * 0.10 + \left(\frac{3}{20} * 60\right) * 0.25$$
   $$= 15 * 0.05 + 36 * 0.10 + 9 * 0.25$$
   $$= 0.75 + 3.60 + 2.25 = 6.60$$

7. Average

7.1 Average

$$\text{Average} = \frac{\text{Sum of all elements}}{\text{Number of elements}}$$

ex.1 If three tickets cost $23.50, $14.99 and $9.87, what is the average cost?

$$\text{the Average Cost} = \frac{\$(23.5+14.99+9.87)}{3} = \$16.12$$

ex.2 In a math test, the average of class A of 17 students was 76, and class B of 25 students was 70.

i) What was the total average from two classes?

a) 73.8   b) 72.4   c) 72.0   d) 71.9   e) 70.7

$$\text{Solution: Average} = \frac{(17*76)+(25*70)}{17+25} = 72.4 \quad \text{answer (b)}$$

ii) If a new student in class A got 51, what was class A's new average?

$$\text{Solution: class A new Average} = \frac{(17*76)+(1*51)}{17+1} = 74.6$$

7.2 Mean, Median and Mode

Mean = the average as mentioned above

Median = the middle number in an ordered list of numbers, when the list has odd number of terms.

or   = the average of the two middle numbers in an ordered list when the list has an even number of terms.

Mode = the value that occurs most frequently in a list of numbers

ex.1 Given: 43, 52, 46, 50, 46, 46, 50, 59, 62, 48

i) find the Mean, Median, and Mode.

Solution:

$$\text{Mean} = \frac{43+52+46+50+46+46+50+59+62+48}{10} = 50.2$$

To find median, order the list: 43, 46, 46, 46, 48, 50, 50, 52, 59, 62

the middle numbers are: 48 & 50,

Median is: (48 + 50) ÷ 2 = 49

Mode is: 46, since it occurs most frequently, 3 times.

ii) if 43 and 62 are removed from the list, which of the following
will change?

a) Mean   b) Median   c) Mode   d) Mean & Mode   e) Median and Mode

Solution: Mean changes, Median is still 49, and Mode is still 46.
The correct answer is (a).

7.3 Distance, Speed and Time

Distance = Speed * Time ,   Speed= $\dfrac{\text{Distance}}{\text{Time}}$,   Time = $\dfrac{\text{Distance}}{\text{Speed}}$

ex.1 A motor boat takes 2 hours to travel 132 miles with the current, and 3
hours on the return trip against the current. What is the speed of the current?

a) 11mi/h   b) 19mi/h   c) 22mi/h   d) 34mi/h   e) 44m/h

Solution: The average speed with the current $= \dfrac{D}{T} = \dfrac{132}{2} = 66$ mi/h

The return speed against the current $= \dfrac{D}{T} = \dfrac{132}{3} = 44$ mi/h

Let S = boat speed,   C = current speed

$\therefore$ S + C = 66 ...(1)   and   S – C = 44 ...(2)

$\therefore$ (1) + (2): 2C = 66 + 44,   C $= \dfrac{66-44}{2} = 11$ mi/h

The correct answer is (a).

ex.2 John visited a university which is 495 miles away. He took a bus to the
University and a train back home with a total traveling time of 12 hours.
The train is 3 times faster than the bus. What is the speed of the bus?

a) 165   b) 95   c) 55   d) 50   e)   48

Solution: Let x = speed of bus, t = time taken by train

	Distance	Speed	Time
bus	495	x	$3t$
train	495	$3x$	t

since the train is 3 times faster, it would take $3t$ time for bus

$\therefore$ $t + 3t = 12$, $4t = 12$, $\therefore$ $t = 3$ (See Algebra 3.1)

$\therefore$ for bus: $495 = x * 3t = x * 3(3)$

$495 = 9x$

$\therefore$ $x = \dfrac{495}{9} = 55$ mi/h

The correct answer is (b).

7.4   Practice and Solutions

1. Pat's past 3 weeks' earnings were $730, $770, and $850, how many hours should he work in the 4th week to make a 4-week average of $800/wk, if he earned $17/h?

2. If a plane's average speed is 950km/h , how long does it take to travel 12000km?

3. Find the Mean, Median and Mode of :   72, 82, 68, 72, 74, 72, 68, 80, 74, 77

4. Ling had an average of 11.4s in her 100m sprint the first five months, and 13.8s the next seven months. What was her average time in 12 months?
   - (A)   12.4
   - (B)   12.6
   - (C)   12.8
   - (D)   13.0
   - (E)   13.2

5. If the cost of a box of 12 mangoes is x dollars, and the cost of a smaller box of 8 mangoes is y dollars, what is the average cost per mango of the two boxes?
   - (A) $\frac{x+y}{2}$
   - (B) $\frac{x+y}{20}$
   - (C) $\frac{12x+8y}{8}$
   - (D) $\frac{12x+8y}{12}$
   - (E) $\frac{12x+8y}{20}$

6. The average cruising speed of a plane RQ is 250mi/h more than for plane RX. If it takes RX 11 hours to travel 7150 miles, how many hours less for RQ to travel that far?
   - (A)   3 hrs
   - (B)   3.5 hrs
   - (C)   4.5 hrs
   - (D)   5 hrs
   - (E)   8hrs

7. Car A's average speed was x mi/h, while car B's was 10mi/h more than A's. They both left from the same place, but B started two hours later than A. Car B caught up with A after B drove for t hours. Which of the following is true?
   - (A) $x = 2t$
   - (B) $x = 5t$
   - (C) $x = 10t$
   - (D) $x = 10(t - 2)$
   - (E) $x = 10t - 2$

8. On the list of: 11, 13, 14, 14, 16, 17, 17, 17, 18, what smallest integer should be added to the list so that their Mean will be greater or equal to the Median?
   - (A)   19
   - (B)   15
   - (C)   13
   - (D)   12
   - (E)   10

Solutions to 7.4 Practice: 1 (50), 2 (12.6), 3 (73.9,73,72), 4(C), 5(B), 6(A),7(B),8(C)

1. Let x = # of hours work in 4th week. $\therefore$ the 4th week earning $= 17x$
    $(730 + 770 + 850 + 17x) \div 4 = 800$, $2350 + 17x = 3200$, $x = 50h$

2. $T = D \div S = 12000 \div 950 = 12.6 \, hours$

3. Mean = average = 73.9, Median $= (72 + 74) \div 2 = 73$, and Mode $= 72$

4. Ling had an average of 11.4s in her 100m sprint the first five months, and 13.8s the next seven months. What was her average time in 12 months?

    (A) 12.4
    (B) 12.6
    (C) 12.8
    (D) 13.0
    (E) 13.2

    $Average \, time \, for \, 12 \, months$
    $= \dfrac{5(11.4) + 7(13.8)}{12}$
    $= 12.8s$

5. If the cost of a box of 12 mangoes is x dollars, and the cost of a smaller box of 8 mangoes is y dollars, what is the average cost per mango of the two boxes?

    (A) $\dfrac{x+y}{2}$
    (B) $\dfrac{x+y}{20}$
    (C) $\dfrac{12x+8y}{8}$
    (D) $\dfrac{12x+8y}{12}$
    (E) $\dfrac{12x+8y}{20}$

    $Average \, cost \, per \, mango \, of \, both \, boxes$
    $= \dfrac{total \, cost \, for \, 2 \, boxes}{total \, number \, of \, mangos} = \dfrac{x + y}{20}$

6. The average cruising speed of a plane RQ is 250mi/h more than for plane RX. If it takes RX 11 hours to travel 7150 miles, how many hours less for RQ to travel that far?

    (A) 3 hrs
    (B) 3.5 hrs
    (C) 4.5 hrs
    (D) 5 hrs
    (E) 8hrs

    $Average \, speed \, of \, RX = \dfrac{7150 \, miles}{11h} = 650mph$
    $Average \, speed \, of \, RQ = (650 + 250)mph = 900mph$
    $Time \, of \, RQ \, travel = \dfrac{7150 \, miles}{900mph} \approx 8h$
    $Difference \, in \, time \approx 11h - 8h = 3h$

7. Car A's average speed was x mi/h, while car B's was 10mi/h more than A's. They both left from the same place, but B started two hours later than A. Car B caught up with A after B drove for t hours. Which of the following is true?

    (A) $x = 2t$
    (B) $x = 5t$
    (C) $x = 10t$
    (D) $x = 10(t - 2)$
    (E) $x = 10t - 2$

    $Distance \, travelled \, by \, car \, A = (t + 2)x \, miles$
    $Distance \, travelled \, by \, car \, B = t(x + 10) \, miles$
    $Use \, (distance = time * speed)$
    $Distances \, are \, equal: (t + 2)x = t(x + 10)$
    $\cancel{tx} + 2x = \cancel{tx} + 10t; \, 2x = 10t; \, x = 5t$

8. On the list of: 11, 13, 14, 14, 16, 17, 17, 17, 18, what smallest integer should be added to the list so that their Mean will be greater or equal to the Median?

    (A) 19
    (B) 15
    (C) 13
    (D) 12
    (E) 10

    $Try \, each \, multiple \, choice \, answers, starting \, with \, the \, smallest:$
    $(E) \, 10: \, Mean = \dfrac{137+10}{10} = 14.7, \, new \, Median = \dfrac{14+16}{2} = 15, \, Mean < Median$
    $(D) \, 12: \, Mean = \dfrac{137+12}{10} = 14.9, \, new \, Median = \dfrac{14+16}{2} = 15, \, Mean < Median$
    $(C) \, 13: \, Mean = \dfrac{137+13}{10} = 15, \, new \, Median = \dfrac{14+16}{2} = 15, \, Mean = Median$

8. Percents: A percent means "per hundred", like $\frac{72}{100}$, *written as* 72%.

1. Percent to Decimal: ex. $27\% = \frac{27}{100} = 0.27$, $4\% = 0.04$

2. p% **of** x means: $\frac{p}{100} * x$:

   30% **of** $150 means: $\frac{30}{100} * \$150 = \$45$ or $0.30 * \$150 = \$45$

ex.1   What percent of $95 is $26?

   a) 25.8%   b) 27.4%   c) 28.3%   d) 29.2%   e) 30%

   Solution: $\frac{26}{95} = 0.274$, $0.274 = 27.4\%$
   The correct answer is (b).

ex.2   Jen got 82% of the 50 points in her unit 4 test, and 15% of the points earned from unit 4 would contribute to her final grade. How many points did she earn for the final from unit 4?

   a) 5.0   b) 6.0   c) 6.2   d) 7.0   e) 8.2
   Solution: 82% of 50:
      $0.82 * 50 = 41$ points
      15% of 41 points:
      $0.15 * 41 = 6.15 \approx 6.2$

   Alternatively, do it in one step:
      $15\% * (82\% * 50) = 0.15 * (0.82 * 50) \approx 6.2$
   The correct answer is (c).

ex.3   Josh sold his bike for $250, and wanted to use 90% of it to buy a scooter, but that amount is only equal to 20% of the cost of a scooter. How much does the scooter cost?

   a) $1125   b) $1299   c) $1525   d) $1725   e) $2025
   Solution: let x = cost of the scooter
         90% of $250: $0.9 * 250 = \$225$
      $\therefore$ $225 is equal to 20% of x
         $20\% * x = 225$,
         $0.2\,x = 225$ divide both sides by 0.2:
            $x = 225 \div 0.2 = 1125$ $\therefore$ The scooter costs $1125

   The correct answer is (a).

8.1 Practice and Solutions

1. What is 43% of 287 ?

2. What percent of $850 is $637.5?

3. What percent is 270 out of 420?

4. 25% of the students in a high school are graduating and 80% of the graduates are going into postsecondary education, and the rest are going to trade schools. If there are 980 students in the school, how many are going to trade schools?
   - (A) 49
   - (B) 56
   - (C) 79
   - (D) 148
   - (E) 245

5. In a test, Tim got 12 out of 15 questions correct in part A, and 15 out of 18 in part B. If each question is worth the same, what is his percentage of correct answers?
   - (A) 78.4%
   - (B) 81.8%
   - (C) 83%
   - (D) 85.2%
   - (E) 86%

6. 180 students from grade 10, 11 and 12 represented the sport team of a high school school. 45% of the team were grade 12 students and there were 27 more grade 12 students than grade 11. What percentage of grade 10 students were on the team?
   - (A) 18%
   - (B) 22%
   - (C) 25%
   - (D) 31%
   - (E) 34%

7. If the price of a fur coat is discounted by a% from its original price of x dollars, what is the discounted price?
   - (A) ax
   - (B) $x - ax$
   - (C) $\dfrac{ax}{100}$
   - (D) $\dfrac{x - ax}{100}$
   - (E) $\dfrac{100x - ax}{100}$

8. Jess sold her cell phone for 40% less than its original price of $380. She spent 75% of the money she got on a new phone and the rest on her phone bill. If she still had $8 left, how much was the phone bill?
   - (A) $25
   - (B) $28
   - (C) $35
   - (D) $49
   - (E) $52

Solutions to 8.1 Practice: 1 (123.41), 2 (75%), 3 (64.3%), 4(A), 5(B), 6(C), 7(E), 8(D)

1. What is 43% of 287 ? $0.43 * 287 = 123.41$

2. What percent of $850 is $637.5? $637.5 \div 850 = 0.75 = 75\%$

3. What percent is 270 out of 420? $270 \div 420 = 0.643 = 64.3\%$

4. 25% of the students in a high school are in graduating class and 80% of the graduates are going to colleges, and the rest are going to trade schools. If there are 980 students in the school, how many are going to trade schools?

   (A) 49
   (B) 56
   (C) 79
   (D) 148
   (E) 245

   > *Number of students graduating* $= 0.25(980) = 245$
   > 20% *of the graduates going to trade schools,*
   > $= 0.2(245) = 49$

5. In a test, Tim got 12 out of 15 questions correct in part A, and 15 out of 18 in part B. If each question is worth the same, what is his percentage of correct answers?

   (A) 78.4%
   (B) 81.8%
   (C) 83%
   (D) 85.2%
   (E) 86%

   > *Overall grade*
   > $= \dfrac{Number\ of\ correct\ answers}{Total\ number\ of\ questions}$
   > $= \dfrac{12+15}{15+18} = \dfrac{27}{33} \approx 81.8\%$

6. 180 students from grade 10, 11 and 12 represented the sport team of a high school school. 45% of the team were grade 12 students and there were 27 more grade 12 students than grade 11. What percentage of grade 10 students were on the team?

   (A) 18%
   (B) 22%
   (C) 25%
   (D) 31%
   (E) 34%

   > *Number of grade* 12 *students* $= 0.45(180) = 81$
   > *Number of grade* 11 *students* $= 81 - 27 = 54$
   > *Number of grade* 10 *students* $= 180 - 81 - 54 = 45$
   > *Percentage of grade* 10 *students* $= \dfrac{45}{180} = 0.25 = 25\%$

7. If the price of a fur coat is discounted by $a\%$ from its original price of x dollars, what is the discounted price?

   (A) ax
   (B) $x - ax$
   (C) $\dfrac{ax}{100}$
   (D) $\dfrac{x-ax}{100}$
   (E) $\dfrac{100x-ax}{100}$

   > *Discount price* $= (100 - a)\%$ *of the original price*
   > $= \dfrac{100-a}{100} * x = \dfrac{100x-ax}{100}$

8. Jess sold her cell phone for 40% less than its original price of $380. She spent 75% of the money she got on a new phone and the rest on her phone bill. If she still had $8 left, how much was the phone bill?

   (A) $25
   (B) $28
   (C) $35
   (D) $49
   (E) $52

   > *Phone sold for* $0.60(380) = \$228$
   > *Cost of phone* $= 0.75(228) = \$171$
   > *left over* $= 228 - 171 = 57$
   > $\$57 - phone\ bill = \$8,\ Phone\ bill = \$57 - \$8 = \$49$

9. Ratios: The comparison of two numbers, A to B, express as A:B or $\frac{A}{B}$

ex.1 If there are 3 dimes and 7 quarters in a box,

then the ratio of dimes(D) to quarters(Q) is: D:Q = 3:7 or $\frac{D}{Q} = \frac{3}{7}$

ex.2 The ratio of boys to girls in a class is 4:3, and there are 24 boys. How many are girls?

    a) 12   b) 14   c) 16   d) 18   e) 19

Solution: Let $x = \#$ of girls, and B:G = 4:3

$\therefore$ $\frac{B}{G} = \frac{4}{3} = \frac{24}{x}$

by cross multiplication:

$\therefore$ $\dfrac{4}{3} \diagdown\!\!\!\!\!\diagup \dfrac{24}{x}$

$4x = 3 * 24$,

$4x = 72$,   (See Algebra 3.1)

$\therefore$ $x = 18$,   answer: 18 girls.

The correct answer is (d).

ex.3   Inside a bag, the ratio of red to green balls is 5:2, and the ratio of green to blue is 4:3. If there are 15 blue balls, how many red balls are there?

    a) 40   b) 50   c) 55   d) 60   c) 65

Solution: $\frac{R}{G} = \frac{5}{2}$ and

$\frac{G}{B} = \frac{4}{3}$

Since $B = 15$, $\therefore$ $\frac{G}{15} = \frac{4}{3}$

by cross multiplication:

$3G = 15 * 4$, $3G = 60$,   and $G = 60 \div 3$

$\therefore$ $G = 20$,   There are green balloons.

Since $\frac{R}{G} = \frac{5}{2}$ $\therefore$ $\frac{R}{20} = \frac{5}{2}$

by cross multiplication:

$2R = 20 * 5$,

$\therefore$ $R = 50$, answer: 50 red balls.

The correct answer is (b).

9.1 Practice and Solutions

1. If the ratio of people to pet dogs in a city is 30 to 1, and the population of the city is 1,200,000 , how many pet dogs are there in the city?
   - (A) 2000
   - (B) 4000
   - (C) 8000
   - (D) 25,000
   - (E) 40,000

2. 42 students joined the track-and-field team with a ratio of girls to boys 3:4. If 2 girls and 4 boys dropped out, what is the new ratio of girls to boys?
   - (A) $\frac{1}{3}$
   - (B) $\frac{3}{5}$
   - (C) $\frac{4}{5}$
   - (D) $\frac{2}{3}$
   - (E) $\frac{1}{1}$

3. If 310 people in total were in a summer camp, and the ratio of adult to children was 1: 9, how many more children were there than adults?
   - (A) 248
   - (B) 252
   - (C) 256
   - (D) 264
   - (E) 279

4. The ratio of large to medium pizzas made each day in a restaurant is 5: 6, and the ratio of medium to small pizzas is 3: 7. What is the ratio of large to small?
   - (A) $\frac{3}{14}$
   - (B) $\frac{5}{14}$
   - (C) $\frac{1}{7}$
   - (D) $\frac{5}{7}$
   - (E) $\frac{6}{7}$

5. The box contains red, blue and yellow crayons in the ratio of 5: 3: 4, and there are 7 more yellow than blue. How many crayons are in the box?
   - (A) 21
   - (B) 35
   - (C) 49
   - (D) 53
   - (E) 84

Solutions to 9.1 Practice: 1(E), 2(C), 3(A), 4(B), 5(E)

1. If the ratio of people to pet dogs in a city is 30 to 1, and the population of the city is 1,200,000 , how many pet dogs are there in the city?

   (A) 2000
   (B) 4000
   (C) 8000
   (D) 25,000
   (E) 40,000

   Let x be the dog population
   $$\frac{people\ population}{dog\ population} = \frac{30}{1} \diagdown \frac{1,200,000}{x}$$
   $30x = 1,200,000,$ dividing both sides by 30:
   $x = 40,000$

2. 42 students joined the track-and-field team with a ratio of girls to boys 3:4. If 2 girls and 4 boys dropped out, what is the new ratio of girls to boys?

   (A) $\frac{1}{3}$
   (B) $\frac{3}{5}$
   (C) $\frac{4}{5}$
   (D) $\frac{2}{3}$
   (E) $\frac{1}{1}$

   $Originally:\ number\ of\ girls = \frac{3}{7} * 42 = 18$
   $$number\ of\ boys = \frac{4}{7} * 42 = 24$$
   $Now: \dfrac{number\ of\ girls}{number\ of\ boys} = \dfrac{18-2}{24-4} = \dfrac{16}{20} = \dfrac{4}{5}$

3. If 310 people in total were in a summer camp, and the ratio of adult to children was 1:9, how many more children were there than adults?

   (A) 248
   (B) 252
   (C) 256
   (D) 264
   (E) 279

   $Number\ of\ adults = \dfrac{1}{10} * 310 = 31$
   $Number\ of\ children = \dfrac{9}{10} * 310 = 279$
   $The\ difference = 279 - 31 = 248$

4. The ratio of large to medium pizzas made each day in a restaurant is 5:6, and the ratio of medium to small is 3:7. What is the ratio of large to small?

   (A) $\frac{3}{14}$
   (B) $\frac{5}{14}$
   (C) $\frac{1}{7}$
   (D) $\frac{5}{7}$
   (E) $\frac{6}{7}$

   $x = number\ of\ large\ pizzas,$ $y = number\ of\ mediums,$
   $z = number\ of\ smalls$
   $Given: \dfrac{x}{y} = \dfrac{5}{6},$ $\dfrac{y}{z} = \dfrac{3}{7}$
   $Cross\ multiply: 6x = 5y,$ $7y = 3z$
   $$x = \frac{5}{6}y,\qquad y = \frac{3}{7}z$$
   $Hence\ x = \frac{5}{6} * \left(\frac{3}{7}z\right) = \frac{15}{42}z = \frac{5}{14}z,\quad \frac{x}{z} = \frac{5}{14}$

5. A box contains red, blue and yellow crayons in the ratio of 5:3:4, and there are 7 more yellow than blue. How many crayons are in the box?

   (A) 21
   (B) 35
   (C) 49
   (D) 53
   (E) 84

   $R:B:Y = 5:3:4,$ $\dfrac{B}{Y} = \dfrac{3}{4},$ $Since\ B + 7 = Y,$
   $\dfrac{B}{Y} = \dfrac{B}{B+7} = \dfrac{3}{4},$ $4B = 3B + 21,$ $B = 21,$ $Y = 28$
   $\dfrac{R}{B} = \dfrac{5}{3} = \dfrac{R}{21},$ $3R = 5 * 21,$ $R = 35,$ $21 + 28 + 35 = 84$

10. Direct and Inverse Relationships (Variation)

10.1 Direct Variation

A Direct Variation is a relationship between two variables x and y, where as x increases y increases, or as x decreases y decreases, at a constant rate.

Direct Variation Formula:

$$\frac{x}{y} = k, \; k \text{ is a non-zero constant,} \quad \text{or} \quad \frac{y_1}{x_1} = \frac{y_2}{x_2} \text{ as in chapter 9. Ratio.}$$

ex.1 The circumference, c, of a circle varies directly as its radius, r. When r is 12cm, the c is 75.40cm, and what is c, when r is 18cm?

Solution: c varies directly as r :

$$\therefore \quad \frac{c_1}{r_1} = \frac{c_2}{r_2} \; , \qquad \frac{75.40}{12} = \frac{c_2}{18}$$

by cross multiplication:

$$18 * 75.40 = 12 * c_2, \qquad 1356.48 = 12c_2, \quad c_2 = 113.1cm$$

10.2 Inverse Variations

Inverse Variation is a relationship in which the variable y varies inversely (indirectly) as x: as x increases, y decreases, and the product of x and y remains a constant.

Indirect Variation Formula:

$$xy = k, \; k \text{ is a non-zero constant, or} \quad x_1 * y_1 = x_2 * y_2$$
ex. $xy = 15$ is an indirect relationship.

ex.1 If m varies inversely as n, and $m = 6$ as $n = 22$, what is m when $n = 12$?

Solution: m varies inversely as n:

$$\therefore \quad m_1 * n_1 = m_2 * n_2, \; 6 * 22 = m_2 * 12, \; \text{divide both sides by 12:}$$

$$\therefore \quad m_2 = \frac{132}{12} = 11$$

ex.2 Speed and time varies inversely, the faster the speed, the less time is needed. If it takes a family 15 hours driving at 55mi/hr to reach a vacation spot, how many hours will it take for driving at 70mi/hr on average?

a) 19.0   b) 16.5   c) 14.2   d) 13.2   e) 11.8

Solution: s varies inversely as t:

$$\therefore \quad s_1 * t_1 = s_2 * t_2, \; 55 * 15 = 70 * t_2, \text{divide both sides by 70:}$$

$$\therefore \quad t_2 = \frac{825}{70} = 11.8h$$

The correct answer is (e).

10.3   Practice and Solutions

1. The number of boxes required to pack oranges varies directly as the quantity of oranges. If packing 600 oranges needs 15 boxes, what is the least number of boxes needed to pack 950 oranges?

    (A)   35
    (B)   27
    (C)   24
    (D)   20
    (E)   19

2. A school claimed to have its teacher to student ratio of 1:15 when it had 600 students. If 270 more students joined, how many more teachers should be hired to maintain that ratio?

    (A)   18
    (B)   15
    (C)   12
    (D)   6
    (E)   3

3. Ian and Josh plan to work 8 hours a day to complete a landscape project in 12 days. Due to the change in weather, they have to finish the work within 4 days, how many people should they ask to help working 8 hours a day?

    (A)   7
    (B)   4
    (C)   3
    (D)   2
    (E)   1

4. If y varies inversely as x, and when $x = 8a$, $y = 3b + 5$, what is y in terms of a and b when x is 2?

    (A) $6ab + 5a$
    (B) $10a(b + 1)$
    (C) $12ab + a$
    (D) $4a(3b + 5)$
    (E) $2a(6b + 5)$

5. If $xy = 15$, which of the following must be true?

    I. y varies inversely as x
    II. y gets bigger as x gets bigger.
    III. When x is 3 times bigger, y is 3 times smaller.

    (A)   I only
    (B)   II only
    (C)   III only
    (D)   I and II only
    (E)   I and III only

Solutions to Practice 10.3: 1(C), 2(A), 3(B), 4(D), 5(E)

1. The number of boxes required to pack oranges varies directly as the quantity of oranges. If packing 600 oranges needs 15 boxes, what is the least number of boxes needed to pack 950 oranges?

   (A) 35
   (B) 27
   (C) 24
   (D) 20
   (E) 19

   Let B = number of boxes, O = number of oranges

   For direct variation: $\frac{O_1}{B_1} = \frac{O_2}{B_2}$, $\frac{600}{15} = \frac{950}{B_2}$

   By cross multiplication: $B_2 = \frac{15*950}{600} = 23.75 \approx 24$

2. A school claimed to have its teacher to student ratio of 1:15 when it had 600 students. If 270 more students joined, how many more teachers should be hired to maintain that ratio?

   (A) 18
   (B) 15
   (C) 12
   (D) 6
   (E) 3

   Let T = number of teachers, S = number of students

   $\frac{T}{S} = \frac{1}{15}$. for 600 students: $\frac{1}{15} = \frac{T}{600}$, $T = \frac{600}{15} = 40$ teachers

   $\frac{1}{15} = \frac{T}{600+270}$, $T = \frac{1*870}{15} = 58$, $58 - 40 = 18$ more Teachers.

3. Ian and Josh plan to work 8 hours a day to complete a landscape project in 12 days. Due to the change in weather, they have to finish the work within 4 days, how many people should they ask to help working 8 hours a day?

   (A) 7
   (B) 4
   (C) 3
   (D) 2
   (E) 1

   Inverse variation: Same project, more people, less days.
   Let P = number of people, D = number of days
   $P_1 * D_1 * 8 = P_2 * D_2 * 8$, $2 * 12 * \cancel{8} = P_2 * 4 * \cancel{8}$,
   $P_2 = \frac{24}{4} = 6$, $6 - 2 = 4$ more people to help

4. If y varies inversely as x, and when $x = 8a$, $y = 3b + 5$, what is y in terms of a and b when x equals 2?

   (A) $6ab + 5a$
   (B) $10a(b+1)$
   (C) $12ab + a$
   (D) $4a(3b+5)$
   (E) $2a(6b+5)$

   For inverse variation: $x_1 * y_1 = x_2 * y_2$
   $8a * (3b + 5) = 2 * y_2$, divide both sides by 2:
   $y_2 = \frac{8a(b+5)}{2} = 4a(3b+5)$

5. If $xy = 15$, which of the following must be true?

   I. y varies inversely as x
   II. y gets bigger as x gets bigger.
   III. When x is 3 times bigger, y is 3 times smaller.

   (A) I only
   (B) II only
   (C) III only
   (D) I and II only
   (E) I and III only

   I. True: Since $xy = a$ constant
   II. False: y should be smaller when x gets bigger
   III. True: for $x * y = 15$, $3x * \frac{y}{3} = 15$
   ∴ I and III only.

11. Number lines

ex.1 $x < 2$:

x is less than -2 (-2 is not included, so it`s an open circle)

ex.2 $x \geq -2.0$:

x is greater than or equal to -2.0 (-2 is included, so it's a closed circle)

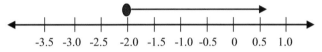

ex.3 $x < -3$ or $x \geq 1$:

x is smaller than-3 or greater or equal to 1

ex.4 $-4 \leq x < 3$:

x is greater or equal to -4 and smaller than 3

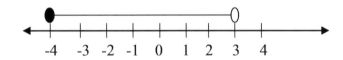

ex.5 $\boxed{|x| \leq 1 \quad \text{means} \quad -1 \leq x \leq 1}$ (see Algebra 9. & 10.)

ex.6 $\boxed{|x| \geq 1 \quad \text{means} \quad x \leq -1 \text{ or } x \geq 1}$ (see Algebra 9. & 10.)

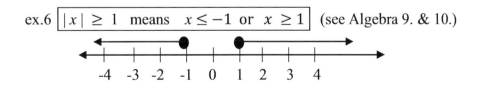

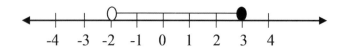

ex.7 Which of the following corresponds to the values represented on the number line above?

a) $x > -2$ b) $x \leq 3$ c) $-2 < x \leq 3$ d) $x < -2$ or $x \geq 3$ e) $x \geq 3$

Solution: Since x is greater than -2 and smaller or equal to 3,
The correct answer is (c).

ex.8 In the number line below, how much longer is $\overline{AB}$ than $\overline{XY}$?

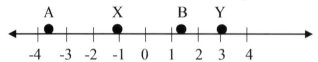

a) 0.5   b) 1.0   c) 1.5   d) 2.0   e) 2.5

Solution: Since A $= -3.5$ and B $= 1.5$, $\therefore$ Length of $\overline{AB}$:
$$1.5 - (-3.5) = 1.5 + 3.5 = 5 \, units$$

Length of $\overline{XY}$:
$$3 - (-1) = 3 + 1 = 4 \, units$$
$$AB - XY = 5 - 4 = 1 \, unit$$

The correct answer is (b).

ex.9 In the number line below, what is the length of $\overline{AB}$?

a) $\dfrac{1}{4}$ b) $\dfrac{3}{4}$ c) 1   d) $\dfrac{3}{2}$ e) $\dfrac{5}{2}$

Solution: From $-\dfrac{3}{4}$ to $\dfrac{1}{4}$, the total length is:

$$\frac{1}{4} - \left(-\frac{3}{4}\right) = \frac{1}{4} + \frac{3}{4} = \frac{4}{4} = 1$$

and there are 4 scales between these two numbers,
$\therefore$ each scale is $1 \div 4 = \dfrac{1}{4}$
There are 6 scales from A to B
$\therefore$ length of AB $= 6 * \dfrac{1}{4} = \dfrac{6}{4} = \dfrac{3}{2}$

The correct answer is (d).

11.1 Practice and Solutions

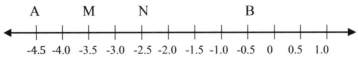

1. On the number line above, MN represents what fraction of AB?

   (A) $\frac{1}{5}$

   (B) $\frac{1}{4}$

   (C) $\frac{2}{5}$

   (D) $\frac{1}{2}$

   (E) $\frac{3}{5}$

2. On the number line above, what is the distance from the mid-point of AM to the mid-point of NB?

   (A) 4.0

   (B) 3.5

   (C) 2.5

   (D) 2.0

   (E) 1.5

3. Which of the following corresponds to the values represented on the number line above?

   (A) $x \leq -3.5 \ \ or \ \ x > -0.5$

   (B) $x < -3.5 \ \ or \ \ x > -0.5$

   (C) $-3.5 \leq x \leq -0.5$

   (D) $-3.5 < x < -0.5$

   (E) $-3.5 \leq x < -0.5$

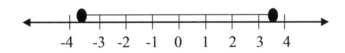

4. Which of the following corresponds to the values represented on the number line above?

   (A) $x \leq -3.5$

   (B) $x \geq 3.5$

   (C) $x \leq -3.5 \ \ or \ \ x \geq 3.5$

   (D) $-3.5 < x \leq 3.5$

   (E) $|x| - 1 \leq 2.5$

Solutions to 11.1 Practice: 1(B), 2(C), 3(A), 4(E)

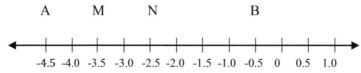

1. On the number line above, MN represents what fraction of AB?

(A) $\frac{1}{5}$

(B) $\frac{1}{4}$

(C) $\frac{2}{5}$

(D) $\frac{1}{2}$

(E) $\frac{3}{5}$

$$AB = -0.5 - (-4.5) = 4.0$$
$$MN = -2.5 - (-3.5)$$
$$= 1.0$$
$$\frac{MN}{AB} = \frac{1}{4}$$

2. On the number line above, what is the distance from the mid-point of AM to the mid-point of NB?

(A)   4.0

(B)   3.5

(C)   2.5

(D)   2.0

(E)   1.5

$$Midpoint\ of\ AM = \frac{(-4.5) + (-3.5)}{2} = -4.0$$
$$Midpoint\ of\ NB = \frac{(-2.5) + (-0.5)}{2} = -1.5$$
$$Distance\ between = |-4.0 - (-1.5)| = 2.5$$

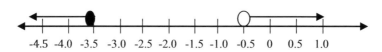

3. Which of the following corresponds to the values represented on the number line above?

(A) $x \le -3.5 \ \ or \ \ x > -0.5$

(B) $x < -3.5 \ \ or \ \ x > -0.5$

(C) $-3.5 \le x \le -0.5$

(D) $-3.5 < x < -0.5$

(E) $-3.5 \le x < -0.5$

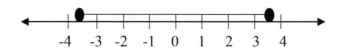

4. Which of the following corresponds to the values represented on the number line above?

(A) $x \le -3.5$

(B) $x \ge 3.5$

(C) $x \le -3.5 \ or \ x \ge 3.5$

(D) $-3.5 < x \le 3.5$

(E) $|x| - 1 \le 2.5$

$$-3.5 \le x \le 3.5$$
$$|x| \le 3.5$$
$$|x| - 1 \le 3.5 - 1$$
$$|x| - 1 \le 2.5$$

12. Sets

Set is a collection of elements.

Union (∪) of two sets : a set of elements which occur in either set or both.
Intersection (∩) of two sets : a set of elements which occur in both sets.

ex.1 Let set A = { 1, 3, 5, 6 }   and   set B = { 2, 4, 6 }

The Union of A and B, or A ∪ B= { 1, 2, 3, 4, 5, 6 }
The Intersection of A and B, or A ∩ B = { 6 }

Venn diagram illustration: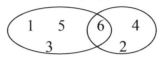

ex.2 Among all the grade ten students in a school, 37 take English, 39 take Math, and 19 take Social Studies. 25 take both English and Math, 7 take both English and Social, and 13 take both Math and Social. 5 students take all three subjects. How many grade ten students are in the school?

a) 95   (b) 90   (c) 71   (d) 68   (e) 55

Solutions: The best way to solve this problem is to draw a Venn diagram with 3 circles as in the following. Then enter the numbers into each area as:

1. First enter 5 for all three subjects in the middle.
2. Then enter English and Math only: $25 - 5 = 20$
3. Then enter English and Social only: $7 - 5 = 2$
4. Then enter Math and Social only: $13 - 5 = 8$
5. Then enter English only: $37 - 5 - 20 - 2 = 10$
6. Then enter Math only: $39 - 5 - 20 - 8 = 6$
7. Then enter Social only: $19 - 5 - 2 - 8 = 4$
8. Add all the numbers: $5 + 20 + 2 + 8 + 10 + 6 + 4 = 55$

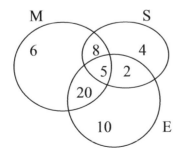

The correct answer is (e).

12.1 Practice and Solutions

1. Set A consists of all the right handed students in a class room, while set B consists of all the students wearing glasses in the room. What is the intersection of A and B?
    - (A) all the right handed students
    - (B) all the students wearing glasses
    - (C) all the right handed students wearing glasses
    - (D) all the right handed students or all the students wearing glasses
    - (E) some right handed students wearing glasses

2. Set A is all the integers from 10 to 20, and set B is all the positive integers less than 30 and divisible by 3. Which of the following represents A ∩ B?
    - (A) { 3, 6, 9, 12, 15, 18, 21, 24, 27 }
    - (B) { 3, 6, 9, 12, 15, 18}
    - (C) { 10, 12, 15, 18, 20 }
    - (D) { 12, 15, 18}
    - (E) { 3 }

3. In the figure on the right, circle S represents students participating in sports, M students in music, and F students in Fine Arts. Which of the following represents students in both music and fine arts but not sports?

    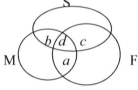

         I. set d II. set a III. set c
    - (A) I only
    - (B) II only
    - (C) III only
    - (D) I and III only
    - (E) II and III only

4. Set A is all real numbers in the range of $-3 \le x \le 12$, and set B is $x \ge 5$. Which of the following represents the union of A and B?
    - (A) $-3 < x \le 5$
    - (B) $5 \le x \le 12$
    - (C) $-3 \le x \le 12$
    - (D) $x > 5$
    - (E) $x \ge -3$

5. A conference room has 97 people. 58 of them speak English, 24 speak French and 35 speak Spanish. 7 of them speak both English and French, 11 speak both English and Spanish, and 5 speak both French and Spanish. 3 speak all three languages. How many people in the room speak only one language?
    - (A) 80
    - (B) 72
    - (C) 65
    - (D) 43
    - (E) 37

Solutions to 12.1 Practice: 1(C), 2 (D), 3(B), 4(E), 5(A)

1. Set A consists of all the right handed students in a class room, while set B consists of all the students wearing glasses in the room. What is the intersection of A and B?

   (A)   all the right handed students
   (B)   all the students wearing glasses
   (C)   all the right handed students wearing glasses
   (D)   all the right handed students or all the students wearing glasses
   (E)   some right handed students wearing glasses

   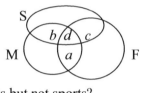

   A:right handed   B:glasses

   right handed with glasses

2. Set A is all the integers from 10 to 20, and set B is all the positive integers less than 30 and divisible by 3. Which of the following represents A ∩ B?

   (A)   { 3, 6, 9, 12, 15, 18, 21, 24, 27 }
   (B)   { 3, 6, 9, 12, 15, 18}
   (C)   { 10, 12, 15, 18, 20 }
   (D)   { 12, 15, 18}
   (E)   { 3 }

   > $A = \{10,11,\underline{12},13,14,\underline{15},16,17,\underline{18},19,20\}$
   > $B = \{3,6,9,\underline{12},\underline{15},\underline{18},21,24,27\}$
   > Since 12,15,18 *are in both sets,* (D) *is* A ∩ B

3. In the figure on the right, circle S represents students participating in sports, M represents students in music, and F represents students in Fine Arts. Which of the following represents students in both music and fine arts but not sports?

   | I. set *d* | II. set *a* | III. set *c* |

   (A)   I only
   (B)   II only
   (C)   III only
   (D)   I and II only
   (E)   II and III only

   > $M \cap F = a \cup d = $ *students in music and art*
   > *Students in set d have to be removed since they*
   > *are in sports so only set a remains.*

4. Set A is all real numbers in the range of $-3 \leq x \leq 10$, and set B is $x \geq 5$. Which of the following represents the union of A and B?

   (A) $-3 < x \leq 5$
   (B) $5 \leq x \leq 10$
   (C) $-3 \leq x \leq 10$
   (D) $x > 5$
   (E) $x \geq -3$

5. A conference room has 97 people. 58 of them speak English, 24 speak French and 35 speak Spanish. 7 of them speak both English and French, 11 speak both English and Spanish, and 5 speak both French and Spanish. 3 speak all three languages. How many people in the room speak only one language?

   (A)   80
   (B)   72
   (C)   65
   (D)   43
   (E)   37

   > 15 *speak only French*
   > 43 *speak only English*
   > 22 *speak only Spanish*
   > 80 *speak only* 1 *language*

   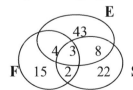

13. Sequences

Arithmetic Sequence:

A sequence in which each term progresses to the next term by **adding** a number.

ex.1　　4, 8, 12, 16, ...　　(adding 4)

ex.2　　15, 10, 5, 0, −5, −10, ... (adding −5)

Geometric Sequence:

A sequence in which each term progresses to the next term by **multiplying** a number.

ex.1　　3, 9, 27, 81, ...　　(multiplied by 3)

ex.2　　$32, 16, 8, 4, 2, \frac{1}{2}, \frac{1}{4}, ...$ (multiplied by $\frac{1}{2}$)

13.1 Arithmetic Sequences

In Arithmetic Sequences, each term progresses to the next by adding a constant number, which is called the **common difference**.

ex. 1.　5, 9, 13, 17, ...　　The common difference $= 4$

Notations:

a = the <u>first term</u>,　　d = the <u>common difference</u> ,

T_n = the nth term ($eg.$　T_4 = the 4th term)

In ex.1 :　$T_1 = 5$,　$T_2 = 9$,　$T_3 = 13$,　$T_4 = 17$,

$\quad\quad\quad a = 5$,　the first term

$\quad\quad\quad \boxed{d = T_2 - T_1} = 9 - 5 = 4$,　　or　　$d = 13 - 9 = 4$

The formula for obtaining any term:　$\boxed{T_n = a + (n - 1)d}$

To find　T_6　or　T_{21}:

$T_6 = a + (n - 1) * d = 5 + (6 - 1) * 4 = 5 + 20 = 25$

$T_{21} = a + (n - 1) * d = 5 + (21 - 1) * 4 = 5 + 80 = 85$

<u>Typical problems in Arithmetic Sequence</u>:

1. <u>Given an arithmetic sequence, find the required term</u>:

ex.2　Given a sequence of　$11, 5, -1, ...,$　find the 13th term:

Since　$a = 11$,　and　$d = 5 - 11 = -6$　or　$(-1) - 5 = -6$

$\therefore\ T_{13} = a + (n - 1) * d = 11 + (13 - 1) * (-6)$

$\quad\quad\quad = 11 + 12 * (-6)$

$\quad\quad\quad = 11 - 72 = -61$

$\therefore\ T_{13} = -61$

2. <u>Given a two terms in an arithmetic sequence, find the required term:</u>

ex.3 Given the second term is 8, and the 5th term is 23,
find the 3rd term in the arithmetic sequence.

Solution: given: $T_2 = 8$ and $T_5 = 23$

$T_2 = a + (2 - 1) * d = 8,$ ∴ $a + d = 8$ (1)
$T_5 = a + (5 - 1) * d = 23,$ ∴ $a + 4d = 23$ (2)
solve for a and d: (See Algebra 3.2)
equations $(2) - (1)$:
$4d - d = 23 - 8$ ∴ $3d = 15,$ $\boxed{d = 5}$
sub $d = 5$ into equation (1): $a + d = 8,$
∴ $a + 5 = 8,$ $\boxed{a = 3}$
∴ $T_n = a + (n - 1) * d = 3 + (n - 1)5,$
$T_3 = 3 + (3 - 1) * 5 = 13$
∴ The 3rd term is 13

13.2 Geometric Sequences

In geometric sequences, each term progresses to the next by multiplying the previous term by a constant number, which is called the **common ratio**.

ex.1 3, 6, 12, 24, 48, … The common ratio $= 2$

Notations:

a = the <u>first term</u> , r = the <u>common ratio</u> ,
T_n = the nth term ($eg.$ $T_4 = 4^{th}$ term)

In ex.1 $T_1 = 3,$ $T_2 = 6,$ $T_3 = 12,$ $T_4 = 24,$ $T_5 = 48$

$a = 3$

$\boxed{r = T_n \div T_{(n-1)}}$: dividing any term by its previous term

∴ $r = T_2 \div T_1 = 6 \div 3 = 2,$ or $r = 48 \div 24 = 2$

The formula for obtaining any term:

$$\boxed{T_n = a * r^{(n-1)}}$$

To find T_6 or T_{11} :
$T_6 = T_5 * 2 = 48 * 2 = 96,$ or $T_6 = a * r^{(6-1)} = 3 * 2^5 = 96$
$T_{11} = a * r^{(11-1)} = 3 * 2^{10} = 3 * 1024 = 3072$

Typical problems in Geometric Sequences:

1. Given a geometric sequence, find the required term:

ex.2 Given a geometric sequence $44, 11, \frac{11}{4}, \dots$, find the 7th term:

$$a = 44, \ \& \ r = 11 \div 44 = \frac{1}{4} \quad \text{or} \quad \frac{11}{4} \div 11 = \frac{11}{4} * \frac{1}{11} = \frac{1}{4}$$

$$\therefore \ T_7 = a * r^{(7-1)} = 44 * \left(\frac{1}{4}\right)^{(7-1)} = 44 * \left(\frac{1}{4}\right)^6 = \frac{44 \times 1}{4096} = \frac{11}{1024}$$

$$\therefore \ T_7 = \frac{11}{1024}$$

2. Given a two terms in a geometric sequence, find the required term:

ex.3 Given $T_2 = 4$ and $T_5 = 32$,
list the first 5 terms of the geometric sequence.

$$T_2 = a * r^{(2-1)} = 4, \qquad a * r = 4 \qquad (1)$$
$$T_5 = a * r^{(5-1)} = 32, \qquad a * r^4 = 32 \quad (2)$$

equations $(2) \div (1)$: $\quad \frac{ar^4}{ar} = \frac{r^4}{r} = \frac{32}{4}$

$$\therefore \ r^3 = 8, \quad \boxed{r = 2}$$

sub $r = 2$ into equation (1):
$$a * r = 4, \quad \therefore \ a * 2 = 4, \quad \boxed{a = 2}$$
$$\therefore \ T_n = a * r^{(n-1)} = 2 * 2^{(n-1)},$$
$$T_3 = 2 * 2^{(3-1)} = 8,$$
$$T_4 = 2 * 2^{(4-1)} = 16, \quad \& \quad T_1 = a = 2$$
$$\therefore \ \text{The first 5 terms are:} \quad 2, \ 4, \ 8, \ 16, \ 32$$

ex.4 If the computer price dropped 50% every year on average, what would a $3499 computer be worth in 9 years?
a) $1749.5 \quad b) $992.93 \quad c) $523.80 \quad d) $89.9 \quad e) $6.83

Solution: This is a geometric sequence, since the price of the subsequent year is obtained by multiplying $\frac{1}{2}$:

3499, 1749.5, 874.75, ...

$n = 10$ (after the 1st term in 9 years will be the 10th term), $a = 3499$, $r = 50\%$ or $\frac{1}{2}$

since $T_n = a * r^{(n-1)} = 3499 * \left(\frac{1}{2}\right)^{n-1}$

$$T_{10} = 3499 * \left(\frac{1}{2}\right)^{10-1} = 3499 * \left(\frac{1}{2}\right)^9$$
$$= \$6.83$$

The correct answer is (e).

13.3 Other Sequences

Some sequences are neither Arithmetic nor Geometric, but sequences which can be determined by a given formula.

ex.1 Each term in a sequence is obtained by squaring the term number and adding 7. Which of the following represents the 11th term in the sequence?

a) 18   b) 49   c) 56   d) 128   e) 142

Solution: Let $n =$ term number ($eg.$ $n = 2$ means the 2nd term)

$$\therefore \quad T_n = n^2 + 7$$
$$\therefore \quad T_{11} = 11^2 + 7 = 128$$

The correct answer is (d).

ex.2 Using the formula in ex.1, list the first 5 terms of the sequence.

Solution: Since $T_n = n^2 + 7$

$$T_1 = 1^2 + 7 = 8$$
$$T_2 = 2^2 + 7 = 11$$
$$T_3 = 3^2 + 7 = 16$$
$$T_4 = 4^2 + 7 = 23$$
$$T_5 = 5^2 + 7 = 32$$
$$\therefore \quad 8, 11, 16, 23, 32, ... \text{ (neither Arithmetic nor Geometric)}$$

ex.3 In a sequence, 5 is the first term, and each term after the first term can be obtained by 2 times the sum of the preceding term and 7.

i.) list the first 3 terms

Solution:

$$T_1 = 5$$
$$T_2 = 2(T_1 + 7) = 2(5 + 7) = 24$$
$$T_3 = 2(T_2 + 7) = 2(24 + 7) = 62$$
$$\therefore \text{ first 3 terms: } 5, 24, 62$$

ii.) Knowing that the 6th term is 594, what is the 5th term?

Solution:

$$\text{Since } T_6 = 2(T_5 + 7)$$
$$T_6 = 2T_5 + 14$$
$$T_5 = \frac{T_6 - 14}{2} = \frac{594 - 14}{2} = 290$$

This is a recursive problem: each term other than the first term can be obtained by using the value in the preceding term.

13.4   Practice and Solutions

1.   In an Arithmetic Sequence, $T_1 = 8$, and $T_4 = 23$, what is T_3 ?

2.   In an sequence of 3, 12, 48, ... , what is T_{12} ?

3.   If $T_n = 3(n-1)$, what is T_6 ?

4.   In a sequence of 6, 13, 20, 27, ... , what is the 26th term?
   (A)   181
   (B)   180
   (C)   177
   (D)   153
   (E)   137

5.   Tim got \$500 from grandma at his 1st birthday and \$50 for each later birthday. How much money would Tim receive from grandma by his 18th birthday?
   (A)   \$1000
   (B)   \$1350
   (C)   \$1400
   (D)   \$2800
   (E)   \$3500

6.   In a sequence of 7, 28, 112, m, n, ..., what is the value of $2m + n$?
   (A)   448
   (B)   1792
   (C)   2240
   (D)   2688
   (E)   7168

7.   A bacteria culture contained 200 cells initially, and would double every 3 hours. How many cells would there be 24 hours later?
   (A)   1600
   (B)   4800
   (C)   19860
   (D)   25600
   (E)   51200

8.   The production of a cell-phone company multiplies every month by the same number in the year of 2005. If it made 300 in February, and 8100 in May, how many cell phones did it make in December of 2005?
   (A)   3600
   (B)   273,000
   (C)   1,968,300
   (D)   7,980,500
   (E)   17,714,700

Solutions to 13.4 Practice: 1 (18), 2 (12582912), 3 (15), 4(A), 5(B), 6(D), 7(E), 8(E)

1. $T_1 = 8$, $T_4 = 23$, $a = 8$, $T_4 = 8 + 3 * d = 23$, $d = 5$, $T_4 = 8 + 2 * 5 = 18$

2. $3, 12, 48, \dots$, $a = 3$, $d = 12 \div 3 = 4$, $\therefore T_{12} = 3 * 4^{11} = 12582912$

3. $T_n = 3(n - 1)$, $T_6 = 3(6 - 1) = 3 * 5 = 15$

4. In a sequence of $6, 13, 20, 27, \dots$, what is the 26th term?

   (A) 181
   (B) 180
   (C) 177
   (D) 153
   (E) 137

   > *The sequence is arithmetic, with the*
   > *first term:* $a = 6$ *and the*
   > *common difference:* $d = 13 - 6 = 7$.
   > *Since* $t_n = a + (n - 1)d$, *for* $n = 26$:
   > $t_{26} = 6 + (26 - 1) * 7 = 6 + 25 * 7 = 6 + 175 = 181$

5. Tim got \$500 from grandma at his 1st birthday and \$50 for each later birthday. How much money in total would Tim receive from grandma by his 18th birthday?

   (A) \$1000
   (B) \$1350
   (C) \$1400
   (D) \$2800
   (E) \$3500

   > *1st birthday* $= \$500$
   > *2nd birthday* $= \$500 + \$50$
   > *3rd birthday* $= \$500 + 2(\$50)$
   > *... following the pattern,*
   > *18th birthday* $= \$500 + 17(\$50) = \$1350$

6. In a sequence of $7, 28, 112, m, n, \dots$, what is the value of $2m + n$?

   (A) 448
   (B) 1792
   (C) 2240
   (D) 2688
   (E) 7168

   > *The sequence is geometric:* $a = 7$ *and* $r = \dfrac{28}{7} = 4$
   > *To find m, we can multiply* 112 *by* $r = 4$
   > $m = 112 * 4 = 448$. *Similarly:* $n = m * 4 = 1792$
   > $2m + n = 896 + 1792 = 2688$

7. A bacteria culture contained 200 cells initially, and would double every 3 hours. How many cells would there be 24 hours later?

   (A) 1600
   (B) 4800
   (C) 19860
   (D) 25600
   (E) 51200

   > *In 24 hours the doubling will happen 8 times*
   > *(since* $24 = 3 * 8$). *This is a geometric sequence*
   > *with* $a = 200$ *and* $d = 2$, *Since* $t_n = a + (n - 1)d$
   > $t_9 = 200 * 2^8 = 51200$ *(note: this is the* 9th *term,* T_9)

8. The production of a cell-phone company multiplies every month by the same number in the year of 2005. If it made 300 in February, and 8100 in May, how many cell phones did it make in December of 2005?

   (A) 3600
   (B) 273,000
   (C) 1,968,300
   (D) 7,980,500
   (E) 17,714,700

   > *The sequence is geometric. Let* $r =$ *the comom ratio*
   > *Feb* $= 300$, *Mar* $= 300r$, *April* $= (300r)r = 300r^2$
   > *May* $= 300r^3 = 8100$, $r^3 = 27$, $r = 3$
   > *Dec* $= 300r^{10} = 200(3)^{10} = 17,714,700$

14. Special Symbols

Some problems with special symbol like ♥ or ◆ are used on the SAT. Though they look bizarre and intimidating, they are actually quite easy to solve. It is important to first understand how the symbols are defined, then work accordingly.

ex.1 If $a \blacklozenge b = a^2 - b^2$, what is the value of $6 \blacklozenge 3$?

Solution: Since $a \blacklozenge b = a^2 - b^2$,

∴ ◆ defines the difference of the squares

∴ $6 \blacklozenge 3 = 6^2 - 3^2$

$= 36 - 9 = 25$

ex.2 If $x \bullet y = \dfrac{xy}{(x+y)}$, which of the following must be equal to $4 \bullet 6$?

a) 2.4 b) 4.2 c) 8.0 d) 16.2 e) 64.6

Solution: since $x \bullet y = \dfrac{xy}{(x+y)}$,

∴ ● defines the product of two operands divided by their sum

∴ $4 \bullet 6 = \dfrac{4*6}{(4+6)} = \dfrac{24}{10} = 2.4$

The correct answer is (a).

ex.3 If $x \leftrightarrow y = (x+y)^2$, for what value of a, $a \leftrightarrow a = 100$?

I. -5

II. 5

III. 10

a) I only b) II only c) III only d) I and II e) II and III

Solution: since $x \leftrightarrow y = (x+y)^2$

∴ $\leftrightarrow$ defines the square of the sum of the two operands

∴ $a \leftrightarrow a = (a+a)^2 = (2a)^2 = 4a^2 = 100$

$4a^2 = 100$, (see Algebra 3.1)

$a^2 = \dfrac{100}{4} = 25$

$a = \pm\sqrt{25}$

$a = \pm 5$

The correct answer is (d).

14.1 Practice and Solutions

1. If $m \propto n = 7(mn - 7)$, what is the value of $9 \propto 2$?
   (A) 77
   (B) 58
   (C) 54
   (D) 38
   (E) 18

2. What is $12 \ \forall \ 36$, if $p \ \forall \ q = (\sqrt{p} + \sqrt{q})^2$?
   (A) 39.5
   (B) 72.8
   (C) 81.0
   (D) 89.6
   (E) 100.0

3. If $x \blacklozenge y = \frac{(x-y)}{4}$, then what is a in terms of b for $a \blacklozenge b = 27$?
   (A) $27 + b$
   (B) $27 - b$
   (C) $108 - b$
   (D) $108 + b$
   (E) $4b$

4. If $a \blacksquare b = \frac{2ab}{(a+2b)}$, what is the value of b for $2 \blacksquare b = 1\frac{3}{5}$?
   (A) 12
   (B) 6
   (C) 4
   (D) 3
   (E) 2

5. If $x \boxplus y = 3(x + y)$, and $x \boxminus y = 3(x - y)$, what is $(a \boxplus b) \boxminus c$?
   (A) $3a + 3b - 3c$
   (B) $9a + 9b - 3c$
   (C) $9a + 9b - 9c$
   (D) $3a + 3b + 3c$
   (E) $9a + 9b + 9c$

Solutions to 14.1 Practice: 1(A), 2(D), 3(D), 4(C), 5(B)

1. If $m \propto n = 7(mn - 7)$, what is the value of $9 \propto 2$?
   (A) 77
   (B) 58
   (C) 54
   (D) 38
   (E) 18

   $m = 9.\ n = 2$
   $9 \propto 2 = 7(9*2 - 7)$
   $= 7(18 - 7)$
   $= 7 * 11 = 77$

2. What is $12 \ \forall \ 36$, if $p \ \forall \ q = (\sqrt{p} + \sqrt{q})^2$?
   (A) 39.5
   (B) 72.8
   (C) 81.0
   (D) 89.6
   (E) 100.0

   $p = 12, \qquad q = 36$
   $p \forall q = (\sqrt{12} + \sqrt{36})^2$ *Use calculator:*
   $= (\sqrt{12} + 6)^2 \approx 89.6$

3. If $x \blacklozenge y = \frac{(x-y)}{4}$, then what is a in terms of b for $a \blacklozenge b = 27$?
   (A) $27 + b$
   (B) $27 - b$
   (C) $108 - b$
   (D) $108 + b$
   (E) $4b$

   $a \blacklozenge b = \frac{a-b}{4} = 27$, *Multiple both sides by* 4:
   $a - b = 108$
   $a = 108 + b$

4. If $a \blacksquare b = \frac{2ab}{(a+2b)}$, what is the value of b for $2 \blacksquare b = 1\frac{3}{5}$?
   (A) 12
   (B) 6
   (C) 4
   (D) 3
   (E) 2

   $a = 2, \qquad 2 \blacksquare b = \frac{2*2*b}{2+2b} = 1\frac{3}{5} = \frac{8}{5}$
   $\frac{4b}{(2+2b)} \diagdown \diagup \frac{8}{5}$ (*by cross multiplication*):
   $20b = 16 + 16b, \quad 4b = 16;\ b = 4$

5. If $x \boxplus y = 3(x + y)$, and $x \boxminus y = 3(x - y)$, what is $(a \boxplus b) \boxminus c$?
   (A) $3a + 3b - 3c$
   (B) $9a + 9b - 3c$
   (C) $9a + 9b - 9c$
   (D) $3a + 3b + 3c$
   (E) $9a + 9b + 9c$

   $(a \boxplus b) \boxminus c = (3(a + b)) \boxminus c$
   $= (3a + 3b) \boxminus c$
   $= 3((3a + 3b) - c)$
   $= 9a + 9b - 3c$

Algebra

1. Algebraic Operations

1.1 Addition and Subtraction (combining like terms)

ex.1 Simplify: $5x^2 + 3 + 2x^2 - 8$

$5x^2$ & $2x^2$ are like terms, so are 3 & -8

$\therefore\ 5x^2 + 3 + 2x^2 - 8\ =\ 7x^2 - 5$ is the simplest form

("$\therefore$" means "Therefore")

ex.2 Simplify: $4x^3 + 2x^2 - 3x^3 + 11 - 6x^2 + 7xy^2 + 5x^3 - 9xy^2 - 23$

$4x^3, -3x^3,$ & $5x^3$ are like terms

$2x^2$ & $-6x^2$ are like terms

$7xy^2$ & $-9xy^2$ are like terms

11 & -23 are like terms

$\therefore\ 4x^3 + 2x^2 - 3x^3 + 11 - 6x^2 + 7xy^2 + 5x^3 - 9xy^2 - 23$

$= 6x^3 - 4x^2 - 2xy^2 - 12$ is the simplest form

ex.3 If $(3x^2 - 5x + 4) - (7x^2 - x - 1) = -4x^2 - 11,$ then $x =$

    a) -4 b) -3 c) 4 d) 5 e) 12

Solution: $(3x^2 - 5x + 4) - (7x^2 - x - 1) = -4x^2 - 11$

$3x^2 - 5x + 4 - 7x^2 + x + 1 = -4x^2 - 11$

$-4x^2 - 4x + 5 = -4x^2 - 11$ (see Algebra 2.1)

$-4x + 5 = -11;\ \ -4x = -11 - 5 = -16,$

divide both sides by -4: $\dfrac{-4x}{-4} = \dfrac{-16}{-4},\ \ \therefore\ x = 4$

The correct answer is (c).

1.2 Multiplication

ex.1 $2x^2 * 5x^3 = 10x^{2+3} = 10x^5$, $3xy^2 * 2xy = 6x^{1+1}y^{2+1} = 6x^2y^3$

(see also Algebra 8.1)

ex.2 $x(4x^2 - 3y) - 4y(x - y)$

$= 4x^3 - 3xy - 4xy + 4y^2$

$= 4x^3 - 7xy + 4y^2$

ex.3 $(x + 2) * (4x - 3) = 4x^2 - 3x + 8x - 6 = 4x^2 + 5x - 6$

ex.4 Which of the following is equivalent to $(2x - 2) * (4x + 2)$?

a) $4x^2 - 4x - 2$ b) $6x^2 + 4x - 4$ c) $8x^2 - 12x - 4$
d) $8x^2 - 4x - 4$ e) $10x^3 - 4x^2 + 4$

Solution: $(2x - 2) * (4x + 2)$
$$= 8x^2 + 4x - 8x - 4$$
$$= 8x^2 - 4x - 4$$

The correct answer is (d).

1.3   Division

ex.1 $\dfrac{x^3}{x^2} = x^{3-2} = x^1 = x$, $14x^3 \div 2x^4 = 7x^{3-4} = 7x^{-1} = \dfrac{7}{x}$

(see also Algebra 8.1)

ex.2 $\dfrac{3x^3 y^{\,5}}{(4x^2 y)^2} = \dfrac{3x^3 y^5}{16x^4 y^2} = \dfrac{3y^3}{16x}$

ex.3 $\dfrac{(5x^3 y^5)(3x^4 y)}{7x^3 y^7} = \dfrac{15x^{3+4} y^{5+1}}{7x^3 y^7} = \dfrac{15}{7} x^{7-3} y^{6-7} = \dfrac{15}{7} x^4 y^{-1} = \dfrac{15x^4}{7y}$

ex.4 If $\dfrac{2x^2 y^3 (3xy)}{(xy^2)^2} = 12$, for $xy \neq 0$, what is the value of x?

a) -4 b) -3 c) -1 d) 1 e) 2

Solution: $\dfrac{2x^2 y^3 (3xy)}{(xy^2)^2} = \dfrac{6x^3 y^4}{x^2 y^4} = 6x$ (see Algebra 8.1)

$\therefore\ 6x = 12$

$\therefore\ x = \dfrac{12}{6} = 2$

The correct answer is (e).

1.4   Practice and Solutions

1. $(2x^2 - 3x + 2) - (7x^2 - x - 7) =$
2. $2(4x^2 - 3y) - 4x(x - y) =$
3. $(3x - 2) * (5x - 3) =$
4. $\dfrac{(2x^3 y^4)(3x^3 y)}{7x^3 y^3} =$

5. If $3(2x^2 + 1) = 6x^2 + x$, what is the value of $2x$?
   (A) 3
   (B) 6
   (C) 8
   (D) 9
   (E) 12

6. Which of the following is equivalent to $\dfrac{4a^4 b^2}{a^2} * \dfrac{a}{2b^2}$?
   (F) $\dfrac{2}{b}$
   (G) $\dfrac{a^2}{2b}$
   (H) $\dfrac{a^2}{b}$
   (I) $\dfrac{2a^2}{b}$
   (J) $2a^3$

7. If $6a = 54$, what is $\dfrac{a^2}{3\sqrt{a}}$ equal to, for $a \neq 0$?
   (A) -9
   (B) -3
   (C) 9
   (D) 12
   (E) 27

8. Which of the following is equivalent to $(4x - 2)(5x + 2)$?
   (A) $20x^2 - 2x - 4$
   (B) $20x^2 - 10x + 2$
   (C) $20x^2 - 18x - 4$
   (D) $20x^2 + 2x + 4$
   (E) $20x^2 + 4x - 4$

9. If $\dfrac{5a^4 b}{(2ab^2)^3} = 2$, what is the value of a in terms of b?
   (A) $a = \dfrac{4}{\sqrt{5}} b^5$
   (B) $a = \dfrac{8}{5} b^4$
   (C) $a = \dfrac{16}{5} b^5$
   (D) $a = \dfrac{16}{2} b^5$
   (E) $a = \dfrac{32}{5} b^5$

Solutions to 1.4 Practice: 5(B), 6(E), 7(C), 8(A), 9(C)

1. $(2x^2 - 3x + 2) - (7x^2 - x - 7) = -5x^2 - 2x + 9$

2. $2(4x^2 - 3y) - 4x(x - y) = 4x^2 - 6y + 4xy$

3. $(3x - 2) * (5x - 3) = 15x^2 - 19x + 6$

4. $\dfrac{(2x^3y^4)(3x^3y)}{7x^3y^3} = \dfrac{6}{7}x^3y^2$, for x, $y \neq 0$

5. If $3(2x^2 + 1) = 6x^2 + x$, what is the value of $2x$?

   (A) 3

   (B) 6

   (C) 8

   (D) 9

   (E) 12

   $$3(2x^2 + 1) = 6x^2 + x$$
   $$6x^2 + 3 = 6x^2 + x$$
   $$3 = x$$
   $$2x = 6$$

6. Which of the following is equivalent to $\dfrac{4a^4b^2}{a^2} * \dfrac{a}{2b^2}$, for a, $b \neq 0$?

   (A) $\dfrac{2}{b}$

   (B) $\dfrac{a^2}{2b}$

   (C) $\dfrac{a^2}{b}$

   (D) $\dfrac{2a^2}{b}$

   (E) $2a^3$

   $$\frac{4a^4b^2}{a^2} * \frac{a}{2b^2}$$
   $$= \frac{4}{2}a^{5-3}b^{2-2}$$
   $$= 2a^3$$

7. If $6a = 54$, what is $\dfrac{a^2}{3\sqrt{a}}$ equal to, for $a \neq 0$?

   (A) -9

   (B) -3

   (C) 9

   (D) 12

   (E) 27

   $$6a = 54$$
   $$a = 9, \quad \sqrt{a} = 3$$
   $$\frac{a^2}{3\sqrt{a}} = \frac{81}{3*3} = 9$$

8. Which of the following is equivalent to $(4x - 2)(5x + 2)$?

   (A) $20x^2 - 2x - 4$

   (B) $20x^2 - 10x + 2$

   (C) $20x^2 - 18x - 4$

   (D) $20x^2 + 2x + 4$

   (E) $20x^2 + 4x - 4$

   $$(4x - 2)(5x + 2)$$
   $$= 20x^2 + 8x - 10x - 4$$
   $$= 20x^2 - 2x - 4$$

9. If $\dfrac{5a^4b}{(2ab^2)^3} = 2$, what is the value of a in terms of b, for a, $b \neq 0$?

   (A) $a = \dfrac{4}{\sqrt{5}}b^5$

   (B) $a = \dfrac{8}{5}b^4$

   (C) $a = \dfrac{16}{5}b^5$

   (D) $a = \dfrac{16}{2}b^5$

   (E) $a = \dfrac{32}{5}b^5$

   $$\frac{5a^4b}{(2ab^2)^3} = 2, \quad \frac{5a^4b}{8a^3b^6} = 2$$
   $$\frac{5a}{8b^5} = 2,$$
   $$5a = 16b^5, \quad a = \frac{16}{5}b^5$$

2. Solving Linear Equations

2.1 One Linear Equation

ex.1 If $x + 8 = 12$, what is the value of $2x + 5$?

    a) -4 b) 4   c) 12   d) 13   e) 15

Solution: solve for: $x + 8 = 12$ Keep x on the left, & move 8 to

$x = 12 - 8$ the right, and 8 changes sign, -8.

$\boxed{x = 4}$

then sub $x = 4$ *into* $2x + 5$

$\therefore\ 2x + 5 = 2(4) + 5 = 8 + 5 = 13$

The correct answer is (d).

ex.2 If $a + 2b = c - 3a$, what is b in terms of a and c?

    a) $\dfrac{4a}{c}$ b) $\dfrac{c-4a}{2}$ c) $\dfrac{c+4a}{2}$ d) $\dfrac{c+4a}{3}$ e) $\dfrac{4a}{3} - c$

Solution: $a + 2b = c - 3a$ Keep b on the left, & move a to right.

$2b = c - 3a - a$ a changes to $-a$.

$2b = c - 4a$

$\therefore\ b = \dfrac{c-4a}{2}$ (divide both sides by 2)

The correct answer is (b).

2.2 Systems of Linear Equations

By Elimination:

ex.1 If $x - y = 3$, *and* $2x + y = 21$, what is x + y equal to?

    a) 5   b) 8   c) 10   d) 11   e) 13

Solution: $x - y = 3$ (1)

$\underline{+\quad 2x + y = 21}$ (2)

$(1) + (2)$: $3x + 0 = 24$

$\therefore\ 3x = 24$

$\boxed{x = 8}$ (divide both sides by 3)

Sub $x = 8$ *into* (1):

$x - y = 3$

$\therefore\ 8 - y = 3,$

$-y = 3 - 8 = -5$ (8 becomes -8 when moves across)

$\boxed{y = 5}$ (divide both sides by -1)

$\therefore\ x + y = 8 + 5 = 13$

The correct answer is (e).

By Substitution:

ex.2 If $x - 2y = 3$, and $2x - 3y = 9$, what is the value of $\dfrac{x}{y}$?

a) 3   b) $\dfrac{8}{3}$ c) $\dfrac{7}{2}$ d) 4   e) $\dfrac{9}{2}$

Solution: $x - 2y = 3$ (1)

$2x - 3y = 9$ (2)

From (1): $x - 2y = 3$,

$\therefore$ $x = 3 + 2y$

Sub $x = 3 + 2y$ *into* (2):

$2x - 3y = 9$

$2(3 + 2y) - 3y = 9$

$6 + 4y - 3y = 9$

$y = 9 - 6 = 3,$ $\therefore$ $\boxed{y = 3}$

Sub $y = 3$ into (1):

$x - 2y = 3$

$x - 2(3) = 3$

$x = 3 + 6 = 9$

$\therefore$ $\boxed{x = 9}$

$\therefore$ $\dfrac{x}{y} = \dfrac{9}{3} = 3$

The correct answer is (a).

ex.3 If $2a - b - c = 2,$ $a + b = -1$ *and* $5b = -3c$, what is the value of abc ?

a) -45 b) -30 c) -8 d) 12   e) 24

Solution: from $a + b = -1,$ $a = -1 - b$ (1)

from $5b = -3c$, $c = -\dfrac{5b}{3}$ (2)

sub (1) and (2) into $2a - b - c = 2$

$\therefore$ $2(-1 - b) - b - (-\dfrac{5b}{3}) = 2$

$-2 - 2b - b + \dfrac{5b}{3} = 2$

$-3b + \dfrac{5b}{3} = 4$

multiplied both sides by 3:

$-9b + 5b = 12,$ $\therefore$ $-4b = 12,$ $\boxed{b = -3}$

sub into (1): $a = -1 - b = -1 - (-3) = 2,$ $\boxed{a = 2}$

sub into (2): $c = -\dfrac{5b}{3} = -\dfrac{5(-3)}{3} = 5,$ $\boxed{c = 5}$

$\therefore$ $abc = a * b * c = 2 * (-3) * 5 = -30$

The correct answer is (b).

2.3   Practice and Solutions

1. Solve for x: $x - 4 = 6 - x$
2. Solve for x: $3x + 5x - 14 = 10x$
3. Solve for a and b: $2a + b = 1$ and $a - b = 11$
4. Solve for x and y: $x - 2y = 15$ and $6x + 2y = 6$
5. Find b: $2a + b + 3c = 11,$ $a - 2b = 0$ and $5b - c = 4$

6. If $x - 4x = 6$, what is the value of x^2?
    (A) -4
    (B) -2
    (C) 4
    (D) 9
    (E) 16

7. If $p - 2q = 2$, and $3p + 2q = 46$, what is the value of $p - q$?
    (A) 2
    (B) 7
    (C) 13
    (D) 38
    (E) 54

8. If $x + 2y = 15$, and $z = 3x$, what is y in terms of z?
    (A) $15 - z$
    (B) $15 - \frac{z}{2}$
    (C) $\frac{45 - z}{3}$
    (D) $\frac{45 - z}{6}$
    (E) $\frac{45 - 3z}{6}$

9. If $a + b + c = 6,$ $a = 2c - 1$ and $c = b + 5$, what is the value of $a + b$?
    (A) -2
    (B) 3
    (C) 5
    (D) 6
    (E) 8

10. If $a^2 - b^2 = 45$, and $a + b = 15$, what is the value of $2(a - b)$?
    (A) -12
    (B) -8
    (C) 6
    (D) 9
    (E) 16

Solutions to 2.3: 1 (5), 2 (−7), 3 (4, −7), 4 (3, −6), 5 (1), 6(C), 7(B), 8(D), 9(B), 10(C)

1. $x - 4 = 6 - x$: $x + x = 6 + 4$, $2x = 10$, $\therefore x = 5$

2. $3x + 5x - 14 = 10x$: $3x + 5x - 10x = 14$, $-2x = 14$, $x = -7$

3. $2a + b = 1$ & $a - b = 11$: $a = 11 + b$, $2(11 + b) + b = 1$, $\boxed{b = -7}$ $\boxed{a = 4}$

4. $x - 2y = 15$ & $6x + 2y = 6$: $7x = 21$, $\boxed{x = 3}$ $3 - 2y = 15$, $\boxed{y = -6}$

5. Find b : $2a + b + 3c = 11$ (1), $a - 2b = 0$ (2) and $5b - c = 3$ (3)
   (2): $a = 2b$, (3): $c = 5b - 3$, $Sub\ into\ (1): 2(2b) + b + 3(5b - 3) = 11$; $b = 1$

6. If $x - 4x = 6$, what is the value of x^2?

   (A) −4
   (B) −2
   (C) 4
   (D) 9
   (E) 16

   $\begin{aligned} x - 4x &= 6 \\ -3x &= 6 \\ x &= -2 \ \ (\textit{divide both sides by} - 3) \\ x^2 &= 4 \end{aligned}$

7. If $p - 2q = 2$, and $3p + 2q = 46$, what is the value of $p - q$?

   (A) 2
   (B) 7
   (C) 13
   (D) 38
   (E) 54

   $p - 2q = 2$ (1) $3p + 2q = 46$ (2)
   (1) + (2) : $4p = 48$, $\therefore p = 12$
   $Sub\ into\ (1)$: $12 - 2q = 2$, $\therefore q = 5$
   $p - q = 12 - 5 = 7$

8. If $x + 2y = 15$, and $z = 3x$, what is y in terms of z?

   (A) $15 - z$
   (B) $15 - \frac{z}{2}$
   (C) $\frac{45 - z}{3}$
   (D) $\frac{45 - z}{6}$
   (E) $\frac{45 - 3z}{6}$

   $x + 2y = 15$, $\therefore 2y = 15 - x$
   $from\ z = 3x$, $x = \frac{z}{3}$
   $2y = 15 - \frac{z}{3} = \frac{45}{3} - \frac{z}{3} = \frac{45 - z}{3}$
   $y = \frac{45 - z}{6}$

9. If $a + b + c = 6$, $a = 2c - 1$ and $c = b + 5$, what is the value of $a + b$?

   (A) −2
   (B) 3
   (C) 5
   (D) 6
   (E) 8

   $a + b + c = 6$ (1), $a = 2c - 1$ (2), $c = b + 5$ (3)
   $From\ (3) : b = c - 5$ (3)
   $Substituting\ (2)$ & (3) $into\ (1)$:
   $(2c - 1) + (c - 5) + c = 6$, $c = 3$
   $Sub\ c = 3\ into\ (1)$: $a + b + 3 = 6$, $a + b = 3$

10. If $a^2 - b^2 = 45$, and $a + b = 15$, what is the value of $2(a - b)$?

    (A) −12
    (B) −8
    (C) 6
    (D) 9
    (E) 16

    $a^2 - b^2 = 45$, $(a + b)(a - b) = 45$
    $Since\ a + b = 15$,
    $\therefore\ 15(a - b) = 45$
    $a - b = 3$
    $2(a - b) = 6$

3. Factoring

3.1 Factoring Binomials (two terms)

$$3x^2 + 6x = 3x(x + 2), \qquad 2x^2 + 3xy = x(2x + 3y)$$

ex.1 For $xy \neq 0$, which of the following is equivalent to $\dfrac{2x^2y^3+4xy}{xy}$?

     a) $4(xy^2 + 2)$ b) $2(xy^2 + 2)$ c) $\dfrac{2(xy+2)}{y}$ d) $\dfrac{x^2+2xy}{y}$ e) $6xy$

     Solution: $\dfrac{2x^2y^3+4xy}{xy} = \dfrac{2xy(xy^2+2)}{xy} = 2(xy^2 + 2)$

     The correct answer is (b).

3.2 Factoring Trinomials (three terms)

$$\boxed{ax^2 + bx + c}$$

To factor $x^2 + bx + c$ into $(x + p)(x + q)$, needs to find p and q

so that $\boxed{p * q = c \ \ and \ \ p + q = b}$

ex.1 Factor $x^2 - 2x - 15$ ($b = -2, \ \ c = -15$)

     Solution: Find 2 numbers, p and q,

           so that they can fill in the following blanks:

              __ $*$ __ $= -15$ ($p * q = c$)

              __ $+$ __ $= -2$ ($p + q = b$)

           Since $\underline{-5} * \underline{\ 3\ } = -15$ and

            $\underline{-5} + \underline{\ 3\ } = -2$

           -5 and 3 (p and q) are the numbers that fill in the blanks

     $\therefore$ $x^2 - 2x - 15 = (x - 5)(x + 3)$

ex.2 If $x^2 + 6x + 9 = 0$, which of the following must be true about the solution of x?

     a) has no value   b) equals zero   c) has one value   d) has two values

           Solution: Factor $x^2 + 6x + 9 = 0$:

                  find p and q, so that $p * q = 9$, & $p + q = 6$

                  since $3 * 3 = 9$

                  and $3 + 3 = 6$, so both p and $q = 3$

              $\therefore$ $x^2 + 6x + 9 = 0 = (x + 3)(x + 3)$ or $(x + 3)^2$

              $\therefore$ $x = -3$ is the only value

     The correct answer is (c).

ex.3 If $y = x^2 + 5x - 6$, what are the x-intercepts of the graph y?

a) $(-6, 0), (1, 0)$ b) $(6, 0), (-1, 0)$ c) $(-2, 0), (-3, 0)$

d) $(2, 0), (-3, 0)$ e) $(-2, 0), (-3, 0)$

Solution: To find x-intercept, set $y = 0$, $\therefore$ $x^2 + 5x - 6 = 0$

Find 2 numbers, p and q, so that $p * q = -6$, & $p + q = 5$

Since $\underline{6}$ * $\underline{-1} = -6$ and $\underline{6} + \underline{-1} = 5$

$\therefore$ 6 and -1 are the two numbers.

$\therefore$ $x^2 + 5x - 6 = (x + 6)(x - 1) = 0$

$x = -6$ & $x = 1$ for $y = 0$

The x-intercepts are at -6 and 1.

The correct answer is (a).

3.3 Factoring the Difference of Two Squares

$$\boxed{a^2 - b^2 = (a + b)(a - b)}$$

ex.1 Factor: $x^2 - 9$

This is a difference of two squares, $x^2 - 3^2$ $(9 = 3^2)$

$a = x$, & $b = 3$ $\therefore$ $x^2 - 9 = x^2 - 3^2 = (x + 3)(x - 3)$

ex.2 $1 - y^2 = 1^2 - y^2 = (1 - y)(1 + y)$

ex.3 If $\dfrac{(x^2 + x - 20)}{x^2 - 16} = 2$, for $x^2 - 16 \neq 0$, what is the value of x ?

a) 3   b) 1   c) -1 d) -3 e) -4

Solution: $\dfrac{(x^2 + x - 20)}{x^2 - 16} = \dfrac{(x+5)(x-4)}{(x+4)(x-4)} = \dfrac{x+5}{x+4} = 2$

$\therefore$ $x + 5 = 2(x + 4) = 2x + 8$

$\therefore$ $5 - 8 = 2x - x$

$\therefore$ $x = -3$

The correct answer is (d).

ex.4 Which of the following is equivalent to $\dfrac{(a^2 + 7a - 8)}{a^2 - 1}$, for $a^2 - 1 \neq 0$?

a) $\dfrac{a+8}{a+1}$ b) $\dfrac{a+4}{a+1}$ c) $\dfrac{-a-8}{a+1}$ d) $\dfrac{a-8}{a-1}$ e) $\dfrac{a+8}{a-1}$

Solution: $(a^2 + 7a - 8) = (a + 8)(a - 1)$

$a^2 - 1 = (a + 1)(a - 1)$

$\therefore$ $\dfrac{(a^2 + 7a - 8)}{a^2 - 1} = \dfrac{(a+8)(a-1)}{(a+1)(a-1)} = \dfrac{a+8}{a+1}$

The correct answer is (a).

3.4   Practice and Solutions

1. Factor: $x^2 + 8x + 15$

2. Factor: $4a^2 - 1$

3. Which of the following is equivalent to $\dfrac{3x^2+6x}{(x^2+x-2)}$, for $x^2 + x - 2 \neq 0$?

   (A) $\dfrac{x+2}{(x-1)}$

   (B) $\dfrac{3x}{(x-1)}$

   (C) $\dfrac{3}{(x-1)}$

   (D) $\dfrac{6}{(x-1)}$

   (E) $\dfrac{3x^2+1}{(x+2)}$

4. If $y = x^2 - 4x - 12$, which of the following is one of the x-intercepts?

   (A) $(-6, 0)$

   (B) $(-4, 0)$

   (C) $(-2, 0)$

   (D) $(3, 0)$

   (E) $(4, 0)$

5. If $\dfrac{(x^2-x-6)}{x^2-9} = 2$, for $x^2 - 9 \neq 0$, what is the value of $3x$?

   (A) -12

   (B) -6

   (C) -1

   (D) 6

   (E) 18

6. If $\dfrac{(a^2-2a-8)}{a^2-4} = b$, for $a^2 \neq 4$, what is a in terms of b?

   (A) $\dfrac{4+2b}{1+b}$

   (B) $\dfrac{4+b}{1+b}$

   (C) $\dfrac{4-2b}{1+b}$

   (D) $\dfrac{4-b}{1-b}$

   (E) $\dfrac{4-2b}{1-b}$

7. Which of the following is the common factor of $x^2 - 3x - 18$
   and $x^2 + 8x + 15$?

   (A) $(x - 6)$

   (B) $(x - 5)$

   (C) $(x + 2)$

   (D) $(x + 3)$

   (E) $(x + 8)$

Solutions to 3.4 Practice: 1 $(x+3)(x+5)$, 2 $(2a+1)(2a-1)$, 3(B), 4(C), 5(A), 6(E), 7(D)

1. Factor: $x^2 + 8x + 15 = (x + 3)(x + 5)$

2. Factor: $4a^2 - 1 = (2a + 1)(2a - 1)$

3. Which of the following is equivalent to $\dfrac{3x^2+6x}{(x^2+x-2)}$, for $x^2 + x - 2 \neq 0$?

   (A) $\dfrac{x+2}{(x-1)}$

   (B) $\dfrac{3x}{(x-1)}$

   (C) $\dfrac{3}{(x-1)}$

   (D) $\dfrac{6}{(x-1)}$

   (E) $\dfrac{3x^2+1}{(x+2)}$

   $$\frac{3x^2 + 6x}{x^2 + x - 2} = \frac{3x(x+2)}{(x - 1)(x+2)}$$
   $$= \frac{3x}{x - 1}$$

4. If $y = x^2 - 4x - 12$, which of the following is one of the x-intercepts?

   (A) $(-6, 0)$

   (B) $(-4, 0)$

   (C) $(-2, 0)$

   (D) $(3, 0)$

   (E) $(4, 0)$

   To find x-intercept, set $y = 0$:
   $x^2 - 4x - 12 = 0$
   $\therefore$ $(x - 6)(x + 2) = 0$ and $x = -2, 6$
   $(-2, 0)$ and $(6, 0)$ are the two x-intercepts.

5. If $\dfrac{(x^2-x-6)}{x^2-9} = 2$, for $x^2 - 9 \neq 0$, what is the value of $3x$?

   (A) -12

   (B) -6

   (C) -1

   (D) 6

   (E) 18

   $$\frac{x^2 - x - 6}{x^2 - 9} = 2$$
   $$\frac{(x-3)(x+2)}{(x-3)(x+3)} = 2, \qquad x + 2 = 2(x + 3)$$
   $$x + 2 = 2x + 6, \qquad x = -4, \qquad 3x = -12$$

6. If $\dfrac{(a^2-2a-8)}{a^2-4} = b$, for $a^2 \neq 4$, what is a in terms of b?

   (A) $\dfrac{4+2b}{1+b}$

   (B) $\dfrac{4+b}{1+b}$

   (C) $\dfrac{4-2b}{1+b}$

   (D) $\dfrac{4-b}{1-b}$

   (E) $\dfrac{4-2b}{1-b}$

   $$\frac{(a+2)(a - 4)}{(a+2)(a - 2)} = b$$
   $$(a - 4) = b(a - 2)$$
   $$a - 4 = ab - 2b,$$
   $$a - ab = 4 - 2b$$
   $$a(1 - b) = 4 - 2b,$$
   $$a = \frac{4 - 2b}{1 - b}$$

7. Which of the following is the common factor of $x^2 - 3x - 18$ and $x^2 + 8x + 15$?

   (A) $(x - 6)$

   (B) $(x - 5)$

   (C) $(x + 2)$

   (D) $(x + 3)$

   (E) $(x + 8)$

   $x^2 - 3x - 18 = (x - 6)(x + 3)$
   $x^2 + 8x + 15 = (x + 5)(x + 3)$
   The common factor is $(x + 3)$

4. Word Problems

4.1 Writing Equations

Jack is three years older than Mary: $j = m + 3$ or $j - 3 = m$

x is 7 less than y: $x = y - 7$ or $y = x + 7$

4 less than a number equal to 12: $n - 4 = 12$ (let n be the number)

twice the number: $2n$
5 times the number: $5n$
45% of the number: $0.45n$
$\frac{2}{3}$ of a number: $\frac{2}{3}n$

6 more than twice a number equal 18: $2n + 6 = 18$

25m less than 3 quarters of a runway is 450m: $\frac{3}{4}r - 25 = 450$

80% of 3 times a number is 50 less than twice that number: $0.8*(3n) = 2n - 50$

4.2 One Variable Word Problems

ex.1 Twice the number increased by 29 is 177. What is the number?

     a) 37   b) 48   c) 59   d) 67   e) 74

Solution: Let $x =$ the number

$$\therefore \quad 2x + 29 = 177$$
$$2x = 177 - 29 = 148$$
$$x = 74$$

The correct answer is (e).

ex.2 If one-fifth of a number is 10 less than one-third of the number, what is the number?

     a) -20 b) -12 c) 34   d) 75   e) 105

Solution: Let $x =$ the number

$$\therefore \quad \frac{x}{5} = \frac{x}{3} - 10$$

multiplied both sides by 15:

$$15 * \frac{x}{5} = 15 * \frac{x}{3} - 15 * 10$$
$$3x = 5x - 150$$
$$150 = 2x$$
$$x = 75$$

The correct answer is (d).

4.3 Two and Three Variables Word Problems

ex.1 Dad's present age is 4 less than three times his son's age. 12 years later, dad is twice as old as his son. How old is dad now?

a) 28   b) 32   c) 34   d) 44   e) 45

Solution: Let x = son's age, y = dad's age

	Son	Dad	Equations
now	x	y	$3x - 4 = y$
12 later	$x + 12$	$y + 12$	$2(x + 12) = y + 12$

$\therefore$ $3x - 4 = y$ .... (1)

$2x + 24 = y + 12$ or $2x + 12 = y$ .... (2)

sub (1) into (2):

$2x + 12 = 3x - 4$ $\therefore$ $x = 16$

sub into (1):

$\therefore$ $3 * (16) - 4 = y$ $\therefore$ $\boxed{y = 44}$

The correct answer is (d).

ex.2 Jen has 16 coins (quarters, dimes, and nickels) with a total value of $2.20. There are 3 more dimes than quarters. How many quarters does Jen has?

a) 2   b) 3   c) 5   d) 7   e) 8

Solution: Let q = # of quarters, d = # of dimes, n = # of nickels

$2.20 = 220$ cents (it's easier to work in cents than dollars)

	Nickels	Dimes	Quarters	Equations
numbers	n	d	q	$n + d + q = 16$....(1) $q = d - 3$ ....(2)
Values,¢	$5 * n$	$10 * d$	$25 * q$	$5n + 10d + 25q = 220$...(3)

sub (2) into (1):

since (1) is: $n + d + q = 16$

$n + d + (d - 3) = 16$

$\therefore$ $n = 19 - 2d$ ....(4)

sub (2) and (4) into (3):

since (3) is: $5n + 10d + 25q = 220$

$\therefore$ $5(19 - 2d) + 10d + 25(d - 3) = 220$

$95 - 10d + 10d + 25d - 75 = 200$

$25d = 200$ $\therefore$ $d = 8$ (8 dimes)

Sub $d = 8$ into (2) :

$q = d - 3 = 8 - 3 = 5$ (5 quarters)

The correct answer is (c).

4.4   Practice and Solutions

1.   The difference between 129 and a number is 76. Find the number.

2.   The sum of 34 and seven times a number is equal to 125. Find the number.

3.   The sum of three consecutive numbers is 345. What is the largest number?
    (A) 125
    (B) 119
    (C) 116
    (D) 108
    (E) 99

4.   The perimeter of a rectangle is 36 cm, and the length is 2cm less than three times the width. What is the area of the rectangle?
    (A) $35cm^2$
    (B) $48cm^2$
    (C) $52cm^2$
    (D) $65cm^2$
    (E) $84cm^2$

5.   Mary left home at 8 a.m. and drove at 60 mi/h, while her brother, John, drove at 75 mi/h and left home at 9 a.m. They drove on the same highway without stopping. By what time would John catch up with Mary to stop for coffee?
    (A) 12 a.m.
    (B) 1 p.m.
    (C) 2 p.m.
    (D) 3 p.m.
    (E) 4 p.m.

6.   A school raised a total of $16458 by selling fruit pies at $6.0 each and meat pies at $10.0 each. The number of fruit pies sold is 18 more than twice the number of meat pies sold. How many pies were sold altogether?
    (A) 228
    (B) 200
    (C) 158
    (D) 108
    (E) 80

7.   The sum of Amy, Bob and Clare's ages is 62. The sum of Amy and Bob's ages is 6 more than Clare's, and Clare's age is 1 less than twice of Amy's. How old is Clare?
    (A) 9
    (B) 15
    (C) 17
    (D) 23
    (E) 29

Solutions to 4.4 Practice: 1 (53), 2 (13), 3(C), 4(D), 5(B), 6(A), 7(B)

1. The difference between 129 and a number is 76. $129 - n = 76$, $n = 53$

2. $34 + 7n = 125$, $7n = 125 - 34$, $7n = 97$, $n = 91 \div 7 = 13$

3. The sum of three consecutive numbers is 345. What is the largest number?

   (A) 125
   (B) 119
   (C) 116
   (D) 108
   (E) 99

   $$Let\ the\ 3\ numbers\ be:\ x, x + 1, x + 2$$
   $$x + (x + 1) + (x + 2) = 345$$
   $$3x + 3 = 345, \quad 3x = 342$$
   $$x = 114$$
   $$\therefore The\ 3\ numbers\ are\ 114, 115, 116$$

4. The perimeter of a rectangle is 36 cm, and the length is 2cm less than three times the width. What is the area of the rectangle?

   (A) $35cm^2$ $A = lw$
   (B) $48cm^2$ $l = 3w - 2$
   (C) $52cm^2$
   (D) $65cm^2$
   (E) $84cm^2$

   $$P = 2(l + w)$$
   $$= 2(3w - 2 + w)$$
   $$= 8w - 4 = 36, \quad 8w = 40, \quad w = 5$$
   $$l = 3 * 5 - 2 = 13$$
   $$Area = 5 * 13 = 65cm^2$$

5. Mary left home at 8 a.m. and drove at 60 mi/h, while her brother, John, drove at 75 mi/h and left home at 9 a.m. They drove on the same highway without stopping. By what time would John catch up with Mary to stop for coffee?

   (A) 12 a.m.
   (B) 1 p.m.
   (C) 2 p.m.
   (D) 3 p.m.
   (E) 4 p.m.

	Mary	John
s (mi/h)	60	75
t (h)	t	$t - 1$
D (mi)	$60t$	$75(t - 1)$

   $60t = 75(t - 1)$, $t = 5$, John will catch up in 4 hours, at 1pm

6. A school raised a total of $1648 by selling fruit pies at $6.0 each and meat pies at $10.0 each. The number of fruit pies sold is 18 more than twice the number of meat pies sold. How many pies were sold altogether?

   (A) 228
   (B) 200
   (C) 158
   (D) 108
   (E) 80

   $$Let\ x = number\ of\ meat\ pies$$
   $$\therefore\ number\ of\ fruit\ pies = 2x + 18$$
   $$(2x + 18) * 6 + x * 10 = 1648; \quad x = 70$$
   $$Total\ number\ of\ pies:\ x + (2x + 18) = 228$$

7. The sum of Amy, Bob and Clare's ages is 62. The sum of Amy and Bob's ages is 6 more than Clare's, and Clare's age is 2 less than twice of Amy's. How old is Amy?

   (A) 9
   (B) 15
   (C) 17
   (D) 23
   (E) 29

   $$Amy's\ age \ldots a, \quad Bob's\ age \ldots b, \quad Clare's\ age \ldots c$$
   $$a + b + c = 62\ (1), \quad a + b = c + 6\ (2), \quad c = 2a - 2\ (3)$$
   $$Replace\ a + b\ by\ c + 6\ in\ (1):\ c + 6 + c = 62, \quad c = 28$$
   $$Substituting\ into\ (3):\ 28 = 2a - 2, \quad a = 15$$

5. Solving Quadratic Equations

ex.1 Solve: $9x^2 - 4 = 32$
$$9x^2 = 32 + 4, \qquad x^2 = \frac{36}{9} = 4, \qquad x = \pm\sqrt{4} = \pm2$$

ex.2 If $2(x + 3)^2 - 6 = 66$, what is the product of the two solutions of x?

a) -42 b) -36 c) -27 d) 9 e) 18

Solution: $2(x + 3)^2 - 6 = 66$
$2(x + 3)^2 = 66 + 6 = 72$
divide both sides by 2:
$(x + 3)^2 = \frac{72}{2} = 36$
$\sqrt{(x + 3)^2} = \sqrt{36}$
$(x + 3) = \pm6, \quad x = \pm6 - 3$
$\therefore \quad x = +6 - 3 = 3 \quad$ or
$x = -6 - 3 = -9$
$\therefore \quad$ the product of the two values of x:
$3 * (-9) = -27$

The correct answer is (c).

ex.3 If $x^2 + 6x - 27 = 0$, what is the sum of the two solutions of x?

a) -9 b) -6 c) 0 d) 3 e) 9

Solution: Solved by Factoring:
Find 2 numbers so that their product equals -27 and sum equals 6
(See Algebra 3.2, Factoring Trinomials)
The 2 numbers are: 9 and -3,
since $9 * (-3) = -27, \quad \& \quad 9 + (-3) = 6$
$\therefore \quad x^2 + 6x - 27 = (x + 9)(x - 3)$
since for $(x + 9)(x - 3) = 0$
$(x + 9) = 0 \quad or \quad (x - 3) = 0$
$\therefore \quad x = -9 \quad \& \quad x = 3$ are the two solutions
The sum of the two solutions:
$-9 + 3 = -6$

The correct answer is (b).

5.1   Practice and Solutions

1. Solve for x: $5x^2 - 4 = 32 + x^2$

2. Solve for x: $6(x - 3)^2 - 54 = 0$

3. Solve for x: $x^2 + 4x = -4$

4. Solve for x: $x^2 - 6x - 16 = 0$

5. Solve for x: $x^2 + 12x + 32 = 0$

6. If $5x^2 - 25 = x^2$, what is the positive value of x?
   - (A) 5
   - (B) 4
   - (C) $\dfrac{25}{4}$
   - (D) $\dfrac{5}{4}$
   - (E) $\dfrac{5}{2}$

7. If $x^2 + 6x - 27 = 0$, what is the smaller value of x?
   - (A) -12
   - (B) -9
   - (C) -3
   - (D) 3
   - (E) 6

8. If $x^2 + kx - 45 = 0$ has solutions 9 and -5, what is the value of k?
   - (A) -4
   - (B) -3
   - (C) 2
   - (D) 3
   - (E) 9

9. Which of the following is the factor of $4x^2 + 8x$ and $x^2 - 7x - 18 = 0$?
   - (A) $(x + 8)$
   - (B) $(x + 4)$
   - (C) $(x + 2)$
   - (D) $(x - 4)$
   - (E) $(x - 8)$

10. Which of the following are the solutions of $3x^2 + x - 2(x^2 - 2x + 12) = 0$?
   - (A) $-6, 4$
   - (B) $6, -4$
   - (C) $6, 4$
   - (D) $8, -3$
   - (E) $-8, 3$

Solutions to 5.1 Practice: 1 (±3), 2 (0, 6), 3 (-2), 4 ($-2, 8$), 5 ($-4, -8$),
6(E), 7(B), 8(A), 9(C), 10(E)

1. $5x^2 - 4 = 32 + x^2$: $5x^2 - x^2 = 32 + 4$, $4x^2 = 36$, $x^2 = 9$, $x = \pm3$
2. $6(x - 3)^2 - 54 = 0$: $6(x - 3)^2 = 54$, $(x - 3)^2 = 9$, $x - 3 = \pm3$, $x = 0, -6$
3. $x^2 + 4x = -4$: $x^2 + 4x + 4 = 0$, $(x + 2)(x + 2) = 0$, $x = -2$
4. $x^2 - 6x - 16 = 0$: $(x + 2)(x - 8) = 0$, $x = -2, 8$
5. $x^2 + 12x + 32 = 0$: $(x + 4)(x + 8) = 0$, $x = -4, -8$

6. If $5x^2 - 25 = x^2$, what is the positive value of x?

    (A) 5
    (B) 4
    (C) $\frac{25}{4}$
    (D) $\frac{5}{4}$
    (E) $\frac{5}{2}$

    $5x^2 - 25 = x^2$

    $4x^2 = 25$, $\qquad x^2 = \dfrac{25}{4}$

    $x = \sqrt{\dfrac{25}{4}} = \dfrac{5}{2}$

7. If $x^2 + 6x - 27 = 0$, what is the smaller value of x?

    (A) -12
    (B) -9
    (C) -3
    (D) 3
    (E) 6

    $x^2 + 6x - 27 = 0$
    $(x - 3)(x + 9) = 0$
    $x = -9, 3$
    The smallest root is -9

8. If $x^2 + kx - 45 = 0$ has solutions 9 and -5, what is the value of k?

    (A) -4
    (B) -3
    (C) 2
    (D) 3
    (E) 9

    Since $x^2 + kx - 45 = 0$ *has solutions* 9 *and* -5,
    Therefore $(x - 9)(x + 5) = 0$
    $(x - 9)(x + 5) = x^2 - 9x + 5x - 45 = x^2 - 4x - 45$
    $\therefore x^2 + kx - 45 = x^2 - 4x - 45$, $\qquad \therefore k = -4$

9. Which of the following is the factor of $4x^2 + 8x$ and $x^2 - 7x - 18$?

    (A) $(x + 8)$
    (B) $(x + 4)$
    (C) $(x + 2)$
    (D) $(x - 4)$
    (E) $(x - 8)$

    $4x^2 + 8x = 4x(x + 2)$
    $x^2 - 7x - 18 = (x + 2)(x - 9)$
    $(x + 2)$ *is the common factor*

10. Which of the following are the solutions of $3x^2 + x - 2(x^2 - 2x + 12) = 0$?

    (A) $-6, 4$
    (B) $6, -4$
    (C) $6, 4$
    (D) $8, -3$
    (E) $-8, 3$

    $3x^2 + x - 2(x^2 - 2x + 12) = 0$
    $3x^2 + x - 2x^2 + 4x - 24 = 0$
    $x^2 + 5x - 24 = 0$
    $(x + 8)(x - 3) = 0$, $\qquad x = -8, 3$

6. Solving Rational Equations

6.1 Add and Subtract Rational Expressions

ex.1 Simplify: $\dfrac{2x+5}{3x} + \dfrac{x-7}{4x}$, for $x \neq 0$

The common denominator is $12x$: (see Basic Math-6.1 Fractions)

$$\therefore \; \frac{2x+5}{3x} + \frac{x-7}{4x} = \frac{4*(2x+5)}{4*3x} + \frac{3*(x-7)}{3*4x}$$

$$= \frac{8x+20+3x-21}{12x}$$

$$= \frac{11x-1}{12x}$$

ex.2 Which of the following is $\dfrac{x-1}{x+1} - \dfrac{3}{x+2}$ for $x \neq -1 \text{ and } x \neq -2$?

a) $\dfrac{x^2-2x-5}{(x+1)(x+2)}$ b) $\dfrac{x^2-2x-5}{(x+2)}$ c) $\dfrac{x^2-2x-5}{(x+1)}$

Solution: The common denominator is: $(x+1)(x+2)$

$$\frac{(x-1)(x+2)}{(x+1)(x+2)} - \frac{3(x+1)}{(x+1)(x+2)}$$

$$= \frac{x^2+2x-x-2}{(x+1)(x+2)} - \frac{3x+3}{(x+1)(x+2)}$$

$$= \frac{x^2+x-2-3x-3}{(x+1)(x+2)} = \frac{x^2-2x-5}{(x+1)(x+2)}$$

The correct answer is (a).

6.2 Multiplying Rational Expressions

Simplify:

ex.1 $\dfrac{x+2}{3(x-1)} * \dfrac{x-3}{2} = \dfrac{(x+2)*(x-3)}{(3x-3)*2} = \dfrac{x^2-3x+2x-6}{6x-6} = \dfrac{x^2-x-6}{6x-6}$, for $x \neq 1$

ex.2 $\dfrac{(x-2)}{(x+3)} * \dfrac{4}{x} = \dfrac{(x-2)4}{(x+3)x} = \dfrac{4x-8}{x^2+3x}$, for $x \neq -3, 0$

ex.3 $3 * \dfrac{7x}{8} = \dfrac{3}{1} * \dfrac{7x}{8} = \dfrac{21x}{8}$

6.3   Dividing Rational Expressions

Simplify:

ex.1 $\dfrac{3(x+2)}{x-1} \div \dfrac{x}{2x-2} = \dfrac{3(x+2)}{x-1} * \dfrac{2x-2}{x} = \dfrac{3(x+2)}{\cancel{(x-1)}} * \dfrac{2\cancel{(x-1)}}{x} = \dfrac{6(x+2)}{x}$,

for $x \ne 0, 1$

ex.2 $\dfrac{\frac{1+x}{2-x}}{\frac{2}{x}} = \dfrac{1+x}{2-x} * \dfrac{x}{2} = \dfrac{(1+x)x}{(2-x)2} = \dfrac{x+x^2}{4-2x}$, for $x \ne 0, 2$

ex.3 $\dfrac{6x-2}{3x} \div 4x = \dfrac{2(3x-1)}{3x} * \dfrac{1}{4x} = \dfrac{2(3x-1)}{12x^2} = \dfrac{3x-1}{6x^2}$, for $x \ne 0$

6.4   Solving Rational Equations

ex.1 If $x - \dfrac{16}{(x+2)} = 4$, for $x \ne -2$, what is the largest value of x?

    a) $\dfrac{1}{4}$ b) $\dfrac{1}{2}$ c) 2   d) 4   e) 6

    Solution: Multiply both sides by $(x+2)$

$$(x+2)*x - \cancel{(x+2)}*\dfrac{16}{\cancel{(x+2)}} = (x+2)*4$$
$$x^2 + 2x - 16 = 4x + 8$$
$$x^2 - 2x - 24 = 0$$
$$(x-6)(x+4) = 0$$
$$\therefore \quad x = 6 \quad or \quad x = -4, \text{ so 6 is the largest root.}$$

The correct answer is (e).

ex.2 If $\dfrac{x+2}{2x+2} = \dfrac{-3}{x+1}$, for $x \ne -1$, what is the value of $2x+1$?

    a) -15 b) -8 c) -3 d) 5   e) 17

    Solution: by **cross multiplication**:

$$\dfrac{(x+2)}{(2x+2)} \diagdown\diagup \dfrac{-3}{(x+1)}$$
$$(x+2)(x+1) = (2x+2)*(-3)$$
$$x^2 + 3x + 2 = -6x - 6$$
$$x^2 + 9x + 8 = 0$$
$$(x+1)(x+8) = 0$$
$$x = -1 \quad or \quad x = -8$$

since $x \ne -1$, $x = -8$ *is the only solution*
$$\therefore \quad 2x + 1 = 2(-8) + 1 = -16 + 1 = -15$$

The answer is (a).

6.5   Practice and Solutions

1. Simplify: $\frac{x+3}{2x} + \frac{2x-3}{4x}$,   for $x \neq 0$

2. Simplify: $\frac{x-2}{x+1} - \frac{2}{x-3}$,   for $x \neq 1$ and $x \neq 3$

3. Simplify: $\frac{x+1}{2(x-4)} * \frac{x-5}{2}$,   for $x \neq 4$

4. Simplify: $\frac{2(x+3)}{x-1} \div \frac{x}{3x-3}$, for $x \neq 0$ and $x \neq 1$

5. If $\frac{(x^2-2x-8)}{x^2-16} = 2$, what is the value of $2x+1$?
    (A) -18
    (B) -11
    (C) -3
    (D) 6
    (E) 15

6. If $\frac{x}{(x-2)} + \frac{3}{(x+1)} = 1$, what is the value of x?
    (A) $\frac{-3}{5}$
    (B) $\frac{-3}{4}$
    (C) 1
    (D) $\frac{4}{5}$
    (E) $\frac{5}{4}$

7. If $\frac{a+6}{b-3} = \frac{a+3}{b}$, what is a in terms of b?
    (A) $-b - 3$
    (B) $\frac{-2b-9}{3}$
    (C) $\frac{-b-9}{3}$
    (D) $b + 3$
    (E) b

8. Which of the following must be the restrictions for $\frac{(x^2-3x-28)}{(y^2+y-12)}$?
    (A) $y \neq -3, -4$
    (B) $y \neq -3, 4$
    (C) $y \neq -4, -3$
    (D) $y \neq -4, 3$
    (E) $y \neq 4, 3$

Solutions to 6.5 Practice: 1 $(\frac{4x+3}{4x})$, 2 $(\frac{(x^2-7x+4)}{(x+1)(x-3)})$, 3 $(\frac{x^2-4x-5}{4x-16})$, 4 $(\frac{6x+18}{x})$,

5(B), 6(D), 7(A), 8(D)

1. $\dfrac{x+3}{2x} + \dfrac{2x-3}{4x} = \dfrac{(x+3)*2}{2x*2} + \dfrac{(2x-3)}{4x} = \dfrac{2x+6+2x-3}{4x} = \dfrac{4x+3}{4x}$

2. $\dfrac{x-2}{x+1} - \dfrac{2}{x-3} = \dfrac{(x-2)(x-3)}{(x+1)(x-3)} - \dfrac{2(x+1)}{(x+1)(x-3)} = \dfrac{x^2-5x+6-2x-2}{(x+1)(x-3)} = \dfrac{(x^2-7x+4)}{(x+1)(x-3)}$

3. $\dfrac{x+1}{2(x-4)} * \dfrac{x-5}{2} = \dfrac{(x+1)(x-5)}{2(x-4)*2} = \dfrac{x^2-4x-5}{4x-16}$

4. $\dfrac{2(x+3)}{x-1} \div \dfrac{x}{3x-3} = \dfrac{2(x+3)}{x-1} * \dfrac{(3x-3)}{x} = \dfrac{2x+6}{x-1} * \dfrac{3(x-1)}{x} = \dfrac{6x+18}{x}$

5. If $\dfrac{(x^2-2x-8)}{x^2-16} = 2$, what is the value of $2x+1$?

   (A) -18

   (B) -11

   (C) -3

   (D) 6

   (E) 15

   $\dfrac{x^2-2x-8}{x^2-16} = \dfrac{(x-4)(x+2)}{(x-4)(x+4)} = 2$

   $\dfrac{x+2}{x+4} = 2, \quad x+2 = 2(x+4), \quad x = -6$

   $2x+1 = 2(-6)+1 = -11$

6. If $\dfrac{x}{(x-2)} + \dfrac{3}{(x+1)} = 1$, what is the value of x?

   (A) $\dfrac{-3}{5}$

   (B) $\dfrac{-3}{4}$

   (C) 1

   (D) $\dfrac{4}{5}$

   (E) $\dfrac{5}{4}$

   $(x-2)(x+1) * \dfrac{x}{x-2} + (x-2)(x+1) * \dfrac{3}{x+1} = (x-2)(x+1)*1$

   $(x+1)*x + (x-2)*3 = (x-2)(x+1)$

   $x^2 + x + 3x - 6 = x^2 + x - 2x - 2$

   $4x - 6 = -x - 2, \quad 5x = 4, \quad x = \dfrac{4}{5}$

7. If $\dfrac{a+6}{b-3} = \dfrac{a+3}{b}$, what is a in terms of b?

   (A) $-b-3$

   (B) $\dfrac{-2b-9}{3}$

   (C) $\dfrac{-b-9}{3}$

   (D) $b+3$

   (E) b

   $\dfrac{a+6}{b-3} = \dfrac{a+3}{b}, \qquad cross\ multiply$

   $b(a+6) = (b-3)(a+3)$

   $ab + 6b = ab + 3b - 3a - 9$

   $3a = -3b - 9, \qquad a = -b - 3$

8. Which of the following must be the restrictions for $\dfrac{(x^2-3x-28)}{(y^2+y-12)}$?

   (A) $y \neq -3, -4$

   (B) $y \neq -3, 4$

   (C) $y \neq -4, -3$

   (D) $y \neq -4, 3$

   (E) $y \neq 4, 3$

   $y^2 + y - 12 \neq 0$

   $(y+4)(y-3) \neq 0$

   $y \neq -4, 3$

7. Solving Radical Equations

7.1 Radical

$\sqrt{x}$: the square root of x,　　ex. $\sqrt{16} = 4$,　　$\sqrt{100} = 10$

$\sqrt[n]{x}$: the nth roots of x,　　ex. $\sqrt[3]{8} = 2$,　　$\sqrt[4]{81} = 3$

$\sqrt[n]{x^m} = x^{\frac{m}{n}}$,　　ex. $\sqrt[3]{27} = 27^{\frac{1}{3}} = 3$　　$\sqrt[3]{8^4} = 8^{\frac{4}{3}} = 16$

(by calculator, $8 \wedge (4 \div 3) = 16$)

$\sqrt{a} * \sqrt{b} = \sqrt{a * b}$

ex.　$\sqrt{28} = \sqrt{7 * 4} = \sqrt{4} * \sqrt{7} = 2\sqrt{7}$

ex.　$2\sqrt{3} * 4\sqrt{12} = 2 * 4\sqrt{3 * 12} = 8\sqrt{36} = 8 * 6 = 48$

$\dfrac{\sqrt{a}}{\sqrt{b}} = \sqrt{\dfrac{a}{b}}$　　ex. $\dfrac{\sqrt{28}}{\sqrt{4}} = \sqrt{\dfrac{28}{4}} = \sqrt{7}$

ex.　$\dfrac{4\sqrt{72}}{7\sqrt{2}*\sqrt{3}} = \dfrac{4}{7}\sqrt{\dfrac{72}{2*3}} = \dfrac{4}{7}\sqrt{12} = \dfrac{4}{7}\sqrt{4*3} = \dfrac{4}{7} * 2 * \sqrt{3} = \dfrac{8}{7}\sqrt{3}$

7.2 Solving Radical Equations

Square of the radicals: $(\sqrt{2})^2 = 2$,　$\left(\sqrt{x}\right)^2 = x$,　$\left(\sqrt{7x}\right)^2 = 7x$, for $x \geq 0$

ex.1　If $\sqrt{3x} = 6$, what is the value of $\dfrac{x}{2}$?

　　a)　2　　　b)　6　　　c)　8　　　d)　9　　　e)　12

　　Solution: square both sides:　$(\sqrt{3x})^2 = 6^2$

　　　　　　　　　　　　　　　$\therefore$　$3x = 36$,　$x = 12$

　　　　　　　　　　　　　$\therefore$　$\dfrac{x}{2} = \dfrac{12}{2} = 6$

　　The correct answer is (b).

ex.2　If $8 + 3\sqrt{2x} = 15$, what is the value of $\dfrac{3x}{7}$?

　　a)　$\dfrac{7}{6}$　　　b)　$\dfrac{14}{6}$　　　c)　3　　　d)　$\dfrac{15}{7}$　　　e)　$\dfrac{43}{7}$

　　Solution:　$3\sqrt{2x} = 15 - 8$

　　　　　　　$3\sqrt{2x} = 7$　　$\sqrt{2x} = \dfrac{7}{3}$

　　　　　　　squaring both sides:　$2x = \dfrac{49}{9}$,　$\therefore$　$x = \dfrac{49}{18}$

　　　　　　$\dfrac{3x}{7} = \dfrac{3}{7} * \dfrac{49}{18} = \dfrac{7}{6}$

　　The correct answer is (a).

7.3   Practice and Solutions

1. Simplify: $\sqrt{50} =$

2. Simplify: $\dfrac{4\sqrt{54}}{7\sqrt{2}*\sqrt{3}} =$

3. Solve for x: $3\sqrt{2x} = 4$

4. Solve for a: $\sqrt{18 - a} = a + 2$

5. Solve for x: $2\sqrt{\dfrac{x}{8}} - 3 = 6$

6. If $x = \sqrt{8}$, and $y = \sqrt{9}$, what is the value of $\sqrt{x^2 y^2}$?

    (A) $6\sqrt{2}$

    (B) $4\sqrt{6}$

    (C) $3\sqrt{8}$

    (D) 3

    (E) $\sqrt{8}$

7. If $4\sqrt{3x} - 7 = 17$, what is the value of $\dfrac{2x}{3}$?

    (A) 6

    (B) 8

    (C) 12

    (D) 24

    (E) 36

8. If $3\sqrt{2a} = 12$, and $\sqrt{b + 9} = 4$, what is the value of $+b$?

    (A) 46

    (B) 38

    (C) 27

    (D) 15

    (E) 6

9. If $4\sqrt{x - 5} = \sqrt{3y}$, which of the following must be true ?

    (A) $4x - 3y = 5$

    (B) $4x + 3y = 20$

    (C) $16x - 3y = 5$

    (D) $16x + 3y = 16$

    (E) $16x - 3y = 80$

10. If $\sqrt{\dfrac{a}{b}} = \dfrac{2a}{3}$, for $a \neq 0, b \neq 0$, what is the value of a in terms of b?

    (A) $\dfrac{3}{2b}$

    (B) $\dfrac{9}{4b}$

    (C) $2b + 3$

    (D) $4b + 9$

    (E) $4b - 9$

Solutions 7.3: 1 ($5\sqrt{2}$), 2 ($\frac{12}{7}$), 3 ($\frac{8}{9}$), 4 ($-2,7$)), 5 (162), 6 (A), 7 (B), 8 (D), 9 (E), 10 (B)

1. Simplify: $\sqrt{50} = \sqrt{25 * 2} = 5\sqrt{2}$ 2. Simplify: $\frac{4\sqrt{54}}{7\sqrt{2}*\sqrt{3}} = \frac{4}{7}\sqrt{\frac{54}{6}} = \frac{4}{7}*3 = \frac{12}{7}$

3. Solve for x: $3\sqrt{2x} = 4$: $\sqrt{2x} = \frac{4}{3}$, $2x = \frac{16}{9}$, $x = \frac{16}{2*9} = \frac{8}{9}$

4. $18 - a = (a + 2)^2 = a^2 + 4a + 4$, $a^2 + 5a - 14 = 0$, $(a - 7)(a + 2) = 0$

5. $2\sqrt{\frac{x}{8}} - 3 = 6$: $2\sqrt{\frac{x}{8}} = 9$, $\sqrt{\frac{x}{8}} = \frac{9}{2}$, $\frac{x}{8} = \frac{81}{4}$, $x = \frac{81*8}{4} = 162$

6. If $x = \sqrt{8}$, and $y = \sqrt{9}$, what is the value of $\sqrt{x^2y^2}$?

   (A) $6\sqrt{2}$

   (B) $4\sqrt{6}$

   (C) $3\sqrt{8}$

   (D) 3

   (E) $\sqrt{8}$

   > $x^2 = 8$, $y^2 = 9$
   > $\sqrt{x^2 * y^2} = \sqrt{8 * 9} = \sqrt{72} = \sqrt{36 * 2} = 6\sqrt{2}$

7. If $4\sqrt{3x} - 7 = 17$, what is the value of $\frac{2x}{3}$?

   (A) 6

   (B) 8

   (C) 12

   (D) 24

   (E) 36

   > $4\sqrt{3x} - 7 = 17$, $4\sqrt{3x} = 24$, (*dividing by 4*)
   > $\sqrt{3x} = 6$ (*squaring both sides*)
   > $3x = 36$, $x = 12$, $\frac{2x}{3} = \frac{2(12)}{3} = \frac{24}{3} = 8$

8. If $3\sqrt{2a} = 12$, and $\sqrt{b + 9} = 4$, what is the value of $+b$?

   (A) 46

   (B) 38

   (C) 27

   (D) 15

   (E) 6

   > $3\sqrt{2a} = 12$ $\sqrt{b + 9} = 4$
   > $\sqrt{2a} = 4$ (*square*) $b + 9 = 16$ (*square*)
   > $2a = 16$ $b = 7$
   > $a = 8$ $\therefore$ $a + b = 8 + 7 = 15$

9. If $4\sqrt{x - 5} = \sqrt{3y}$, which of the following must be true ?

   (A) $4x - 3y = 5$

   (B) $4x + 3y = 20$

   (C) $16x - 3y = 5$

   (D) $16x + 3y = 16$

   (E) $16x - 3y = 80$

   > $4\sqrt{x - 5} = \sqrt{3y}$ (*square*)
   > $16(x - 5) = 3y$
   > $16x - 80 = 3y$
   > $16x - 3y = 80$

10. If $\sqrt{\frac{a}{b}} = \frac{2a}{3}$, for $a \neq 0, b \neq 0$, what is the value of a in terms of b?

    (A) $\frac{3}{2b}$

    (B) $\frac{9}{4b}$

    (C) $2b + 3$

    (D) $4b + 9$

    (E) $4b - 9$

    > $\sqrt{\frac{a}{b}} = \frac{2a}{3}$ (*square*)
    > $\frac{a}{b} = \frac{4a^2}{9}$, $\frac{1}{b} = \frac{4a}{9}$ (*cross multiply*)
    > $9 = 4ab$,   (*divide both sides by 4b*) $a = \frac{9}{4b}$

8. Solving Equations Involving Exponents

8.1 Exponents

x^n : Products of n copies of x

  ex. $5^2 = 5 * 5 = 25,$ $3^4 = 3 * 3 * 3 * 3 = 81$

$x^m * x^n = x^{m+n}$

  ex. $x^2 * x^5 = x^{2+5} = x^7,$ $3^2 * 3^3 = 3^5 = 243$

$\dfrac{x^m}{x^n} = x^{m-n}$

  ex. $\dfrac{x^5}{x^2} = x^{5-2} = x^3,$ $5^6 \div 5^4 = 5^{6-4} = 5^2 = 25$

$(x^m)^n = x^{m*n}$

  ex. $(x^7)^3 = x^{7*3} = x^{21},$ $(2^3)^2 = 2^{3*2} = 2^6 = 64$

$(xy)^m = x^m y^m$

  ex. $(5\sqrt{3})^2 = 5^2(\sqrt{3})^2 = 25 * 3 = 75$

$\left(\dfrac{x}{y}\right)^m = \dfrac{x^m}{y^m}$

  ex. $\left(\dfrac{x}{y^2}\right)^3 = \dfrac{x^3}{y^{2*3}} = \dfrac{x^3}{y^6}$, $\left(\dfrac{\sqrt{5}}{7}\right)^2 = \dfrac{(\sqrt{5})^2}{7^2} = \dfrac{5}{49}$

$x^{-m} = \dfrac{1}{x^m}$

  ex. $x^{-3} = \dfrac{1}{x^3},$ $\left(\dfrac{3}{5}\right)^{-2} = \left(\dfrac{5}{3}\right)^2 = \dfrac{5^2}{3^2} = \dfrac{25}{9} = 2\dfrac{7}{9}$

8.2 Solving Equations Involving Exponents

I. <u>When both sides have the same base: Equate the exponents:</u>

ex.1 $7^{(3x-5)} = 7^{10}$

Solution: Both sides have the same base of 7,

$\therefore$ Equate the exponents:

$$3x - 5 = 10$$
$$3x = 10 + 5$$
$$x = 5$$

ex.2 If $2^{5x+9} = 16^{2x}$, what is the value of 3x?

a) $\frac{3}{4}$ b) 3   c) 9   d) 12   e) 15

Solution: See if both sides can be written using the same base:

since $16 = 2^4$ $\therefore$ $16^{2x} = (2^4)^{2x} = 2^{8x}$

$\therefore$ $2^{5x+9} = 2^{8x}$

$\therefore$ $5x + 9 = 8x$ and $\therefore$ $9 = 3x$

The correct answer is (c).

II. <u>When the exponent is a rational, as $\frac{3}{4}$ in $x^{\frac{3}{4}}$:</u>

Raise both sides to the power of the reciprocal of the given exponent (ex. $\frac{4}{3}$).

ex.3 If $x^{\frac{3}{4}} = 27$, what is x equal to?

a) 3   b) 9   c) 27   d) 32   e) 81

Solution: Since $x^{\frac{3}{4}} = 27$, raise both sides to the power of $\frac{4}{3}$:

$$(x^{\frac{3}{4}})^{\frac{4}{3}} = 27^{\frac{4}{3}}$$

$\therefore$ $x = 27^{\frac{4}{3}} = 81$

note: $27^{\frac{4}{3}} = (3^3)^{\frac{4}{3}} = 3^4 = 81$

or by calculator: $27\wedge(4 \div 3) = 81$

The answer is (e).

ex.4 If $(2x - 6)^{\frac{3}{5}} = 8$, what is the value of $x + 4$?

a) 12   b) 19   c) 23   d) 32   e) 38

Solution: $((2x - 6)^{\frac{3}{5}})^{\frac{5}{3}} = 8^{\frac{5}{3}}$

$2x - 6 = 8^{\frac{5}{3}}$ (by calculator: $8 \wedge (5 \div 3) = 32$)

$2x - 6 = 32$

$2x = 32 + 6 = 38$

$x = 19$ $\therefore$ $x + 4 = 23$

The correct answer is (c).

8.3   Practice and Solutions

1. Solve for x: $7^x 7^3 = 7^{(2x+5)}$

2. Solve for x: $x^{\frac{2}{3}} = 25$

3. Solve for a: $6^5 = (\frac{1}{6})^{(2a+1)}$

4. Solve for x: $(a + 2)^x = a^2 + 4a + 4$

5. If $x^{\frac{2}{3}} = 16$, what is the value of x?
   (A) 4
   (B) 16
   (C) 24
   (D) 48
   (E) 64

6. $9^{(3b-7)} = \frac{3^a}{3^2}$, what is the value of a in terms of b?
   (A) $(3b - 7)$
   (B) $(b - 2)$
   (C) $6(b - 2)$
   (D) $(b + 3)$
   (E) $(b + 7)$

7. If $3^x = 27\sqrt{3}$, what is the value of x?
   (A) $\frac{3}{2}$
   (B) $\frac{7}{2}$
   (C) $\frac{9}{2}$
   (D) 3
   (E) 4

8. If $(\frac{2}{3})^{3p-q} = (\frac{4}{9})^{k+m}$, which of the following must be true?
   (A) $3p + 2k = 2m - q$
   (B) $3p + 2k = m + q$
   (C) $3p - 2k = 2m + q$
   (D) $3p - 2k = 2m - q$
   (E) $3p - 2k = m - 2q$

9. If $(ab)^x = \sqrt{ab}$, what is 4^{4x} equal to?
   (A) 2
   (B) 8
   (C) 16
   (D) 26
   (E) 64

Solutions to 8.3 Practice: 1 (−2), 2 (125), 3 (−3), 4 (2) , 5(E), 6(C), 7(B), 8(C), 9(C)

1. Solve for x: $7^x 7^3 = 7^{(2x+5)}$ Solution: $x + 3 = 2x + 5$, $\therefore$ $x = -2$

2. Solve for x: $x^{\frac{2}{3}} = 25$ Solution: $x = 25^{\frac{3}{2}} = 125$

3. Solve for a: $6^5 = (\frac{1}{6})^{(2a+1)}$ $6^5 = (\frac{1}{6})^{(2a+1)} = 6^{-(2a+1)}$, $5 = -2a - 1$, $a = -3$

4. Solve for x: $(a + 2)^x = a^2 + 4a + 4$ Solution: $a^2 + 4a + 4 = (a + 2)(a + 2)$
   $\therefore$ $(a + 2)^x = (a + 2)^2$, $\therefore$ $x = 2$

5. If $x^{\frac{2}{3}} = 16$, what is the value of x?
   - (A) 4
   - (B) 16
   - (C) 24
   - (D) 48
   - (E) 64

   $x = 16^{\frac{3}{2}} = (\sqrt{16})^3 = 4^3 = 64$
   $x = 64$ (or by calculator $16 \wedge (3 \div 2) = 64$)

6. $9^{(3b-7)} = \frac{3^a}{3^2}$, what is the value of a in terms of b?
   - (A) $(3b - 7)$
   - (B) $(b - 2)$
   - (C) $6(b - 2)$
   - (D) $(b + 3)$
   - (E) $(b + 7)$

   $9^{(3b-7)} = 3^{(a-2)}$
   $(3^2)^{(3b-7)} = 3^{(a-2)}$
   $3^{6b-14} = 3^{a-2}$
   $6b - 14 = a - 2$
   $6b - 12 = a$

7. If $3^x = 27\sqrt{3}$, what is the value of x?
   - (A) $\frac{3}{2}$
   - (B) $\frac{7}{2}$
   - (C) $\frac{9}{2}$
   - (D) 3
   - (E) 4

   $3^x = 27\sqrt{3}$
   $3^x = 3^3 * 3^{\frac{1}{2}}$, $3^x = 3^{3+\frac{1}{2}}$
   $x = 3 + \frac{1}{2} = \frac{7}{2}$

8. If $(\frac{2}{3})^{3p-q} = (\frac{4}{9})^{k+m}$, which of the following must be true?
   - (A) $3p + 2k = 2m - q$
   - (B) $3p + 2k = m + q$
   - (C) $3p - 2k = 2m + q$
   - (D) $3p - 2k = 2m - q$
   - (E) $3p - 2k = m - 2q$

   $\left(\frac{2}{3}\right)^{3p-q} = ((\frac{2}{3})^2)^{k+m}$
   $3p - q = 2(k + m)$
   $3p - q = 2k + 2m$
   $3p - 2k = 2m + q$

9. If $(ab)^x = \sqrt{ab}$, what is 4^{4x} equal to?
   - (A) 2
   - (B) 8
   - (C) 16
   - (D) 26
   - (E) 64

   $(ab)^x = (ab)^{\frac{1}{2}}$
   $x = \frac{1}{2}$, $4x = 4\left(\frac{1}{2}\right) = \frac{4*1}{2} = 2$
   $4^{4x} = 4^2 = 16$

9. Solving Absolute Value Equations

Defining Absolute Value: $|x| = \begin{cases} x, \text{ if } x \text{ is positive, (case 1)} \\ -x, \text{ if } x \text{ is negative. (case 2)} \\ 0, \text{ if } x \text{ is 0.} \end{cases}$

ex.1 $|3| = 3$ *and* $|-3| = 3$

ex.2 $|x| = 3$ means: case 1: $x = 3$,   case 2: $-x = 3$ or $x = -3$

ex.3   Solve for x, if $|x - 6| + 3 = 11$

Solution: $|x - 6| = 11 - 3$

$|x - 6| = 8$

case 1: $x - 6 = 8$,

$x = 8 + 6$

$\therefore \boxed{x = 14}$

case 2: $-(x - 6) = 8$,

$-x + 6 = 8$

$-x = 8 - 6, \quad -x = 2$

$\therefore \boxed{x = -2}$

answer: $x = -2$ *or* $x = 14$

ex.4   What is the sum of the solutions of $|x + 3| = |2x + 5|$?

a) $\dfrac{-14}{3}$ b) -4 c) $\dfrac{-8}{3}$ d) -2 e) $\dfrac{4}{3}$

Solution:

case 1: $x + 3 = 2x + 5$

$x - 2x = 5 - 3$

$-x = 2, \quad \therefore \boxed{x = -2}$

case 2: $-(x + 3) = (2x + 5)$ or $x + 3 = -(2x + 5)$

$x + 3 = -2x - 5$

$x + 2x = -5 - 3$

$3x = -8, \quad \therefore \boxed{x = -\dfrac{8}{3}}$

$\therefore \quad x = -2$ *and* $-\dfrac{8}{3}$ are the two solutions,

$\therefore \quad$ sum of two solutions $= -2 + \left(-\dfrac{8}{3}\right)$

$= \dfrac{-6}{3} - \dfrac{8}{3} = \dfrac{-14}{3}$

The correct answer is (a).

9.1 Practice and Solutions

1. If $|x + 3| = 12$, which of the following is true?

   I. x could be greater than zero
   II. x could be smaller than zero
   III. x could be zero

   (A) I only
   (B) II only
   (C) III only
   (D) I and II
   (E) I and III

2. Which of the following has the largest value?
   (A) $-3 + |-7|$
   (B) $|-3| + |-7|$
   (C) $|-3| + (-7)$
   (D) $(-3) + (-7)$
   (E) $-3 + 7$

3. What is the sum of the solutions of $|x - 4| + 2 = 15$?
   (A) -9
   (B) -4
   (C) 0
   (D) 8
   (E) 18

4. What are the solutions of $|x - 3| = |2x + 7|$?
   (A) $-10, \frac{-4}{3}$
   (B) $-4, \frac{-5}{3}$
   (C) $\frac{-10}{3}, \frac{-5}{3}$
   (D) $2, \frac{-4}{3}$
   (E) $2, 5$

5. What are the coordinates of the intersection of $3x = -12$ and $y = |x - 12|$?
   (A) $(4, 16)$
   (B) $(4, -12)$
   (C) $(-4, -8)$
   (D) $(-4, 12)$
   (E) $(-4, 16)$

Solutions to 9.1 Practice: 1(D), 2(B), 3(D), 4(A), 5(E)

1. If $|x + 3| = 12$, which of the following is true?

   I. x could be greater than zero
   II. x could be smaller than zero
   III. x could be zero

   (A) I only
   (B) II only
   (C) III only
   (D) I and II
   (E) I and III

   > $|x + 3| = 12$
   > case 1: $x + 3 = 12$; $\boxed{x = 9}$
   > case 2: $-(x + 3) = 12$; $-x - 3 = 12$; $\boxed{x = -15}$
   > 0 *does not work*

2. Which of the following has the largest value?

   (A) $-3 + |-7|$
   (B) $|-3| + |-7|$
   (C) $|-3| + (-7)$
   (D) $(-3) + (-7)$
   (E) $-3 + 7$

   > $-3 + |-7| = -3 + 7 = 4$
   > $|-3| + |-7| = 3 + 7 = 10$
   > $|-3| + (-7) = 3 - 7 = -4$
   > $(-3) + (-7) = -3 - 7 = -10$
   > $-3 + 7 = 4$
   > *The largest value is* 10

3. What is the sum of the solutions of $|x - 4| + 2 = 15$?

   (A) -9
   (B) -4
   (C) 0
   (D) 8
   (E) 18

   > $|x - 4| = 13$
   > case 1: $x - 4 = 13$; $x = 17$
   > case 2: $-x + 4 = 13$; $x = -9$
   > *The sum is* $17 + (-9) = 8$

4. What are the solutions of $|x - 3| = |2x + 7|$?

   (A) $-10, \dfrac{-4}{3}$
   (B) $-4, \dfrac{-5}{3}$
   (C) $\dfrac{-10}{3}, \dfrac{-5}{3}$
   (D) $2, \dfrac{-4}{3}$
   (E) $2, 5$

   > $|x - 3| = |2x + 7|$
   > case 1: $x - 3 = 2x + 7$; $-7 - 3 = 2x - x$; $x = -10$
   > case 2: $-x + 3 = 2x + 7$; $3 - 7 = 2x + x$; $x = \dfrac{-4}{3}$

5. What are the coordinates of the intersection of $3x = -12$ and $y = |x - 12|$?

   (A) $(4, 16)$
   (B) $(4, -12)$
   (C) $(-4, -8)$
   (D) $(-4, 12)$
   (E) $(-4, 16)$

   > *To find intersection is to solve for x & y:*
   > $3x = -12$; $x = -4$
   > $y = |x - 12| = |-4 - 12| = 16$
   > *Point of intersection is* $(-4, 16)$

10. Solving Inequalities

$x > y$: *x is greater than y*

$x < y$: *x is smaller than y*

$x \geq y$: *x is greater than or equal to y*

$x \leq y$: *x is smaller than or equal to y*

ex.1 If $2x + 7 > 13$, which of the following must be true?

    a) $x < -2$ b) $x < 0$ c) $x = 2$ d) $x > 3$ e) $x = 6$

        Solution: $2x + 7 > 13$ keep $2x$ on the left, & move 7 to the right,

                     $2x > 13 - 7$ 7 becomes -7 when it moves across.

           $\therefore$ $2x > 6$, $x > 3$

        The correct answer is (d).

ex.2 If $3(x - 4) \geq 4x + 9$, which of the following must be true?

        I. $-35 \leq x < -21$

        II. $x \leq -21$

        III. $x > 0$

    a) I only   b) II only   c) III only   d) I and II   e) I and III

        Solution: $3x - 12 \geq 4x + 9$ move $4x$ to left, & -12 to right:

                 $3x - 4x \geq 9 + 12$ $4x$ becomes $-4x$, -12 becomes 12.

                     $-x \geq 21$

    Note: multiply both sides by -1 and reverse the inequality sign:

         $\therefore$ $x \leq -21$

    The correct answer is (b).

ex.3 *Solve*: $\frac{1}{2}|x - 3| > 2$

        solution: multiply both sides by 2: $|x - 3| > 4$

        case 1: $(x - 3) > 4$

                    $x > 7$

        case 2: $-(x - 3) > 4$

                    $-x + 3 > 4$

                    $-x > 1$

        multiply both sides by -1 and reverse the inequality sign:

                    $x < -1$

         $\therefore$ $x < -1$ *or* $x > 7$

        Expressed on a number line:

10.1 Practice and Solutions

1. Solve for x, $\quad 2x + \frac{1}{3} < 7$

2. Solve for x, $\quad 2x + 9 \geq x - 6$

3. Solve for a, $\quad 3a + 12 \geq 7a + 3$

4. If $4x - 5 > 13$, which of the following must be true?
   (A) $x < 4$
   (B) $x > -5$
   (C) $x > \frac{13}{4}$
   (D) $x > \frac{9}{2}$
   (E) $x > 8$

5. $2(x - 5) \geq 3x + 7$, what is the value of x?
   (A) $x \leq -17$
   (B) $x \leq -2$
   (C) $x > -5$
   (D) $x \geq 5$
   (E) $x \geq 17$

6. If $a - 4 > b + 3$, which of the following must always be true?
   I. $a > b$
   II. $a - b > 7$
   III. $b < -7$
   (A) I only
   (B) II only
   (C) III only
   (D) I and II only
   (E) II and III only

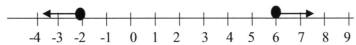

-4 -3 -2 -1 0 1 2 3 4 5 6 7 8 9

7. Which of the following has a solution set represented on the number line above?
   (A) $x + 4 \leq 2$
   (B) $x - 7 \leq 1$
   (C) $x - 1 \geq 5$
   (D) $|x + 2| \geq 4$
   (E) $|x - 2| \geq 4$

Solutions to 10.1 Practice: 1 ($x < \frac{10}{3}$), 2 ($x \geq -15$), 3 ($a \leq \frac{9}{4}$),

4(D), 5(A), 6(D), 7(E)

1. Solve for x, $2x + \frac{1}{3} < 7$; $x < 7 - \frac{1}{3}$; $2x < \frac{20}{3}$; $x < \frac{10}{3}$

2. Solve for x, $2x + 9 \geq x - 6$; $2x - x \geq -6 - 9$; $x \geq -15$

3. Solve for a, $3a + 12 \geq 7a + 3$; $3a - 7a \geq 3 - 12$; $-4a \geq -9$; $a \leq \frac{9}{4}$

4. If $4x - 5 > 13$, which of the following must be true?

   (A) $x < 4$

   (B) $x > -5$

   (C) $x > \frac{13}{4}$

   (D) $x > \frac{9}{2}$

   (E) $x > 8$

   $4x - 5 > 13$
   $4x > 13 + 5$
   $4x > 18$, $x > \frac{18}{4}$, $x > \frac{9}{2}$

5. $2(x - 5) \geq 3x + 7$, what is the value of x?

   (A) $x \leq -17$

   (B) $x \leq -2$

   (C) $x > -5$

   (D) $x \geq 5$

   (E) $x \geq 17$

   $2(x - 5) \geq 3x + 7$
   $2x - 10 \geq 3x + 7$
   $-7 - 10 \geq 3x - 2x$
   $-17 \geq x$

6. If $a - 4 > b + 3$, which of the following must always be true?

   I. $a > b$

   II. $a - b > 7$

   III. $b < -7$

   (A) I only

   (B) II only

   (C) III only

   (D) I and II only

   (E) II and III only

   $a - 4 > b + 3$
   $a > b + 3 + 4$, $\therefore$ $a > b + 7$, $\therefore$ I is true
   since $a > b + 7$, $a - b > 7$, $\therefore$ II is true
   since b can be any real number, ex. $a = 9$ and $b = 1$.
   $\therefore$ III. is false.

   -4 -3 -2 -1 0 1 2 3 4 5 6 7 8 9

7. Which of the following has a solution set represented on the number line above?

   (A) $x + 4 \leq 2$

   (B) $x - 7 \leq 1$

   (C) $x - 1 \geq 5$

   (D) $|x + 2| \geq 4$

   (E) $|x - 2| \geq 4$

   It can't be (A), (B) and (C), since each has only one half-line solution, not two like in the number line above.
   for (E): $|x - 2| \geq 4$:
   case 1: $x - 2 \geq 4$, $x \geq 6$ or
   case 2: $-(x - 2) \geq 4$, $-x + 2 \geq 4$, $x \leq -2$

11. Functions and Their Graphs, Domain and Range

Domain: D = { set of possible values of x for a given function }

Range: R = { set of possible values of y for a given function }

11.1 Linear Functions and Their Graphs, Domain and Range

Linear Functions (straight lines):

$$y = mx + b$$

$$m = \text{slope}$$

(m = positive : *an ascending line,* ╱)

(m = negative: *a descending line,* ╲)

($m = 0$: *a horizontal line parallel to x axis*)

b = y-intercept (where the line intersects the y-axis)

ex. $y = 2x + 1$,

slope: $m = 2$ (an ascending line, ╱)

y-intercept: $b = 1$

Domain and Range:

The domain and range of any linear function whose graph is not parallel to either axis are:

D = { $x \in$ Real } and **R = { $y \in$ Real }**

ex. 1. The domain and range of
$y = 2x + 1$:
D = { $x \in$ Real} and R = { $y \in$ Real }

When the graph is parallel to the x-axis:

ex. 2. $y = 5$, D = { $x \in$ Real} and R = { $y = 5$ }

When the graph is parallel to the y-axis:

ex. 3. $x = -3$, D = { $x = -3$} and R = { $y \in$ Real }

<u>Graph of Linear Functions</u>: Straight line

ex. 1. Graph $y = 0.5x + 2$, $y = 0.5x - 2$, $y = 0.5x - 4$, and find their Domain and Range.

All three lines have the same slope, since $m_1 = m_2 = m_3 = 0.5$, so they are parallel.

Top graph: $y = 0.5x + 2$, y-int $= 2$ and $D = \{ x \in \text{Real} \}$ and $R = \{ y \in \text{Real} \}$

Middle graph: $y = 0.5x - 2$, y-int $= -2$ and $D = \{ x \in \text{Real} \}$ and $R = \{ y \in \text{Real} \}$

Bottom graph: $y = 0.5x - 4$, y-int $= -4$ and $D = \{ x \in \text{Real} \}$ and $R = \{ y \in \text{Real} \}$

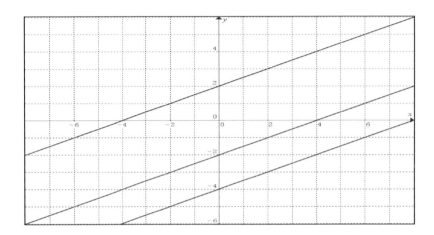

ex. 2. Which of the following is the graph of $y = -x + 2$?

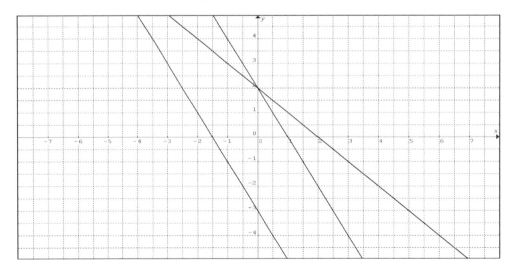

Solution: The equation $y = -x + 2$, has y-intercept $= 2$,

∴ the far left graph cannot be, since its y-intercept $= -3$.

Find the x-intercept for the graph of $y = -x + 2$ by setting $y = 0$,

∴ $0 = -x + 2$, therefore $x = 2$ is the x-intercept.

From the graphs above, the far right one has the x-intercept $= 2$,

∴ The far right graph represents the equation $y = -x + 2$.

11.2 Quadratic Functions and Their Graphs, Domain and Range

$y = x^2$: parabola passes through the origin, opening upward

$y = -x^2$: parabola passes through the origin, opening downward

$y = (x - p)^2 + q$:

    when q is positive, move up.   ex. $y = x^2 + 2$, up 2 units from $y = x^2$,

    when q is negative, move down. ex. $y = x^2 - 2$, down 2 units from $y = x^2$,

    when p is positive, move right. ex. $y = (x - 4)^2$, right 4 units from $y = x^2$,

    when p is negative, move left.

           ex. $y = (x - (-5))^2 = (x + 5)^2$, left 5 units from $y = x^2$.

ex. comparing $y_2 = (x + 2)^2 - 3$ with $y_1 = x^2$,

    Graph of y_2 is obtained by moving y_1 2 units left, 3 units down.

The Domain of a quadratic function is always: **D** = { $x \in$ **Real**}

The Range of a quadratic function is always:

    R = { $y \geq q$ }   for $y = (x - p)^2 + q$, the graph opens up

               or

    R = { $y \leq q$ }   for $y = -(x - p)^2 + q$, the graph opens down

Graph of quadratic function is called ***parabola***.

ex.1   Graphs: Top: $y = x^2$ (opening up),   Bottom: $y = -x^2$ (opening down)

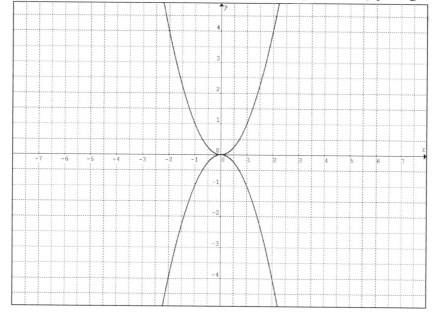

    Top Graph: D = { $x \in$ Real }   and   R = { $y \geq 0$}

    Bottom Graph: D = { $x \in$ Real }   and   R = { $y \leq 0$}

ex.2   Graphs: Top: $y = x^2 + 2$,   Middle: $y = x^2$,   Bottom: $y = x^2 - 4$

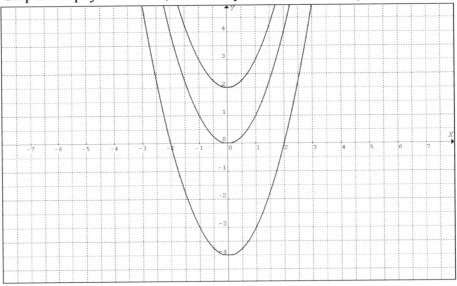

Domain and Range:

Top: $y = x^2 + 2$,   D = $\{\, x \in \text{Real}\}$ and R = $\{\, y \geq 2\, \}$

Middle: $y = x^2$,   D = $\{\, x \in \text{Real}\}$ and R = $\{\, y \geq 0\, \}$

Bottom: $y = x^2 - 4$,   D = $\{\, x \in \text{Real}\}$ and R = $\{\, y \geq -4\, \}$

ex.3. Graphs: Left: $y = (x + 5)^2$ Middle: $y = x^2$ Right: $y = (x - 3)^2$

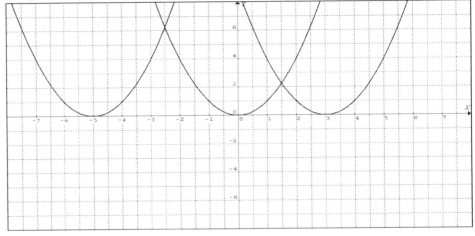

Domain and Range:

Left: $y = (x + 5)^2$,   D = $\{\, x \in \text{Real}\}$ and R = $\{\, y \geq 0\, \}$

Middle: $y = x^2$,   D = $\{\, x \in \text{Real}\}$ and R = $\{\, y \geq 0\, \}$

Right: $y = (x - 3)^2$,   D = $\{\, x \in \text{Real}\}$ and R = $\{\, y \geq 0\, \}$

ex.4. Graphs: Top: Left: $y = (x + 5)^2 + 1$, Middle: $y = x^2$, Right: $y = (x - 3)^2 - 3$
Bottom: Left: $y = -(x + 2)^2$, Right: $y = -x^2 - 2$

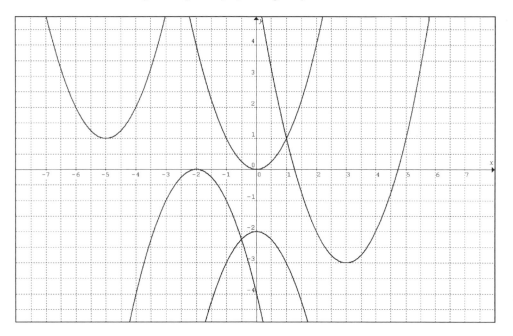

Domain and Range:

Top Left:	$y = (x + 5)^2 + 1$,	$D = \{ x \in \text{Real} \}$ and $R = \{ y \geq 1 \}$
Top Middle:	$y = x^2$,	$D = \{ x \in \text{Real} \}$ and $R = \{ y \geq 0 \}$
Top Right:	$y = (x - 3)^2 - 3$,	$D = \{ x \in \text{Real} \}$ and $R = \{ y \geq -3 \}$
Bottom Left:	$y = -(x + 2)^2$,	$D = \{ x \in \text{Real} \}$ and $R = \{ y \leq 0 \}$
Bottom Right:	$y = -x^2 - 2$,	$D = \{ x \in \text{Real} \}$ and $R = \{ y \leq -2 \}$

11.3 Absolute Value Functions and Their Graphs, Domain and Range

$y = |x|$: passes through the origin, opening upward
$y = -|x|$: passes through the origin, opening downward
$y = |x| + q$: when q is positive, up q units from $y = |x|$
 when q is negative, down q units from $y = |x|$
$y = |x - p|$:
if p is positive, move p units to the right from $y = |x|$
ex. $y = |x - 4|$, move 4 units right
if p is negative, move p units to the left from $y = |x|$
ex. $y = |x - (-4)| = |x + 4|$, move 4 units left

Domain of an absolute value function is always: $D = \{ x \in \text{Real} \}$

Range of an absolute value function:
$R = \{ y \geq q \}$ for $y = |x - p| + q$, the graph opens upward.
   or
$R = \{ y \leq q \}$ for $y = -|x - p| + q$, the graph opens downward.

ex.1   Graph: $y = |x|$ and $D = \{\, x \in \text{Real}\}$ and $R = \{\, y \geq 0 \,\}$

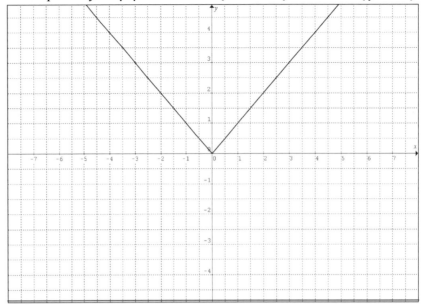

ex.2   Graph: $y = -|x|$ and $D = \{\, x \in \text{Real}\}$ and $R = \{\, y \leq 0 \,\}$

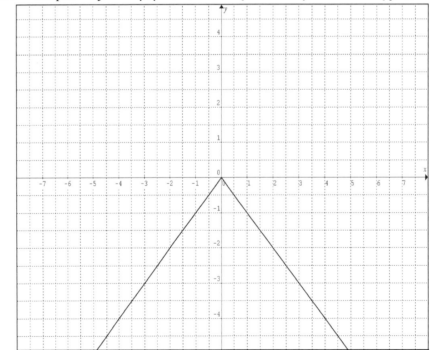

ex.3   Graphs: Left: $y = |x + 4| + 1$ Right: $y = -|x - 3| + 1$

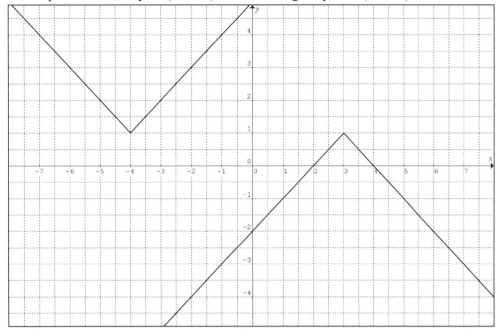

Domain and Range:

Top Left: $y = |x + 4| + 1,$ $D = \{x \in \text{Real}\}$ and $R = \{y \geq 1\}$

Bottom Right: $y = -|x - 3| + 1,$ $D = \{x \in \text{Real}\}$ and $R = \{y \leq 1\}$

11.4   Radical Functions and Their Graphs, Domain and Range

$y = \sqrt{x}$:   a curved line that starts at the origin and gradually curves up:

$y = -\sqrt{x}$:   a curved line that starts at the origin and gradually curves down:

$y = \sqrt{x} + q$:   when q is positive, up q units from $y = \sqrt{x}$

when q is negative, down q units from $y = \sqrt{x}$

$y = \sqrt{x - p}$:

If p is positive, move p units to the right from $y = \sqrt{x}$

ex. $y = \sqrt{x - 4}$, move 4 units right

If p is negative, move p units to the left from $y = \sqrt{x}$

ex. $y = \sqrt{x - (-4)} = \sqrt{x + 4}$, move 4 units left

Domain of radical functions: $\mathbf{D = \{x \geq p\}}$ for $y = \pm\sqrt{x - p} + q$

Range of a radical function is always:

$\mathbf{R = \{y \geq q\}}$ for $y = \sqrt{x - p} + q$

or

$\mathbf{R = \{y \leq q\}}$ for $y = -\sqrt{x - p} + q$

ex.1 $y = \sqrt{x}$,

     $D = \{ x \geq 0 \}$ & $R = \{ y \geq 0 \}$

ex.2 $y = -\sqrt{x}$,

     $D = \{ x \geq 0 \}$ & $R = \{ y \leq 0 \}$

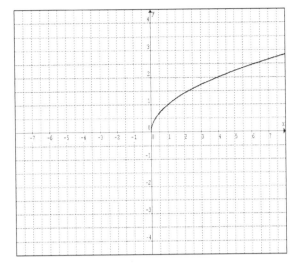

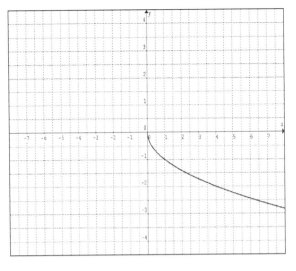

ex.3   Top Left: $y = \sqrt{x + 5} + 2$, $D = \{x \geq -5\}$ and $R = \{y \geq 2\}$

       Top Right: $y = \sqrt{x - 3}$, $D = \{x \geq 3\}$ and $R = \{y \geq 0\}$

       Bottom: $y = -\sqrt{x + 1} - 2$, $D = \{x \geq -1\}$ and $R = \{y \leq -2\}$

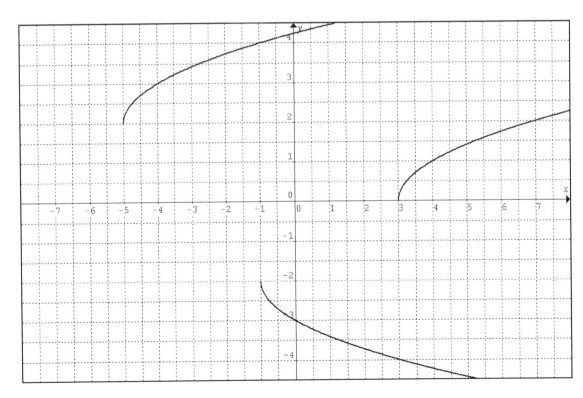

11.5   Practice and Solutions

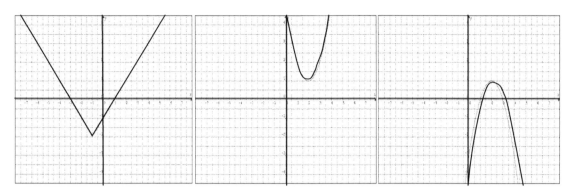

Graph 1   Graph 2   Graph 3

1. For $a > 0$ and $b > 0$, which of the following represents the Graph 1 above?
    (A) $y = |x|$
    (B) $y = |x + a| - b$
    (C) $y = -|x + a| - b$
    (D) $y = ax + b$
    (E) $y = ax^2 + b$

2. For $a > 0$ and $b > 0$, which of the following represents the Graph 2 above?
    (A) $y = ax + by$
    (B) $y = |x + a| + b$
    (C) $y = -(x - a)^2 + b$
    (D) $y = (x - a)^2 - b$
    (E) $y = (x - a)^2 + b$

3. Which of the following represents the range of the Graph 3 above?
    (A) $y \geq 0$
    (B) $y \leq 0$
    (C) $0 \leq y \leq 1$
    (D) $y \leq 1$
    (E) y can be any real number.

4. If $y = -2x^2 + 2x + 3$, which of the following must be true about
    the graph of y?
    (A) It is a straight line, y-intercept = 3.
    (B) It is a parabola, opening up, y-intercept = 2.
    (C) It is a parabola, opening up, y-intercept = 3.
    (D) It is a parabola, opening down, y-intercept = 2.
    (E) It is a parabola, opening down, y-intercept = 3.

5. Which of the following functions represents Graph 1?
   (A) $y = 2x - 2$
   (B) $y = 2x$
   (C) $y = 2x^2 - 2$
   (D) $y = |x| - 2$
   (E) $y = \sqrt{x} - 2$

Graph 1:

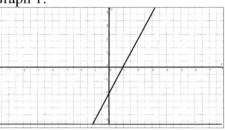

6. Which of the following represents the Range of Graph 4?
   (A) $y \leq 1$
   (B) $-5 \leq y \leq -1$
   (C) $y \geq -2$
   (D) $y \geq 1$
   (E) $y \geq 2$

Graph 2:

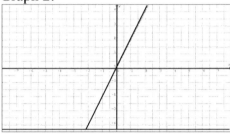

7. If $h > 0$ and $k > 0$, which Graph represents the function
   $y = |x + h| - k$?
   (A) Graph 1
   (B) Graph 2
   (C) Graph 3
   (D) Graph 4
   (E) Graph 5

Graph 3:

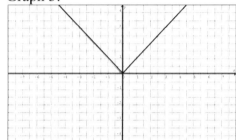

8. Which of the following functions represents Graph 5?
   (A) $y = 2x$
   (B) $y = |x - 2|$
   (C) $y = (x - 2)^2$
   (D) $y = (x - 2)^2 + 7$
   (E) $y = \sqrt{x - 2}$

Graph 4:

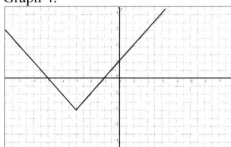

9. If Graph 5 is translated so the vertex moves from $(2, 0)$ to $(4, -3)$, which of the following represents the translated graph?
   (A) $y = 2(x - 4) - 3$
   (B) $y = |x - 4| - 3$
   (C) $y = \sqrt{x + 4} - 3$
   (D) $y = (x + 4)^2 - 3$
   (E) $y = (x - 4)^2 - 3$

Graph 5:

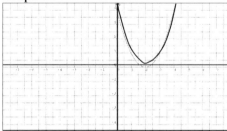

Solutions to 11.5 Practice: 1(B), 2(E), 3(D), 4(E), 5(A), 6(C), 7(D), 8(C), 9(E)

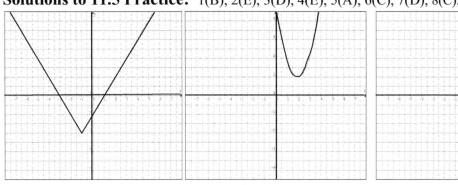

Graph 1   Graph 2   Graph 3

1. For $a > 0$ and $b > 0$, which of the following represents the Graph 1 above?

(A) $y = |x|$

(B) $y = |x + a| - b$

(C) $y = -|x + a| - b$

(D) $y = ax + b$

(E) $y = ax^2 + b$

> $Graph\ 1\ is\ a\ Absolute\ Value\ Function,\ \ y = |x|$
> $translated\ left\ to\ y = |x + a|\ \ for\ \ a > 0$
> $and\ down\ to\ y = |x + a| - b\ \ for\ \ b > 0$

2. For $a > 0$ and $b > 0$, which of the following represents the Graph 2 above?

(A) $y = ax + by$

(B) $y = |x + a| + b$

(C) $y = -(x - a)^2 + b$

(D) $y = (x - a)^2 - b$

(E) $y = (x - a)^2 + b$

> $Graph\ 2\ corresponds\ to\ a\ Quadratic$
> $Function\ y = x^2\ translated\ right$
> $to\ (x - a)^2\ for\ \ a > 0\ and$
> $up\ to\ y = (x - a)^2 + b\ \ for\ \ b > 0$

3. Which of the following represents the range of the Graph 3 above?

(A) $y \geq 0$

(B) $y \leq 0$

(C) $0 \leq y \leq 1$

(D) $y \leq 1$

(E) y can be any real number.

> $All\ points\ on\ Graph\ 3\ are\ below\ the$
> $line\ y = 1\ with\ the\ vertex\ on\ y = 1$

4. If $y = -2x^2 + 2x + 3$ which of the following must be true about
    the graph of y? It is a:

(A) straight line, y-intercept = 3.

(B) parabola, opening up, y-intercept = 2.

(C) parabola, opening up, y-intercept = 3.

(D) parabola, opening down, y-intercept = 2.

(E) parabola, opening down, y-intercept = 3.

> $The\ function\ is\ a\ quadratic\ function$
> $and\ hence\ the\ graph\ is\ a\ parabola.$
> $The\ coefficient - 2\ at\ the\ front\ of$
> $x^2\ means\ the\ graph\ opens\ down.$
> $y - intercept\ is\ 3\ since\ y = 3\ for\ x = 0$

5. Which of the following functions represents Graph 1?

Graph 1:

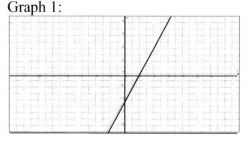

(A) $2x - 2$
(B) $2x$
(C) $2x^2 - 2$
(D) $|x| - 2$
(E) $\sqrt{x} - 2$

Equation of line is: $y = mx + b$
(A) & (B) are lines.
(A): $y = 2x - 2$
has y intercept at
-2 as in Graph 1.

6. Which of the following represents the Range of Graph 4?

Graph 2:

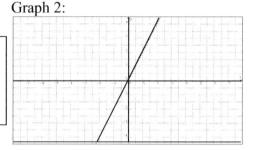

(A) $y \leq 1$
(B) $-5 \leq y \leq -1$
(C) $y \geq -2$
(D) $y \geq 1$
(E) $y \geq 2$

All points on Graph 4 are above $y = -2$.
$\therefore y \geq -2$

7. If $h > 0$ and $k > 0$, which Graph represents the function $y = |x + h| - k$?

Graph 3:

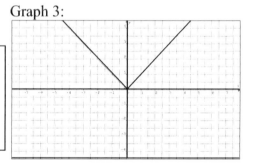

(A) Graph 1
(B) Graph 2
(C) Graph 3
(D) Graph 4
(E) Graph 5

Graphs 3 and 4 are absolute functions, but only graph 4 has the translation of h units left & k units down.

8. Which of the following functions represents Graph 5? $y =$

Graph 4: represent

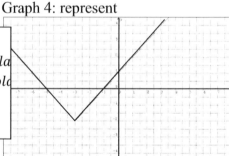

(A) $2x$
(B) $|x - 2|$
(C) $(x - 2)^2$
(D) $(x - 2)^2 + 7$
(E) $\sqrt{x - 2}$

(C) or (D)
represents parabola
but (D) is a parabola
that shifed 7 up.
(C) is correct.

9. If Graph 5 is translated so the vertex moves from $(2, 0)$ to $(4, -3)$, which of the following represents the translated graph? $y =$

Graph 5:

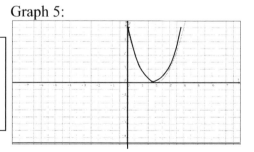

(A) $2(x - 4) - 3$
(B) $|x - 4| - 3$
(C) $\sqrt{x + 4} - 3$
(D) $(x + 4)^2 - 3$
(E) $(x - 4)^2 - 3$

parabola $y = x^2$
translated 4
units right and
3 units down.

12. Composition of Functions

12.1 Function Notations

In Algebra, f(x) and g(x) are often used to represent functions.

ex.1 $f(x) = 4x^2 - 5x + 2$

$f(2) = 4(2)^2 - 5(2) + 2 = 8$

f(2) means to substitute 2 for every x in the function.

ex.2 If $f(x) = -2x^2 + x - 3$, what is the value of $f(\sqrt{3})$?

    a) $-9 + \sqrt{3}$ b) $-6 + \sqrt{3}$ c) $\sqrt{3}$ d) $2 + \sqrt{3}$ e) 3

    Solution: to find $f(\sqrt{3})$, replace every x by $\sqrt{3}$:

$$\therefore \quad f(\sqrt{3}) = -2(\sqrt{3})^2 + (\sqrt{3}) - 3 = -2(3) + \sqrt{3} - 3$$
$$= -9 + \sqrt{3}$$

    The answer is (a).

12.2 Function Operations

Let $f(x) = -7x + 2$, $g(x) = 3x + 4$

Find   1. $(f + g)(x)$,   2. $(f - g)(x)$ 3. $(fg)(x)$ 4. $\left(\dfrac{f}{g}\right)(x)$

1. Add: $(f + g)(x) = f(x) + g(x) = (-7x + 2) + (3x + 4) = -4x + 6$

2. Subtract: $(f - g)(x) = f(x) - g(x) = (-7x + 2) - (3x + 4) = -10x - 2$

3. Multiply: $(fg)(x) = f(x) * g(x) = (-7x + 2) * (3x + 4) = -21x^2 - 22x + 8$

4. Divide: $\left(\dfrac{f}{g}\right)(x) = \dfrac{f(x)}{g(x)} = \dfrac{-7x+2}{3x+4}$

Use the functions above, find $(f + g)(5)$ and $\left(\dfrac{f}{g}\right)(-2)$:

     $(f + g)(5) = -4x + 6 = -4(5) + 6 = -14,$ and

$$\left(\tfrac{f}{g}\right)(-2) = \dfrac{-7x+2}{3x+4} = \dfrac{-7(-2)+2}{3(-2)+4} = \dfrac{16}{-2} = -8$$

12.3   Composition of Functions

If $f(x)$ and $g(x)$ are two functions, the composite functions of them are expressed as $f(g(x))$ or $g(f(x))$:

ex.1 Let $f(x) = x^2 + 3$ and $g(x) = 3x + 2$

    1. Find $f(g(x))$:

$$f(x) = x^2 + 3$$

Substitute $g(x)$ for every x in $f(x)$.

$$f(g(x)) = (g(x))^2 + 3$$
$$= (3x + 2)^2 + 3$$
$$= (3x + 2)(3x+2) + 3$$
$$= 9x^2 + 12x + 7$$

    2. Find $g(f(x))$:

since $g(x) = 3x + 2$ and $f(x) = x^2 + 3$

$\therefore$ $g(f(x)) = 3(x^2 + 3) + 2$, substitute $f(x)$ for every x in $g(x)$.

$$= 3x^2 + 11$$

ex.2 If $f(x) = x^2 + 3$, and $g(x) = 2x - 4$, what is the value of $g(f(6))$?

    a) 12   b) 27   c) 39   d) 60   e) 74

Solution: $f(6) = 6^2 + 3 = 39$

$\therefore$ $g(f(6)) = g(39) = 2*39 - 4 = 74$

The correct answer is (e).

ex.3 Let $f(x) = x^2 - 3$ and $g(x) = \dfrac{x}{3}$

What is the smallest value of x such that $g(f(x)) = 11$?

    a) -8 b) -6 c) -3 d) 0   e) 3

Solution: $g(f(x)) = \dfrac{(x^2 - 3)}{3}$ and since $g(f(x)) = 11$

$\therefore$ $\dfrac{x^2 - 3}{3} = 11$

$\therefore$ $x^2 - 3 = 33,$ $x^2 = 36$

$x = -6$ or $6,$

$\therefore$ The smallest value is -6.

The correct answer is (b).

12.4   Practice and Solutions

1. For $f(x) = 3 - x$, find $f(-2)$:

2. For $f(x) = -6x - 5$, and $g(x) = 2x + 3$, find $(f + g)(3)$:

3. For $f(x) = 2x - 3$, and $g(x) = 4x + 1$, find $\left(\dfrac{f}{g}\right)(5)$:

4. If $f(x) = x^2 + 4$, and $g(x) = 3x - 1$, what is the value of $g(f(4))$?

5. If $f(x) = x^2 - 4$ and $g(x) = \dfrac{x}{2}$, what is the value of $f(g(-6))$?

6. If $f(x) = 6x^2 - kx$, and $f(-2) = 12$, what is the value of k?
   - (A) -12
   - (B) -6
   - (C) 9
   - (D) 18
   - (E) 22

7. If $f(x) = x\sqrt{2x^2 + 4}$, what is the value of $f(2)$?
   - (A) 2
   - (B) $3\sqrt{2}$
   - (C) $4\sqrt{3}$
   - (D) 5
   - (E) $6\sqrt{2}$

8. If $f(x) = 2x - 3$, and $g(x) = x + 1$, what is the value of $g(f(3))$?
   - (A) 4
   - (B) 5
   - (C) 12
   - (D) 14
   - (E) 21

9. If $f(x) = x^2 + 3x - 4$, and $g(x) = x^2 - 1$, which of the following is $\left(\dfrac{f}{g}\right)(x)$?
   - (A) $\dfrac{x-4}{x^2-1}$

   - (B) $\dfrac{x-4}{x+1}$

   - (C) $\dfrac{x-4}{x+1}$

   - (D) $\dfrac{x-1}{x-2}$

   - (E) $\dfrac{x+4}{x+1}$

Solutions to 12.4 Practice: 1 (5), 2 (−14), 3 ($\frac{1}{3}$), 4 (59), 5 (5), 6(B), 7(C), 8(A), 9(E)

1. $f(x) = 3 - x$: $f(-2) = 3 - (-2) = 3 + 2 = 5$

2. $f(x) = -6x - 5$, $g(x) = 2x + 3$: $(f + g)(x) = -6(3) - 5 + 2(3) + 3 = -14$

3. $f(x) = 2x - 3$, $g(x) = 4x + 1$: $\frac{f}{g}(5) = \frac{2(5)-3}{4(5)+1} = \frac{7}{21} = \frac{1}{3}$

4. $f(x) = x^2 + 4$, $g(x) = 3x - 1$: $g(f(4)) = 3(4^2 + 4) - 1 = 59$

5. $f(x) = x^2 - 4$, $g(x) = \frac{x}{2}$: $f(g(-6)) = (\frac{-6}{2})^2 - 4 = \frac{36}{4} - \frac{16}{4} = \frac{20}{4} = 5$

6. If $f(x) = 6x^2 - kx$, and f(−2) = 12, what is the value of k?

   (A) −12

   (B) −6

   (C) 9

   (D) 18

   (E) 22

   $$f(-2) = 6(-2)^2 - k(-2) = 12$$
   $$24 + 2k = 12$$
   $$k = -6$$

7. If $f(x) = x\sqrt{2x^2 + 4}$, what is the value of $f(2)$?

   (A) 2

   (B) $3\sqrt{2}$

   (C) $4\sqrt{3}$

   (D) 5

   (E) $6\sqrt{2}$

   $$f(2) = 2\sqrt{2 * 4 + 4}$$
   $$= 2\sqrt{12}$$
   $$= 2\sqrt{4 * 3}$$
   $$= 2 * 2\sqrt{3}$$
   $$= 4\sqrt{3}$$

8. If $f(x) = 2x - 3$, and $g(x) = x + 1$, what is the value of $g(f(3))$?

   (A) 4

   (B) 5

   (C) 12

   (D) 14

   (E) 21

   $$f(3) = 2 * 3 - 3 = 3$$
   $$g(f(3)) = g(3)$$
   $$= 3 + 1$$
   $$= 4$$

9. If $f(x) = x^2 + 3x - 4$, and $g(x) = x^2 - 1$, which of the following is $\left(\frac{f}{g}\right)(x)$?

   (A) $\frac{x-4}{x^2-1}$

   (B) $\frac{x-4}{x+1}$

   (C) $\frac{x-4}{x+1}$

   (D) $\frac{x-1}{x-2}$

   (E) $\frac{x+4}{x+1}$

   $$\left(\frac{f}{g}\right)(x) = \frac{f(x)}{g(x)}$$
   $$= \frac{x^2 + 3x - 4}{x^2 - 1}$$
   $$= \frac{(x + 4)(x - 1)}{(x + 1)(x - 1)}$$
   $$= \frac{x + 4}{x + 1} \quad for \ x \neq \pm 1$$

13. Remainder Theorem

When a polynomial f(x) is divided by a linear divisor $(x - a)$, the remainder is equal to f(a).

ex.1 Determine the remainder when $f(x) = x^3 - 2x^2 + 3x - 4$ is divided
by (1) $x - 3$ and (2) $x + 1$
Solution: (1) Divided by $x - 3$
The remainder can be obtained by finding f(3):
$f(3) = 3^3 - 2(3)^2 + 3(3) - 4 = 14$
∴ 14 is the remainder
(2) Divided by $x + 1$
Since $x + 1$ is $x - (-1)$ the remainder is f(-1):
$f(-1) = (-1)^3 - 2(-1)^2 + 3(-1) - 4$
$= -10$
∴ -10 is the remainder.

ex.2 When $x^2 - qx + 14$ is divided by $x + 2$, the remainder is 6.
What is the value of q ?
a) $- 5$ b) -1 c) 6   d) 9   e) 13
Solution: since $x + 2$ is $x - (-2)$, the remainder is f(-2)
By the Remainder Theorem, the remainder is:
$f(-2) = (-2)^2 - q(-2) + 14 = 6$
∴ $4 + 2q + 14 = 6$ ∴ $q = -6$
The correct answer is (c).

ex.3 Let $f(x) = ax^2 + bx - 4$. When f(x) is divided by $x - 1$,
the remainder is 4, and when f(x) is divided by $x + 3$,
the remainder is -4. Which of the following is f(x) ?

a) $2x^2 + 6x - 4$ b) $4x^2 - 2x - 4$ c) $4x^2 + 3x - 4$
Solution: By the Remainder Theorem
$a(1)^2 + b(1) - 4 = 4$ ∴ $a + b = 8$ (1)
$a(-3)^2 + b(-3) - 4 = -4$ ∴ $9a - 3b = 0$ (2)
from (2): $9a = 3b$ ∴ $b = 3a$
sub into (1): $a + (3a) = 8$
∴ $a = 2$ ∴ $b = 6$
∴ $f(x) = 2x^2 + 6x - 4$

The correct answer is (a).

13.1 Practice and Solutions

Using Remainder Theorem, find the remainder of:

1. $(x^2 + 6x - 27) \div (x - 2)$

2. $(3x^3 - x^2 + 3x - 9) \div (x + 1)$

3. $(x^3 - 4x^2 + x - 2) \div (x - 5)$

4. What is the remainder when $f(x) = 2x^2 + 3x - 9$ is divided by $(x - 3)$?
   (A) 18
   (B) 7
   (C) $\dfrac{25}{4}$
   (D) $\dfrac{12}{5}$
   (E) $\dfrac{5}{3}$

5. When $2x^2 - qx + 9$ is divided by $x + 2$, the remainder is 45, what is the value of q?
   (A) -22
   (B) -14
   (C) -3
   (D) 8
   (E) 14

6. Let $f(x) = x^2 - kx + 4$. When $f(x)$ is divided by $x + 1$, the remainder is 13, what is the remainder when $f(x)$ is divided by $(x - 2)$?
   (A) -26
   (B) -12
   (C) -8
   (D) 8
   (E) 32

7. If $f(x) = 3x^2 - 6x + 1$, then $f(x)$ is divided by which of the following to give a remainder of 10?
   (A) $(x + 8)$
   (B) $(x + 6)$
   (C) $(x + 2)$
   (D) $(x - 1)$
   (E) $(x - 3)$

Solutions to 13.1 Practice: 1 (-11), 2 (-16), 3 (28), 4(A), 5(E), 6(C), 7(E)

Using Remainder Theorem, find the remainder of:

1. $(x^2 + 6x - 27) \div (x - 2)$: $f(2) = 2^2 + 6(2) - 27 = -11$

2. $(3x^3 - x^2 + 3x - 9) \div (x + 1)$: $f(-1) = 3(-1)^3 - (-1)^2 + 3(-1) - 9 = -16$

3. $(x^3 - 4x^2 + x - 2) \div (x - 5)$: $f(5) = 5^3 - 4(5)^2 + 5 - 2 = 28$

4. What is the remainder when $f(x) = 2x^2 + 3x - 9$ is divided by $(x - 3)$?

    (A) 18
    (B) 7
    (C) $\dfrac{25}{4}$
    (D) $\dfrac{12}{5}$
    (E) $\dfrac{5}{3}$

    $Remainder = f(3)$
    $= 2*9 + 3*3 - 9$
    $= 18$

5. When $2x^2 - qx + 9$ is divided by $x + 2$, the remainder is 45, what is the value of q?

    (A) -22
    (B) -14
    (C) -3
    (D) 8
    (E) 14

    $Remainder = f(-2)$
    $= 2(-2)^2 - q(-2) + 9$
    $= 8 + 2q + 9$
    $= 17 + 2q = 45$
    $2q = 28, \quad q = 14$

6. Let $f(x) = x^2 - kx + 4$. When $f(x)$ is divided by $x + 1$, the remainder is 13, what is the remainder when $f(x)$ is divided by $(x - 2)$?

    (A) -26
    (B) -12
    (C) -8
    (D) 8
    (E) 32

    $Remainder\ 13 = f(-1)$
    $13 = (-1)^2 - k(-1) + 4$
    $13 = 5 + k, \quad k = 8$
    $f(x) = x^2 - 8x + 4$
    $The\ remainder\ of\ f(x) \div (x - 2)$
    $is\ f(2) = 4 - 16 + 4 = -8$

7. If $f(x) = 3x^2 - 6x + 1$, then $f(x)$ is divided by which of the following to give a remainder of 10?

    (A) $(x + 8)$
    (B) $(x + 6)$
    (C) $(x + 2)$
    (D) $(x - 1)$
    (E) $(x - 3)$

    $Remainder = f(a) = 10$
    $Find\ a$:
    $3a^2 - 6a + 1 = 10$
    $3a^2 - 6a - 9 = 0$
    $a^2 - 2a - 3 = 0$
    $(a + 1)(a - 3) = 0$
    $a = -1, 3$

Data Analysis

1. Fundamental Counting Principle (FCP)

FCP states that if a task is to be accomplished in steps, the first step in a different ways, the second step in b different ways, and the third in c different ways and so on, then the number of possible ways to accomplish the task is:

$$a * b * c * ...$$

ex.1   Getting from point M to N must pass through point O. There are 4 possible ways to get from point M to O, and 3 ways from O to N. How many possible ways are there to get from M to N?

   a) 4   b) 7   c) 9   d) 12   e) 16

  Solution: For each of the 4 ways from M to O,
     there are 3 possible ways from O to N,
    ∴ Use FCP to find the total possible number of ways from M to N:
     4 * 3 = 12
   ("∴" means "Therefore")

M   N

  The route-map above, verifies the number of possible ways.

Point M

Point O

Point N

  The tree diagram above verifies the number of possible ways to be 12.
 The correct answer is (d).

ex.2   A student needs to take three courses, a math, a science, and a language; one out of four math courses, one out of nine science courses, and one out of five language courses. How many possible selections are there?

   a) 120   b) 180   c) 225   d) 345   e) 480

  Solution: Use FCP to find the number of possible selections:
     4 * 9 * 5 = 180
  The correct answer is (b).

ex.3 The student council has 3 people running for president, 2 for vice-president, and 2 for secretary. How many ways can the positions be filled?

a) 7   b) 12   c) 18   d) 22   e) 24

Solution: number of choices for president = 3
number of choices for vice-president = 2
number of choices for secretary = 2
Use FCP to find the number of ways to fill the 3 positions:
3 * 2 * 2 = 12

The correct answer is (b).

The following tree diagram verifies the FCP result to be 12:

Let the 3 people running for president be: Amy, Bob and Charlie (A, B, C)
the 2 people running for vice-president be: Mary and Norm (M, N)
and the 2 people running for secretary be: Xin and Young (X, Y)

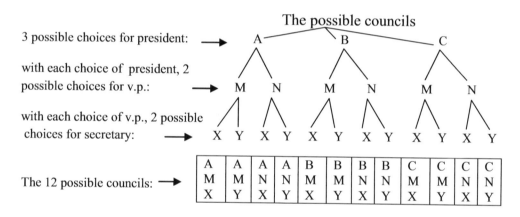

ex.4 A math quiz consists of 5 multiple choice questions, each with 4 possible answers A, B, C, and D. If every question must be answered, how many ways can this math quiz be completed?

a) 20   b) 80   c) 240   d) 512   e) 1024

Solution: Let the answer be represented by the following blanks:
1. __ , 2. __ , 3. __ , 4. __ , 5. __
   4   4   4   4   4

each blank has 4 choices.
Use FCP to find the number of possible ways to complete the quiz:
4 * 4 * 4 * 4 * 4 = 1024

The correct answer is (e).

1.1 Practice

1. A school lunch combo includes a sandwich, a drink and a fruit. There are 3 types of sandwiches, 4 kinds of drinks, and 5 kinds of fruits available. How many possible lunch combos are there?
   - (A) 12
   - (B) 15
   - (C) 20
   - (D) 35
   - (E) 60

2. How many different caps can you get from 4 styles, each with 12 different colors?
   - (A) 60
   - (B) 48
   - (C) 24
   - (D) 12
   - (E) 7

3. A restaurant offers $5 one-topping pizzas, choosing from 2 different shapes, 3 kinds of crusts, and 14 toppings. How many possible $5 pizzas are there?
   - (A) 84
   - (B) 60
   - (C) 42
   - (D) 30
   - (E) 28

4. A chemist produced a total of 168 different mixtures; each was the combination of solutions A, B and C in different concentrations. He used 8 different concentrations of solution A, and 7 of B. How many different concentrations of C did he use?
   - (A) 3
   - (B) 5
   - (C) 7
   - (D) 8
   - (E) 9

5. Jason constructed 24 model airplanes from x number of styles, each style with $3y$ number of colors. What is x in terms of y?
   - (A) $\dfrac{24}{y}$
   - (B) $\dfrac{12}{y}$
   - (C) $\dfrac{8}{y}$
   - (D) $24y$
   - (E) $8y$

Solutions to Practice 1.1:   1(E), 2(B), 3(A), 4(A),5(C)

1. A school lunch combo includes a sandwich, a drink and a fruit. There are 3 types of sandwiches, 4 kinds of drinks, and 5 kinds of fruits available. How many possible lunch combos are there?

   (A) 12
   (B) 15
   (C) 20
   (D) 35
   (E) 60

   > Choose a sandwich ... 3 choices
   > Choose a drink ... 4 choices
   > Choose a fruit ... 5 choices
   > Use FCP to find number of combos possible:
   > 3*4*5 = 60

2. How many different caps can you get from 4 styles, each with 12 different colors?

   (A) 60
   (B) 48
   (C) 24
   (D) 12
   (E) 7

   > Choose a style ... 4 ways
   > Choose a color ... 12 ways
   > Total number of selections is
   > 4 * 12 = 48

3. A restaurant offers $5 one-topping pizzas, choosing from 2 different shapes, 3 kinds of crusts, and 14 toppings. How many possible $5 pizzas are there?

   (A) 84
   (B) 60
   (C) 42
   (D) 30
   (E) 28

   > Using FCP:
   > number of different pizzas is
   >
   > 2 * 3 * 14 = 84

4. A chemist produced a total of 168 different mixtures; each was the combination of solutions A, B and C in different concentrations. He used 8 different concentrations of solution A, and 7 of B. How many different concentrations of C did he use?

   (A) 3
   (B) 5
   (C) 7
   (D) 8
   (E) 9

   > Let x = number of concentrations of C
   > by FCP, the number of mixtures:
   > $7 * 8 * x = 168$, $56x = 168$,
   > $x = 168 \div 56 = 3$, $\therefore$ $x = 3$

5. Jason constructed 24 model airplanes from x number of styles, each style with $3y$ number of colors. What is x in terms of y?

   (A) $\dfrac{24}{y}$
   (B) $\dfrac{12}{y}$
   (C) $\dfrac{8}{y}$
   (D) $24y$
   (E) $8y$

   > $x * (3y) = 24$
   > $x = \dfrac{24}{3y} = \dfrac{8}{y}$

2. Permutations

A permutation is an arrangement of elements in which **the order of elements is important**. For example, 123, 132, 213, 231, 312, 321 are the 6 possible permutations for the three digits 1, 2 and 3.

The Permutation formula, nPr, is used to calculate the number of permutations possible when arranging r elements taken from a pool of n elements:

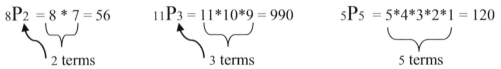

$$nPr = n(n-1)(n-2)\ldots(n-r+1)$$

r terms, n and r are integers, and $1 \le r \le n$

Examples:

$$8P2 = 8 * 7 = 56$$

2 terms

$$11P3 = 11*10*9 = 990$$

3 terms

$$5P5 = 5*4*3*2*1 = 120$$

5 terms

ex.1 How many four-digit numbers can be made from the digits 1, 2, 3 and 4, if no digit can be repeated?

a) 32   b) 24   c) 12   d) 8   e) 4

    Solution: There are 4 digits to choose from ($n = 4$)
           to form 4-digit numbers ($r = 4$).

        Use nPr to find the number of possible permutations:

$$4P4 = 4 * 3 * 2 * 1 = 24$$

The correct answer is (b).

ex.2 How many different six-letter passwords can be made from 26 alphabet letters if no letter may be repeated? (M = millions)

a) 24M   b) 200M   c) 166M   d) 92M   e) 80M

    Solution: There are 26 letters to choose from ($n = 26$)
           to form 6-letter passwords ($r = 6$).

        Use nPr to find the number of possible permutations:

$$26P6 = 26 * 25 * 24 * 23 * 22 * 21$$
$$= 165{,}765{,}600$$
$$= 166M$$

The correct answer is (c).

2.1 Practice

1. Find the value of $_{11}P_2$.

2. Find the value of $_9P_4$.

3. An advertising page in a phone book has 6 spots for advertisements. In how many ways can 6 companies' ads be put into these 6 spots?
   (A) 720
   (B) 424
   (C) 320
   (D) 118
   (E) 36

4. How many different four-digit numerals can be formed from the digits 2, 4, 5, 7 and 8?
   (A) 12
   (B) 48
   (C) 86
   (D) 120
   (E) 150

5. In an Olympic game of 16 competitors, how many possible outcomes are there of winning a gold medal, a silver medal, and a bronze medal?
   (A) 4240
   (B) 3360
   (C) 2486
   (D) 1296
   (E) 720

6. How many ways are there to line up a sports team of seven (2 coaches and 5 players) for a photograph, if the two coaches are at opposite ends of the line-up and the 5 players are in between?
   (A) 60
   (B) 120
   (C) 240
   (D) 360
   (E) 480

7. The student-IDs at a university consist of 3 letters followed by 4 digits. About how many different IDs can be made if no letter and no digit may be repeated?
   (A) 200M (million)
   (B) 120M
   (C) 98.2M
   (D) 78.6M
   (E) 9.5M

Solutions to 2.1 Practice: 1 (110), 2 (3024), 3(A), 4(D), 5(B), 6(C), 7(E)

1. Find the value of $_{11}P_2 = 11 * 10 = 110$

2. Find the value of $_9P_4 = 9 * 8 * 7 * 6 = 3024$

3. An advertising page in a phone book has 6 spots for advertisements.
   In how many ways can 6 companies' ads be put into these 6 spots?

   (A) 720
   (B) 424
   (C) 320
   (D) 118
   (E) 36

   > The number of ways to place the advertisements is $_6P_6$.
   >
   > $_6P_6 = 6 * 5 * 4 * 3 * 2 * 1 = 720$

4. How many different four-digit numerals can be formed from the digits
   2, 4, 5, 7 and 8?

   (A) 12
   (B) 48
   (C) 86
   (D) 120
   (E) 150

   > Total of 5 digits to choose from: $n = 5$
   > To form the four-digit numerals: $r = 4$
   > The order of the digits is important:
   > The total possible numerals is $_5P_4 = 120$

5. In an Olympic game of 16 competitors, how many possible outcomes are
   there of winning a gold medal, a silver medal, and a bronze medal?

   (A) 4240
   (B) 3360
   (C) 2486
   (D) 1296
   (E) 720

   > 16 competitors to choose from: $n = 16$
   > To fill the 3 winning positions, and the order
   > of gold, silver and bronze matters, $r = 4$
   > Total possible outcomes is
   > $_{16}P_3 = 16 * 15 * 14 = 3360$

6. How many ways are there to line up a sports team of seven (2 coaches
   and 5 players) for a photograph, if the two coaches are at opposite ends
   of the line-up and the 5 players are in between?

   (A) 60
   (B) 120
   (C) 240
   (D) 360
   (E) 480

   > Place coaches at the ends...2 ways
   > Order 5 players between...$_5P_5$ ways
   > Total number of orders is $2 * _5P_5 = 240$

7. The student-IDs at a university consist of 3 letters followed by 4 digits. About
   how many different IDs can be made if no letter and no digit may be repeated?

   (A) 200M (million)
   (B) 120M
   (C) 98.2M
   (D) 78.6M
   (E) 11.2M

   > Select 3 letters out of 26... $_{26}P_3$
   > Select 3 digits out of 10... $_{10}P_3$
   > The total number of ID's is
   > $(_{26}P_3)(_{10}P_3) = (26 * 25 * 24)(10 * 9 * 8) = 11,232,000 = 11.2M$

3. Combinations

A combination is an arrangement of elements in which **the order of elements is not important**. For example, Joey decided to use 3 different colors out of of 12 available colors to complete his coloring sheet. In this case, the order of the colors is not important.

The Combination formula, nCr, is used to calculate the number of possible combinations when selecting r elements from a pool of n elements:

$$nCr = \frac{n(n-1)(n-2)...(n-r+1)}{r*(r-1)\,...\,2*1}$$

where n and r are integers, and $1 \leq r \leq n$

Example of applying the formula for nCr:

$$_{11}C_3 = \frac{\overbrace{11*10*9}^{3 \text{ terms} \quad (_{11}P_3)}}{\underbrace{3*2*1}} = 165 \qquad _{25}C_4 = \frac{\overbrace{25*24*23*22}^{4 \text{ terms}}}{\underbrace{4*3*2*1}} = 12650$$

$$_8C_5 = \frac{8*7*6*5*4}{5*4*3*2*1} = 56 \qquad _{111}C_2 = \frac{111*110}{2*1} = 6105$$

ex.1 A father won two hockey game tickets and decided to give the tickets to two of his five children. How many ways can the two children be chosen?

    a) 60   b) 30   c) 20   d) 16   e) 10

        Solution: Since he is choosing 2 from a pool of 5,
                $n = 5$ and $r = 2$.
            Since the order of the 2 chosen is not important,
            use nCr:

$$_5C_2 = \frac{5*4}{2*1} = 10$$

        The correct answer is (e).

ex.2 Ten different points are marked on the circumference of a circle. How many triangles can be drawn using the marked points as vertices?

a) 10   b) 30   c) 56   d) 120   e) 124

Solution: There are 10 points to chose from ($n = 10$).
It takes 3 points to form each triangle ($r = 3$).
The order in which the 3 points are chosen of the triangle is not important.

∴ use $n\mathbf{C}r$:

$$_{10}C_3 = \frac{10*9*8}{3*2*1} = 120$$

The correct answer is (d).

ex.3 Eleven students, 5 male and 6 female, are trying out for 4 main roles in a play, 2 female roles and 2 male roles. In how many ways can the four roles be filled?

a) 30   b) 60   c) 150   d) 160   e) 180

Solution: Out of the 5 males, select 2. Order is not important:

$$_5C_2 = \frac{5*4}{2*1} = 10$$

Out of the 6 females, select 2. Order is not important:

$$_6C_2 = \frac{6*5*4}{3*2*1} = 15$$

Use FCP to find the combinations for 4 roles formed with 2 males and 2 females

$$_5C_2 * {}_6C_2 = 10 * 15 = 150$$

The correct answer is (c).

3.1 Practice

1. Find the value of $_6C_2$.

2. Find the value of $_9C_4$.

3. Find the value of $_7C_3 * {}_3C_2$.

4. Three students are randomly chosen from a class of 15 to meet with a visiting guest in the school. In how many ways can the three students be chosen?
   (A) 720
   (B) 455
   (C) 320
   (D) 118
   (E) 75

5. If 14 people in a conference room shake hands with one another, how many handshakes are there?
   (A) 14
   (B) 28
   (C) 56
   (D) 91
   (E) 110

6. Jen wants to give 5 music CDs to her mom, choosing from her 12 Blues and 11 Jazz. In how many ways can the 5 CDs be chosen if two are Jazz?
   (A) 36460
   (B) 14400
   (C) 12100
   (D) 1296
   (E) 121

7. A cell-phone promotional package offers one free phone choosing from four available models, and three free features selecting from seven available features. In how many ways can a customer choose the package?
   (A) 11
   (B) 28
   (C) 60
   (D) 108
   (E) 140

8. On a book sale list, there are 15 mystery, 12 science fiction, and 9 adventure books. If Cole is buying 2 books from each category, how many possible ways can he choose?
   (A) 249480
   (B) 2246
   (C) 1620
   (D) 108
   (E) 8

Solutions to 3.1 Practice: 1 (15), 2 (126), 3 (105), 4(B), 5(D), 6(C), 7(E), 8(A)

1. Find the value of $_6C_2 = \frac{6*5}{2*1} = 15$

2. Find the value of $_9C_4 = \frac{9*8*7*6}{4*3*2*1} = 126$

3. Find the value of $_7C_3 * _3C_2 = \frac{7*6*5}{3*2*1} * \frac{3*2}{2*1} = 105$

4. Three students are randomly chosen from a class of 15 to meet with a visiting guest in the school. In how many ways can the three students be chosen?

   (A) 720
   (B) 455
   (C) 320
   (D) 118
   (E) 75

   > Order in which we choose students is not important.
   >
   > The number of choices is $_{15}C_3 = \frac{15*14*13}{3*2*1} = 455$

5. If 14 people in a conference room shake hands with one another, how many handshakes are there?

   (A) 14
   (B) 28
   (C) 56
   (D) 91
   (E) 110

   > The number of handshakes is
   >
   > $_{14}C_2 = \frac{14*13}{2*1} = 91$

6. Jen wants to give 5 music CDs to her mom, choosing from her 12 Blues and 11 Jazz. In how many ways can the 5 CDs be chosen if two are Jazz?

   (A) 36460
   (B) 14400
   (C) 12100
   (D) 1296
   (E) 121

   > Choose 2 Jazz CD's out of 11... $_{11}C_2$
   >
   > Choose 3 Blues CD's out of 12... $_{12}C_3$
   >
   > The number of ways to choose 5 CD's is
   >
   > $(_{11}C_2)(_{12}C_3) = \frac{11*10}{2*1} * \frac{12*11*10}{3*2*1} = 12100$

7. A cell-phone promotional package offers one free phone choosing from four available models, and three free features selecting from seven available features. In how many ways can a customer choose the package?

   (A) 11
   (B) 28
   (C) 60
   (D) 108
   (E) 140

   > The cell-phone package can be selected
   >
   > $(_4C_1)(_7C_3) = 4 * \frac{7*6*5}{3*2*1} = 140$ ways.

8. On a book sale list, there are 15 mystery, 12 science fiction, and 9 adventure books. If Cole is buying 2 books from each category, how many possible ways can he choose?

   (A) 249480
   (B) 2246
   (C) 1620
   (D) 108
   (E) 8

   > Using FCP, the number of book selections is
   >
   > $(_{15}C_2)(_{12}C_2)(_9C_2) = \frac{15*14}{2*1} * \frac{12*11}{2*1} * \frac{9*8}{2*1} = 249480$

4. Probability

Probability is a measure of the chance that an event will occur. For example, the probability of getting a head when tossing a coin is $\frac{1}{2}$.

Probability Formula:

$$P(\text{some event occurs}) = \frac{Number\ of\ ways\ an\ Event\ occurs\ (E)}{Total\ number\ of\ possible\ outcomes\ (T)} = \frac{E}{T}$$

ex.1   Find the probability of each of the following when tossing a die:
   a) Getting a 2.
   b) Getting an even number.
   Solutions:
   a) $E = 1$,   since there is only one 2 on a die
       $T = 6$,   since there are 6 total possible outcomes: 1, 2, 3, 4, 5, 6
       $\therefore$ $P(2) = \frac{E}{T} = \frac{1}{6}$
   b) $E = 3$,   since there are 3 even numbers on a die: 2, 4, 6
       $T = 6$,   since there are 6 total possible outcomes: 1, 2, 3, 4, 5, 6
       $\therefore$ $P(even\ number) = \frac{E}{T} = \frac{3}{6} = \frac{1}{2}$

ex.2   Two students from a class of 18 are randomly chosen to join the principal's luncheon meeting. What is the probability that the twins Jack and Jill are chosen?

   a) $\frac{1}{180}$ b) $\frac{1}{153}$ c) $\frac{1}{72}$ d) $\frac{1}{36}$ e) $\frac{1}{18}$

   Solution: Use the nCr formula to find the total possible outcomes
   of choosing 2 from 18, so $n = 18$ and $r = 2$:
   $$nCr = 18C2 = \frac{18*17}{2*1} = 153$$
   $\therefore$ the total number of outcomes, $T = 153$
   $\therefore$ number of event with Jack and Jill be chosen, $E = 1$
   $$P(\text{the twins chosen}) = \frac{E}{T} = \frac{1}{153}$$
   The correct answer is (b).

ex.3 From past experience, a school predicts the probability of its students passing a state-wide Math test as $\frac{4}{5}$. If there are 185 students taking the next Math test, how many students are expected to fail?

a) 30   b) 37   c) 39   c) 45   e) 47

Solution: Since the probability of passing is $\frac{4}{5}$,

the probability of failing is $1 - \frac{4}{5} = \frac{1}{5}$.

$\therefore$ number of students failing $= \frac{1}{5} * 185$

$$= \frac{185}{5} = 37$$

The correct answer is (b).

ex.4 Two color pencils are drawn at random from a box containing six red, five blue and four yellow. What is the probability of getting a red and a blue?

a) $\frac{1}{15}$ b) $\frac{2}{15}$ c) $\frac{2}{7}$ d) $\frac{1}{7}$ e) $\frac{1}{3}$

Solution: This problem can be solved by FCP or Combinations:

1. By FCP

since there are 15 color pencils in total, and 6 red, 5 blue:

$\therefore$ P (first red, then a blue) $= \frac{6}{15} * \frac{5}{14} = \frac{1}{7}$

$\therefore$ P (first blue, then a red) $= \frac{5}{15} * \frac{6}{14} = \frac{1}{7}$

P(a red and a blue) $= \frac{1}{7} + \frac{1}{7} = \frac{2}{7}$

2. By nCr

Total number of possible outcomes of drawing 2 pencils from 15:

choosing 2 pencils from 15: $_{15}C_2 = = \frac{15 * 14}{2 * 1} = 105$

Total number of possible ways of getting a red and a blue:

choosing 1 red from 6: $_6C_1 = 6$

choosing 1 blue from 5: $_5C_1 = 5$

$\therefore$ total for a red and a blue (FCP): $6 * 5 = 30$

$\therefore$ P(a red and a blue) $= \frac{_6C_1 * _5C_1}{_{15}C_2} = \frac{30}{105} = \frac{2}{7}$

The correct answer is (d).

4.1 Practice

1. When tossing a coin and a die, what is the probability of getting a head on the coin and an even number on the die?

    (A) $\frac{1}{8}$

    (B) $\frac{1}{4}$

    (C) $\frac{1}{2}$

    (D) $\frac{3}{4}$

    (E) $\frac{2}{3}$

2. What is the probability of getting a sum of four when rolling two dice?

    (A) $\frac{1}{36}$

    (B) $\frac{1}{18}$

    (C) $\frac{1}{12}$

    (D) $\frac{1}{6}$

    (E) $\frac{1}{4}$

3. Three students are randomly selected from a class of 21, and two of them are sick. What is the probability that none of the students selected is sick?

    (A) 0.84

    (B) 0.73

    (C) 0.68

    (D) 0.65

    (E) 0.58

4. A case contains 6 cans of Cokes and 10 cans of Pepsi. If 2 cans are drawn from the case without replacement, what is the probability of getting 2 Pepsi?

    (A) $\frac{1}{32}$

    (B) $\frac{1}{16}$

    (C) $\frac{1}{8}$

    (D) $\frac{1}{4}$

    (E) $\frac{3}{8}$

5. In a high school of 780 senior graduates, the probability of a student going to college is $\frac{41}{50}$. How many students are not expected to go to college?

    (A) 140

    (B) 121

    (C) 108

    (D) 84

    (E) 58

Solutions to Practice 4.1: 1(B), 2(C), 3(B), 4(E), 5(A)

1. When tossing a coin and a die, what is the probability of getting a head on the coin and an even number on the die?

    (A) $\dfrac{1}{8}$

    (B) $\dfrac{1}{4}$

    (C) $\dfrac{1}{2}$

    (D) $\dfrac{3}{4}$

    (E) $\dfrac{2}{3}$

    > T = 12 since there are 12 possible outcomes:
    >   H1, H2, H3, H4, H5, H6, T1, T2, T3, T4, T5, T6
    > E = 3, for head on the coin, and an even number on the dice are: H2, H4, H6
    > P (H on coin, even on dice) $= \dfrac{3}{12} = \dfrac{1}{4}$

2. What is the probability of getting a sum of four when rolling two dice?

    (A) $\dfrac{1}{36}$

    (B) $\dfrac{1}{18}$

    (C) $\dfrac{1}{12}$

    (D) $\dfrac{1}{6}$

    (E) $\dfrac{1}{4}$

    > T = 36 since we can get 1, 2, 3, 4, 5 or 6 on either dice, the number of outcomes is 6 * 6 = 36
    > E = 3 since we can get the sum of 4 three different ways
    >   (3 + 1 = 1 + 3 = 2 + 2)
    > P (sum = 4) $= \dfrac{3}{36} = \dfrac{1}{12}$

3. Three students are randomly selected from a class of 21, and two of the 21 are sick. What is the probability that none of the students selected is sick?

    (A) 0.84

    (B) 0.73

    (C) 0.68

    (D) 0.65

    (E) 0.58

    > $T = {}_{21}C_3 = \dfrac{21*20*19}{3*2*1}$
    > $E = {}_{19}C_3 = \dfrac{19*18*17}{3*2*1}$
    > P (none are sick) $= \dfrac{19*18*17}{21*20*19} = 0.729$

4. A case contains 6 cans of Cokes and 10 cans of Pepsi. If 2 cans are drawn from the case without replacement, what is the probability of getting 2 Pepsi?

    (A) $\dfrac{1}{32}$

    (B) $\dfrac{1}{16}$

    (C) $\dfrac{1}{8}$

    (D) $\dfrac{1}{4}$

    (E) $\dfrac{3}{8}$

    > $T = {}_{16}C_2 = \dfrac{16*15}{2*1} = 120$, the number of selections of 2 cans out of 16.
    > $E = {}_{10}C_2 = \dfrac{10*9}{2*1} = 45$, the number of selections of 2 Pepsi cans out of 10 Pepsi cans.
    > P (2 Pepsi) $= \dfrac{45}{120} = \dfrac{3}{8}$

5. In a high school of 780 senior graduates, the probability of a student going to college is $\dfrac{41}{50}$. How many students are not expected to go to college?

    (A) 140

    (B) 121

    (C) 108

    (D) 84

    (E) 58

    > The probability of a student not going to college is
    > $1 - \dfrac{41}{50} = \dfrac{9}{50} = 18\%$
    > 18% of 780 students is 0.18 * 780 = 140

5. Data Analysis

When given a table, graph or chart, it is important to study the data carefully, understand and analyze the data, recognize the trend, and perform the required task.

The total number of bikes sold in a store in 2009

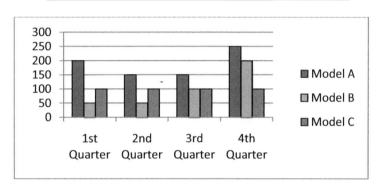

ex.1 From the chart above, what was the percentage of total sales in the 4th quarter to the total sales in the whole year?

a) 26.0%   b) 30.9%   c) 35.5%   d) 38.5%   e) 43.3%

Solution: Total sales in 1st Q $= 200 + 50 + 100 = 350$
Total sales in 2nd Q $= 150 + 50 + 100 = 300$
Total sales in 3rd Q $= 150 + 100 + 100 = 350$
Total sales in 4th Q $= 250 + 200 + 100 = 550$

Total sales in 2009 $= 350 + 300 + 350 + 550 = 1550$
Percentage of 4th to Total $= \dfrac{550}{1550} * 100\% = 35.5\%$

The correct answer is (c).

ex.2 From the chart above, what fraction of the total number of Model A sold in 2009 is to the total?

a) $\dfrac{1}{4}$ b) $\dfrac{2}{5}$ c) $\dfrac{3}{7}$ d) $\dfrac{13}{15}$ e) $\dfrac{15}{31}$

Solution: Total sales for Model A $= 200 + 150 + 150 + 250 = 750$
Total sales for Model B $= 50 + 50 + 100 + 200 = 400$
Total sales for Model C $= 100 + 100 + 100 + 100 = 400$
Total sales in 2009 $= 750 + 400 + 400 = 1550$

Fraction of Model A to Total $= \dfrac{750}{1550} = \dfrac{75}{155} = \dfrac{15}{31}$

The correct answer is (e).

5.1 Practice: 1(e), 2(c), 3(a), 4(d), 5(d), 6(b)

Age Population Demography of the City of Ambrose

Age	0 - 20	21 - 40	41 - 60	61 – 80	above 80
Population	270,000	250,000	230,000	240,000	10,000

1. When a telemarketer makes a phone call in the evening in Ambrose, according to the table above, what is the probability that he/she reaches a person aged 60 or under?
   (A) 45%
   (B) 52%
   (C) 66%
   (D) 70%
   (E) 75%

Results of a School Math Exam

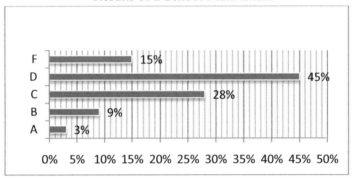

2. The chart above shows the percentage of students achieving a grade of A, B, C, D and F in a school Math Exam. What percentage of students achieved C or better?
   (A) 28%
   (B) 31%
   (C) 40%
   (D) 45%
   (E) 60%

3. The chart above shows the percentage of students achieving a grade of A, B, C, D and F in a school Math Exam. If 45 students got F, how many students achieved C or better?
   (A) 120
   (B) 116
   (C) 108
   (D) 95
   (E) 84

	Apples	Oranges	Pears	Plums
Number of boxes	14	15	12	10
Number of fruits per box	15	12	x	24

4. In the table above, if the total number of fruits is 870, what is x?

(A) 8

(B) 12

(C) 15

(D) 20

(E) 24

Cost of T-shirt Orders

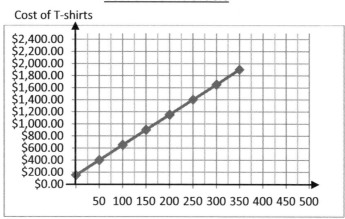

5. The graph above represents the total cost of T-shirt orders in different quantities, with minimum order of 50. What is the expected cost of ordering 450 T-shirts?

(A) 1900

(B) 2000

(C) 2200

(D) 2400

(E) 2500

6. Which of the following equations best represents the chart above, Cost of T-shirt Orders?

(A) $y = 2x + 50$

(B) $y = 5x + 150$

(C) $y = 10x + 150$

(D) $y = 2x^2 + 50$

(E) $y = 5x^2 + 150$

Solutions to 5.1 Practice: 1(E), 2(C), 3(A), 4(D), 5(D), 6(B)

Age Population Demography of the City of Ambrose

Age	0 - 20	21 - 40	41 - 60	61 – 80	above 80
Population	270,000	250,000	230,000	240,000	10,000

1. When a telemarketer makes a phone call in the evening in Ambrose, according to the table above, what is the probability that he/she reaches a person aged 60 or under?

    (A) 45%
    (B) 52%
    (C) 66%
    (D) 70%
    (E) 75%

    T (total population) = 10,000 (27 + 25 + 23 + 24 + 1) = 1,000,000
    E (population aged 60 or under) = 10,000 (27 + 25 + 23) = 750,000
    $P \ (\text{age} \leq 60) = \frac{750,000}{1,000,000} = 75\%$

Results of a School Math Exam

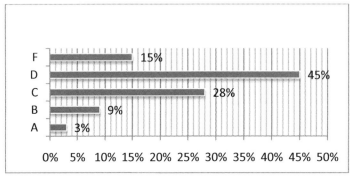

2. The chart above shows the percentage of students achieving a grade of A, B, C, D and F in a school Math Exam. What percentage of students achieved C or better?

    (A) 28%
    (B) 31%
    (C) 40%
    (D) 45%
    (E) 60%

    28% (C) + 9% (B) + 3% (A) = 40% achieved a 'C' or higher.

3. The chart above shows the percentage of students achieving a grade of A, B, C, D and F in a school Math Exam. If 45 students got F, how many students achieved C or better?

    (A) 120
    (B) 116
    (C) 108
    (D) 95
    (E) 84

    Let x = the number of students achieving a 'C' or higher.
    45 students got F, representing 15%,
    x students got C or above, representing 40%
    $\frac{15}{45} = \frac{40}{x}$; by cross multiplication: $x = \frac{45*40}{15} = 120$

	Apples	Oranges	Pears	Plums
Number of boxes	14	15	12	10
Number of fruits per box	15	12	x	24

4. In the table above, if the total number of fruits is 870, what is x?

   (A) 8
   (B) 12
   (C) 15
   (D) 20
   (E) 24

   $14 * 15 + 15 * 12 + 12 * x + 10 * 24 = 870$
   $12x + 630 = 870$
   $12x = 240$
   $x = 20$

Cost of T-shirt Orders

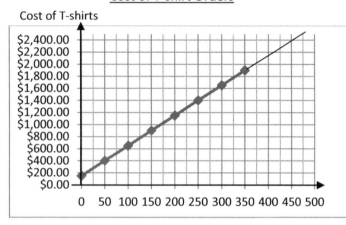

5. The graph above represents the total cost of T-shirt orders in different quantities, with minimum order of 50. What is the expected cost of ordering 450 T-shirts?

   (A) 1900
   (B) 2000
   (C) 2200
   (D) 2400
   (E) 2500

   By extending the graph we estimate that the cost of ordering 450 T-shirts is $2400

6. Which of the following equations best represents the chart above, Cost of T-shirt Orders?

   (A) $y = 2x + 50$
   (B) $y = 5x + 150$
   (C) $y = 10x + 150$
   (D) $y = 2x^2 + 50$
   (E) $y = 5x^2 + 150$

   (See Geometry 7.2 & 7.3)
   The graph is a line so the equation has the form $y = mx + b$ where m is the slope and b is the y-intercept. (only (A), (B), or (C) can be right)
   Choose 2 points on the line, say (50, 400) and (450, 2400). Slope $m = \frac{2400-400}{450-50} = 5$

Geometry

1. Geometry Terms and Notations

∴ : A symbol means "Therefore".   ex. ∴ $x = 2$ ⟶ *Terefore x = 2*

Δ : Triangle,   ex. ΔABC: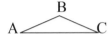

∠ : The angle or the measure of the angle.   ex.   ∠D = 35°
∠BDC means the angle of the middle letter, D.

   ∠BDC is ∠D

≅ : Congruent, or same shape and size.   ex. ΔABC ≅ ΔXYX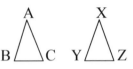

$\overleftrightarrow{AB}$: A line containing points A and B:

$\overline{AB}$: A line segment that has endpoints A and B: A————————B

AB: When there is no bar on top, AB means the length of the line segment $\overline{AB}$

⊥ : Perpendicular,   ex. $\overline{RS}$ is perpendicular to $\overline{TS}$, $\overline{RS} \perp \overline{TS}$

   ∠RST=90°

‖ : Parallel,   ex. line *m* is parallel to line *n*,   *m* ‖ *n*

Bisect: to divide into two equal parts: ex. P bisects line segment $\overline{AB}$,
∴ AP = BP

A————————+————————B

Hypotenuse: the side opposite to the right angle in a right triangle:

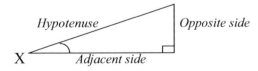

2. Angle Relationships

2.1 Angles on one side of a straight line add to 180°

$$x + y = 180$$
$$x = 180 - y \quad or \quad y = 180 - x$$

2.2 There are 360° in a circle

$$x + y + z + a + b = 360$$

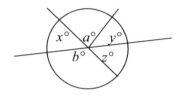

2.3 Opposite angles are equal

Angles that are opposite to each other when two lines intersect have the same measure.

a is opposite to b, and p is opposite to q.

∴ $\underline{a = b}$ (opposite angles)

$\underline{p = q}$ (opposite angles)

ex.1 In the figure below, if $a = 72$ and $c = 45$, what is the value of b?

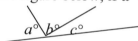

Note: Figure not drawn to scale.

a) 45   b) 63   c) 73   d) 89   e) 108

Solution: since $a + b + c = 180$

∴ $b = 180 - a - c = 180 - 72 - 45 = 63$

The correct answer is (b).

ex.2 In the figure below, if $n = 35$, what is the sum of a, b and c ?

Note: Figure not drawn to scale.

a) 290   b) 300   c) 310   d) 315   e) 325

Solution: since m and n are opposite angles,

∴ $m = n = 35$

since $a + b + c + m + n = 360$

∴ $a + b + c = 360 - m - n$

∴ $= 360 - 35 - 35 = 290$

The correct answer is (a).

2.4 Angles in Parallel lines

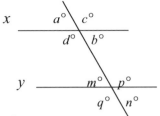

When $x \parallel y$, then

$\quad$ $a = m$, $\quad$ $c = p$,

and $\quad d = q$, $\quad b = n$

also $\quad b = m$ (alternate angles) $\quad$ so $\quad a = b = m = n$

and $\quad d = p$ (alternate angles) $\quad$ so $\quad c = d = p = q$

$\therefore \quad d + m = 180$

and $\quad b + p = 180$

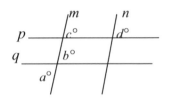

ex.3 In the figure on the right, if $p \parallel q$,
$m \parallel n$, and $\quad d = 50$,
what is the value of a?

$\quad$ a) 50 $\qquad$ b) 80 $\qquad$ c) 100 $\qquad$ d) 120 $\qquad$ e) 130

$\qquad$ Solution: since $m \parallel n$, $\quad \therefore c = d = 50$,

$\qquad\qquad\qquad$ since $p \parallel q$, $\quad \therefore b = c = 50$,

$\qquad\qquad\qquad$ since a and b are in opposite angles,

$\qquad\qquad\qquad\qquad \therefore a = b = 50$

$\qquad$ The correct answer is (a).

2.5 The sum of the measures of the three angles of any triangle is 180°

$$\boxed{\angle A + \angle B + \angle C = 180°}$$

2.6 The sum of the measures of the interior angles of a polygon with n sides is: $\boxed{180° * (n - 2)}$

n (# of sides)	Name	Formula	Sum of Interior Angles
3	triangle	180°* (3−2)	180°
4	quadrilateral	180°* (4−2)	360°
5	pentagon	180°* (5−2)	540°
6	hexagon	180°* (6−2)	720°
7	heptagon	180°* (7−2)	900°
8	octagon	180°* (8−2)	1080°

ex.4   In the figure on the right, $\angle PBA = 145°$,
and $\angle A = 105°$, what is the
measure of $\angle C$?

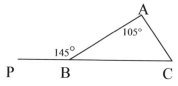

Note: Figure not drawn to scale.

a) 25°   b) 35°   c) 40°   d) 50°   e) 55°

Solution: $\angle ABC = 180° - \angle PBA = 180° - 145° = 35°$
since: $\angle BAC + \angle ABC + \angle ACB = 180°$
$\therefore \angle ACB = 180° - (\angle BAC + \angle ABC)$
$= 180° - (105° + 35°) = 40°$
$\therefore \angle C = 40°$

The correct answer is (c).

ex.5   In the figure on the right, $\overline{AB} \parallel \overline{XY}$,
which of the following must be equal to q?

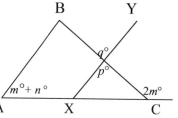

a) $180 - m - n$ b) $180 - 3m - n$ c) $2m - n$ d) $m - n$ e) $2m$

Solution:

$\qquad$ since $\angle ACB = 180° - 2m°$
$\qquad$ since $\overline{AB} \parallel \overline{XY}$
$\qquad \angle YXC = \angle BAC = m° + n°$
$\qquad$ since $\angle YXC + \angle ACB + p° = 180°$
$\qquad\qquad p° = 180° - \angle YXC - \angle ACB$
$\qquad\qquad\quad = 180° - (m° + n°) - (180° - 2m°)$
$\qquad\qquad\quad = 180° - m° - n° - 180° + 2m°$
$\qquad\qquad\quad = m° - n°$
$\qquad \therefore \quad p = m - n$

$\qquad$ since p and q are in opposite angles,
$\qquad \therefore \quad q = p = m - n$
The correct answer is (d).

ex.6   In the figure below, what is the value of x?

Note: Figure not drawn to scale.

a) 61   b) 105   c) 136   d) 176   e) 210

Solution: since the shape has 5 sides, a pentagon and $n = 5$,
so the sum of the interior angles is:
$180 * (n - 2) = 180 * (5 - 2) = 540$
$\therefore\ 120 + 176 + 108 + x + y = 540$
since $y = 180 - 105 = 75$
$\therefore\ 120 + 176 + 108 + x + 75 = 540$
$x = 540 - 120 - 176 - 108 - 75$
$= 61$

The correct answer is (a).

ex.7   In the figure below, what is the value of $a + b$ in terms of x and y?

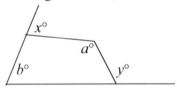

a) $180 - x$ b) $180 - y$ c) $180 - x - y$ d) $x + y$ e) $x + y + 180$

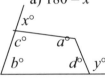

Solution: since the shape is a quadrilateral, so $n = 4$,
the sum of interior angles $= 180 *(4 - 2) = 360$.
Let label the other two angles as c, and d.

$\therefore\qquad a + b + c + d = 360$
$\therefore\qquad a + b = 360 - c - d$
and $\quad c = 180 - x,$
$\qquad d = 180 - y$
$\therefore\qquad a + b = 360 - (180 - x) - (180 - y)$
$\qquad\qquad = 360 - 180 + x - 180 + y$
$\qquad\qquad = x + y$

The correct answer is (d).

2.7   Practice and Solutions

1. If a, b, c, and d are the angles of a quadrilateral, and $a + b + c = 295°$, then what is the value of d?

2. If the sum of the interior angles of a polygon is $1620°$, how many sides are there?

3. If $p = 25°$, q, $r = 68°$, and s are angles on one side of a straight line, then what is the value of $q + s$?

4. In two intersecting lines, x and y are opposite angles, m and n are opposite angles. If $x = 25°$, then what is the value $m - n$?

5. In the figure on the right, what is the value of $m + n$?
    - (A) 38
    - (B) 60
    - (C) 80
    - (D) 126
    - (E) 152

Note: Figure not drawn to scale.

6. In the figure on the right, which of the following is true?
    - (K) $a - b = x - y$
    - (L) $a - b = x + y$
    - (M) $a + b = 180 + x - y$
    - (N) $a + b = 180 - x - y$
    - (O) $a + b = 360 - x - y$

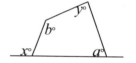

7. In the figure on the right, $p \parallel q$, what is the value of $a + b$?
    - (A) 218
    - (B) 180
    - (C) 146
    - (D) 107
    - (E) 98

8. In the figure on the right, $l_1 \parallel l_2$, what is c in terms of a and b?
    - (F) $180 - a - b$
    - (G) $180 - a + b$
    - (H) $90 - a - b$
    - (I) $90 - a + b$
    - (J) $a + b$

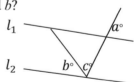

9. In the figure on the right, $m \parallel n$, what is the value of x?
    - (F) 135
    - (G) 121
    - (H) 104
    - (I) 98
    - (E) 94

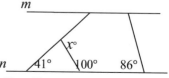

Note: Figure not drawn to scale.

Solutions to 2.7 Practice: 1 (65), 2 (11), 3 (87), 4 (0), 5(E), 6(C), 7(B), 8(A), 9(B)

1. For a quadrilateral, $n = 4$, so sum of the interior angles $= 180 * (4 - 2) = 360$
   $a + b + c + d = 360$, since $a + b + c = 295°$, $\therefore$ $d = 360 - 295 = 65$

2. Since sum of the interior angles of a polygon: $180 * (n - 2) = 1620$, $n = 11$

3. $p + q + r + s = 180$, $q + s = 180 - p - r = 180 - 25 - 68 = 87$

4. Since m and n are opposite angles, $m = n$; $\therefore$ $m - n = 0$

5. In the figure on the right, what is the value of $m + n$?

   (A) 38
   (B) 60
   (C) 80
   (D) 126
   (E) 152

   $n + 36 + 68 = 180$
   $n = 76$
   $\angle n, \angle m$ are opposite
   $\therefore m = n = 76$
   $m + n = 152$

   Note: Figure not drawn to scale.

6. In the figure on the right, which of the following is true?

   (A) $a - b = x - y$
   (B) $a - b = x + y$
   (C) $a + b = 180 + x - y$
   (D) $a + b = 180 - x - y$
   (E) $a + b = 360 - x - y$

   By section 2.6, the sum of
   the interior angles of a
   quadrilateral is 360°:
   $(180 - x) + a + b + y = 360$
   $a + b = 180 + x - y$

   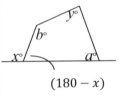

   $(180 - x)$

7. In the figure on the right, $p \parallel q$, what is the value of $a + b$?

   (A) 218
   (B) 180
   (C) 146
   (D) 107
   (E) 98

   By section 2.4,
   b and x are alternate angles,
   so $x = b$; $a + x = a + b = 180$

   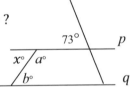

8. In the figure on the right, $l_1 \parallel l_2$, what is c in terms of a and b?

   (A) $180 - a - b$
   (B) $180 - a + b$
   (C) $90 - a - b$
   (D) $90 - a + b$
   (E) $a + b$

   See section 2.4,
   $a + b + c = 180$
   $c = 180 - a - b$

   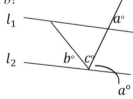

9. In the figure on the right, $m \parallel n$, what is the value of x?

   (A) 135
   (B) 121
   (C) 104
   (D) 98
   (E) 94

   See sections 2.4 and 2.6: the sum of
   the interior angles of a pantagon:
   $180° * (5 - 2) = 540°$
   $x = 540 - 100 - 86 - 94 - 139 = 121$

   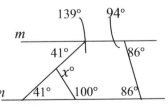

   Note: Figure not drawn to scale.

3. Pythagorean Theorem

In a right angle triangle, the square of the hypotenuse, c, is equal to the sum of the squares of the other two sides, a and b. (*Note*: Hypotenuse is the longest side.)

$$c^2 = a^2 + b^2$$

ex.1 In the figure on the right, solve for x to the nearest hundredth.

Solution:

by Pythagorean Theorem:
$$6^2 = 4^2 + x^2$$
$$x^2 = 6^2 - 4^2$$
$$= 36 - 16 = 20$$
$$x = 4.72 \text{ m}$$

ex.2 In the figure below, if AC = 11 and BC = 4, how much longer is $\overline{AB}$ than $\overline{AC}$?

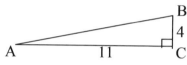

Note: Figure not drawn to scale.

a) 0.7   b) 1.2   c) 3.6   d) 5.3   e) 7

Solution: by Pythagorean Theorem:
$$AB^2 = AC^2 + BC^2$$
$$AB^2 = 11^2 + 4^2$$
$$= 121 + 16$$
$$= 137$$
$$AB = \sqrt{137} = 11.7$$
$$AB - AC = 11.7 - 11 = 0.7$$

The correct answer is (a).

The typical right angle triangle ratios often used:

5: 4: 3   since $5^2 = 4^2 + 3^2$

where the hypotenuse is 5 and the two other sides are 4 and 3.

and more:

10 : 8 : 6   since $10^2 = 8^2 + 6^2$

13 :12: 5   since $13^2 = 12^2 + 5^2$

3.1   Practice and Solutions

1. In the figure on the right, what is the value of x rounded to nearest tenth?

    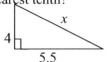

    (A) 6.1

    (B) 6.9

    (C) 7.3

    (D) 8.2

    (E) 9.0

    Note: Figure not drawn to scale.

2. In the figure on the right, what is the length of a?

    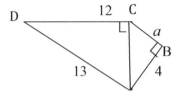

    (A) 3.0

    (B) 3.5

    (C) 4.8

    (D) 5.0

    (E) 7.2

    Note: Figure not drawn to scale.

3. In the right-angle triangle on the right, what is m in terms of n ?

    (A) $\sqrt{n^2 + 121}$

    (B) $\sqrt{n^2 - 121}$

    (C) $n - 11$

    (D) $n^2 + 121$

    (E) $n^2 - 121$

4. In the figure on the right, a, b, x and y are the lengths of the sides indicated
    Which of the following is true?

    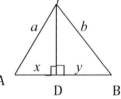

    (A) $a^2 - b^2 = x^2 + y^2$

    (B) $a^2 + b^2 = x^2 - y^2$

    (C) $a^2 - x^2 = y^2 - b^2$

    (D) $a^2 + y^2 = b^2 + x^2$

    (E) $a^2 + y^2 = b^2 - x^2$

5. The circle below with center O, has a radius of 12.5 cm. AB is 15 cm,
    $\overline{OP} \perp \overline{AB}$, and bisects $\overline{AB}$ at X. What is the length XP?

    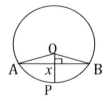

    (A)   2.5cm

    (B)   3.5cm

    (C)   4.2cm

    (D)   4.6cm

    (E)   5.0cm

    Note: Figure not drawn to scale.

Solutions to 3.1 Practice: 1(B), 2(A), 3(B), 4(D), 5(A)

1. In the figure on the right, what is the value of x rounded to nearest tenth?

   (A) 6.1

   (B) 6.8

   (C) 7.3

   (D) 8.2

   (E) 9.0

   $$x^2 = 5.5^2 + 4^2$$
   $$x = \sqrt{5.5^2 + 4^2}$$
   $$= \sqrt{46.25} = 6.8$$

   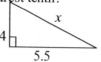

   Note: Figure not drawn to scale.

2. In the figure on the right, what is the length of a?

   (A) 3.0

   (B) 3.5

   (C) 4.8

   (D) 5.0

   (E) 7.2

   ΔACD is a right Δ:
   $$CA^2 = 13^2 - 12^2 = 25$$
   ΔABC is a right Δ:
   $$CA^2 = AB^2 + BC^2$$
   $$25 = 16 + a^2$$
   $$a^2 = 25 - 16 = 9; \quad a = 3$$

   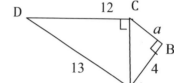

   OR:

   ΔACD has ratio $13:12:5, \therefore CA = 5$
   ΔABC has ratio $5:4:3; \therefore a = 3$

3. In the right-angle triangle on the right, what is m in terms of n?

   (A) $\sqrt{n^2 + 121}$

   (B) $\sqrt{n^2 - 121}$

   (C) $n - 11$

   (D) $n^2 + 121$

   (E) $n^2 - 121$

   By Pythagorean Th.:
   $$m^2 + 11^2 = n^2$$
   $$m^2 = n^2 - 11^2 = n^2 - 121$$
   $$m = \sqrt{n^2 - 121}$$

4. In the figure on the right, a, b, x and y are the lengths of the sides indicated. Which of the following is true?

   (A) $a^2 - b^2 = x^2 + y^2$

   (B) $a^2 + b^2 = x^2 - y^2$

   (C) $a^2 - x^2 = y^2 - b^2$

   (D) $a^2 + y^2 = b^2 + x^2$

   (E) $a^2 + y^2 = b^2 - x^2$

   ΔACD is a right Δ:
   $$CD^2 = a^2 - x^2$$
   ΔBCD is a right Δ:
   $$CD^2 = b^2 - y^2$$
   $$\therefore a^2 - x^2 = b^2 - y^2$$
   $$a^2 + y^2 = b^2 + x^2$$

   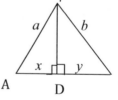

5. The circle below with center O, has a radius of 12.5 cm. AB is 15 cm, $\overline{OP} \perp \overline{AB}$, and bisects $\overline{AB}$ at X. What is the length XP?

   (A) 2.5cm

   (B) 3.5cm

   (C) 4.2cm

   (D) 4.6cm

   (E) 5.0cm

   $$OP = radius = 12.5cm$$
   ΔAXO is a right Δ:
   $$OX^2 = OA^2 - AX^2 \quad (AX = 15 \div 2 = 7.5)$$
   $$= 12.5^2 - 7.5^2 = 100$$
   $$OX = 10cm$$
   $$XP = OP - OX = 12.5 - 10 = 2.5cm$$

   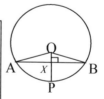

4. Special Triangles

4.1 Equilateral Triangle

An equilateral triangle is a triangle with three equal sides. In an equilateral triangle each angle is equal to 60°.

AB = AC = BC
and
$\angle A = \angle B = \angle C = 60°$

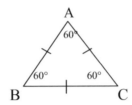

ex.1 In the triangle on the right,
if each side is equal to 12,
what is the height, AO, of the triangle?

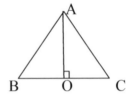

a) 6.0   b) 8.2   c) 9.0   d) 10.4   e) 11.0

Solution: since

AB = AC = BC = 12, $\triangle ABC$ is an equilateral triangle,
so $\overline{AO}$ is at the midpoint of $\overline{BC}$, and $\overline{AO} \perp \overline{BC}$,

$$\therefore \quad OC = \frac{1}{2}(BC) = \frac{1}{2}(12) = 6$$

by Pythagorean Theorem, in the $\triangle AOC$,

$AC^2 = AO^2 + OC^2$
$AO^2 = AC^2 - OC^2$
$\quad = 12^2 - 6^2$
$\quad = 144 - 36$
$\quad = 108$

$AO = \sqrt{108}$
$\quad = 10.4$

The correct answer is (d).

4.2 Isosceles Triangle

An isosceles triangle is a triangle with two equal sides. In an isosceles triangle the two angles opposite the equal sides are also equal.

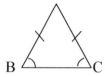

$$AB = AC$$
$$\angle B = \angle C$$

ex.2   In the figure below, if $XY = XZ$, and $\angle Z = 38°$, and $\angle AXY = 25°$, what is the measure of $\angle BXZ$?

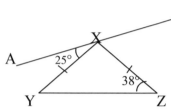

Note: Figure not drawn to scale.

a) 51°   b) 60°   c) 64°   d) 65°   e) 72°

Solution:

Since $XY = XZ$, ΔXYZ is an isosceles triangle,

∴ $\angle Y = \angle Z = 38°$

∴ $\angle YXZ = 180° - 2 * 38° = 104°$

Since AB is a straight line,

$\angle BXZ = 180° - \angle AXY - \angle YXZ$

$= 180° - 25° - 104° = 51°$

The correct answer is (a).

ex.3   If $RS = BS$, and $\overline{AB} \parallel \overline{CD}$, what is the measure of $\angle B$?

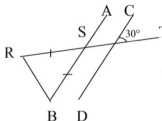

Note: Figure not drawn to scale.

a) 30°   b) 45°   c) 75°   d) 80°   e) 86°

Solution: Since $\overline{AB} \parallel \overline{CD}$,   ∴ $\angle AST = 30°$ (See Section 2.4)

Since $\angle AST$ and $\angle RSB$ are opposite angles,

∴ $\angle RSB = \angle AST = 30°$

Since $RS = BS$, ΔRSB is an isosceles triangle,

∴ $\angle B = \angle R = (180° - 30°) \div 2 = 75°$

The correct answer is (c).

4.3 Special Right-Angled Triangles

45°-45°-90°

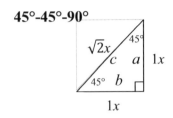

To understand this ratio, think of this 45°-45°-90° triangle as half of a square, so the two sides of the square are equal, in 1 to 1 ratio, and the hypotenuse, c, is found by: $c^2 = a^2 + b^2$

$$\therefore \quad c = \sqrt{(1x)^2 + (1x)^2} = \sqrt{2}x$$

30°-60°-90°

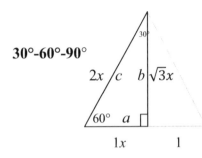

Think of this 30°-60°-90° triangle as half of the equilateral triangle with each side 2, so the hypotenuse is 2, and the bottom is half of the hypotenuse, which is 1, and the third side, b, is therefore:

$$b = \sqrt{c^2 - a^2} = \sqrt{(2x)^2 - (1x)^2} = \sqrt{3}x$$

ex.4. In the figure below, if AB is 8, and ∠BAC equals to 60°, what is the combined length of $\overline{AC}$ and $\overline{BC}$?

a) 4.0   b) 6.9   c) 8.2   d) 9.0   e) 10.9

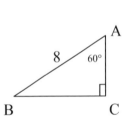

Solution: since ΔABC is a 30°-60°-90° special triangle,

$\therefore$ AB: AC: BC = $2x : 1x : \sqrt{3}x$

$\dfrac{AB}{AC} = \dfrac{2}{1} \diagdown \dfrac{8}{AC}$, $2AC = 8$, $AC = 4$

$\dfrac{AC}{BC} = \dfrac{1}{\sqrt{3}} = \dfrac{4}{BC}$, $BC = 4 * \sqrt{3} = 6.9$

$\therefore$ The combined length of $\overline{AC}$ and $\overline{BC}$ is:
AC + BC = 4 + 6.9 = 10.9

The correct answer is (e).

4.4 Congruent Triangles

Two triangles are congruent if they have the same shape and size.
All the corresponding sides and angles are equal.

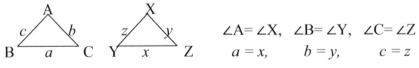

∠A= ∠X, ∠B= ∠Y, ∠C= ∠Z
$a = x$, $b = y$, $c = z$

Triangle ABC is congruent to triangle XYZ: ΔABC ≅ Δ XYZ

---

ex.5 In the figure below, if △ABO ≅ △XYO, and AB is 4.5
and ∠A is 60°, what is the length AX?

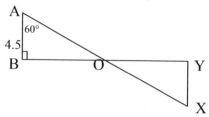

a) 4.5   b) 9.0   c) 12.5   d) 18.0   e) 24.0

Solution: since ∠A = 60°,

$$\frac{AO}{AB} = \frac{2}{1}$$

△ABO is a 30°-60°-90° triangle,

∴ $AO:AB:BO = 2x : 1x : \sqrt{3}x$

by cross multiplication:

AO = AB * 2

since AB = 4.5

∴ AO = 4.5 * 2 = 9.0

since △ABO ≅ △XYO,

AB = XY, AO = XO, and BO = YO

∴ XO = AO = 9.0

∴ AX = AO + XO

= 9.0 + 9.0 = 18.0

The correct answer is (d).

4.5 Similar Triangles

Two triangles are similar if they have the same shape, but may be of different
sizes; all the corresponding angles are the same, and the corresponding sides are
in proportion as in the following:

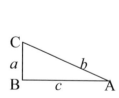 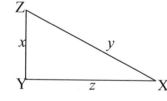

△ABC & △XYZ are similar:

∠A = ∠X, ∠B = ∠Y, ∠C = ∠Z

$$\frac{a}{x} = \frac{b}{y} = \frac{c}{z}$$

ex.6 The following triangles △ABC and △RST are similar, because:

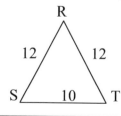

$$\frac{AB}{RS} = \frac{6}{12} = \frac{1}{2};\quad \frac{AC}{RT} = \frac{6}{12} = \frac{1}{2}$$

$$\frac{BC}{ST} = \frac{5}{10} = \frac{1}{2};\quad The\ proportion = \frac{1}{2}$$

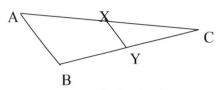

ex.7 In the figure above, $\overline{AB} \parallel \overline{XY}$, and XY = 3.5, XC = 5, and AB = 7, what is the length AC?

a) 4.3   b) 6.2   c) 7.7   d) 9.5   e) 10.0

Solution: since $\overline{AB} \parallel \overline{XY}$,

∴   ∠A = ∠CXY and   ∠B = ∠CYX   (See section 2.4)

and △ABC and △XYC share the third common angle, ∠C,

∴   △ABC and △XYC have the same shape, but different size,

∴   △ABC and △XYC are similar triangles.

Since the corresponding sides of two similar triangles are in proportion:

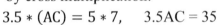

∴ $\dfrac{XY}{AB} = \dfrac{XC}{AC}$

given : $\dfrac{XY}{AB} = \dfrac{3.5}{7}$, $\dfrac{XC}{AC} = \dfrac{5}{AC}$

∴ $\dfrac{3.5}{7} = \dfrac{5}{AC}$,

by cross multiplication:

$3.5 * (AC) = 5 * 7$, $3.5AC = 35$

∴ $AC = 10.0$

The correct answer is (e).

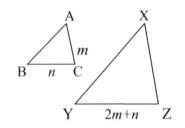

ex.8. In the figures on the right, if △ ABC is similar to △ XYZ, what is the length XZ in terms of m and n?

a) $m + n$ b) $\dfrac{2m^2}{n}$ c) $\dfrac{2m^2+mn}{n}$ d) $\dfrac{2m^2+mn}{m}$ e) $2m^2 + mn$

Solution: since △ABC and △XYZ are similar,

∴ $\dfrac{BC}{YZ} = \dfrac{AC}{XZ}$

∴ $\dfrac{n}{2m+n} = \dfrac{m}{XZ}$

∴   by cross multiplication

$n * XZ = m * (2m + n)$

∴ $XZ = \dfrac{2m^2+mn}{n}$

The correct answer is (c).

4.6   Practice and Solutions

1. In the figure on the right, if ΔABC is an equilateral triangle with each side equal to 9, what is the length of the height AO?

    (A) 5.3
    (B) 6.2
    (C) 7.8
    (D) 8.1
    (E) 8.4

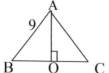

Note: Figure not drawn to scale.

2. In the figure on the right, if ΔXYZ is an isosceles triangle, XY = XZ, what is measure of ∠Y?

    (F) 32°
    (G) 49°
    (H) 51°
    (I)   62°
    (J) 71°

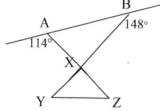

Note: Figure not drawn to scale.

3. In the figure on the right, if $\overline{AB} \parallel \overline{XY}$, what is m in terms of n ?

    (A) $m = \frac{3}{5}n$

    (B) $m = \frac{2}{3}n$

    (C) $m = n$

    (D) $m = \frac{5}{3}n$

    (E) $m = \frac{3}{2}n$

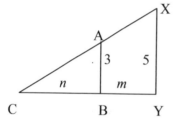

Note: Figure not drawn to scale.

4. ABCD forms a parallelogram as shown. What is x in terms of a, b and c ?

    (A) $360 - a - b - c$
    (B) $360 - a + b + c$
    (C) $180 - a - b - c$
    (D) $a + b + c - 180$
    (E) $a + b + c$

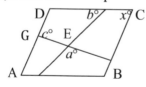

5. In the figure on the right, ∠CAB = 45°, ∠DAB = 60°, $\overline{DE}$ bisects $\overline{AB}$, and $\overline{DE} \perp \overline{AB}$. If AB = 2x, what is DC in terms of x?

    (A) $\sqrt{3}x - x$

    (B) $\sqrt{3}x - \frac{x}{2}$

    (C) $\sqrt{3}x - \sqrt{2}x$

    (D) $\frac{\sqrt{3}}{2}x - x$

    (E) $\frac{\sqrt{3}}{2}x - \frac{x}{2}$

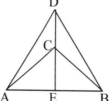

Note: Figure not drawn to scale.

Solutions to 4.6 Practice: 1(C), 2(B), 3(B), 4(D), 5(A)

1. In the figure on the right, if ΔABC is an equilateral triangle with each side equal to 9, what is the length of the height AO?

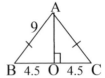

(A) 5.3

(B) 6.2

(C) 7.8

(D) 8.1

(E) 8.4

> O is the midpoint of $\overline{BC}$:
>
> $OB = OC = 4.5$
>
> ΔAOB is a right Δ: by Pythagorean:
>
> $AB^2 = OB^2 + AO^2$, $\ 9^2 = 4.5^2 + AO^2$
>
> $AO = \sqrt{9^2 - 4.5^2} \approx 7.8$

Note: Figure not drawn to scale.

2. In the figure on the right, if ΔXYZ is an isosceles triangle, XY = XZ, what is measure of ∠Y?

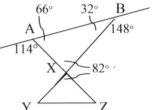

(A) 32°

(B) 49°

(C) 51°

(D) 62°

(E) 71°

> $\angle ABX = 180° - 148° = 32°$
>
> $\angle BAX = 180° - 114° = 66°$
>
> $\angle AXB = 180° - 32° - 66° = 82°$
>
> $\angle YXZ = \angle AXB \ (opposite \ \angle) = 82°$
>
> $\angle Y = \angle Z = \dfrac{1}{2}(180° - 82°) = 49°$

Note: Figure not drawn to scale.

3. In the figure on the right, if $\overline{AB} \parallel \overline{XY}$, what is m in terms of n ?

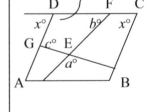

(A) $m = \dfrac{3}{5}n$

(B) $m = \dfrac{2}{3}n$

(C) $m = n$

(D) $m = \dfrac{5}{3}n$

(E) $m = \dfrac{3}{2}n$

> ΔCAB and ΔCXY are similar:
>
> $\dfrac{XY}{AB} = \dfrac{CY}{CB}; \ \dfrac{5}{3} = \dfrac{m+n}{n}$
>
> $5n = 3(m+n)$
>
> $5n = 3m + 3n \ ; \ 5n - 3n = 3m$
>
> $m = \dfrac{2}{3}n$

Note: Figure not drawn to scale.

4. ABCD forms a parallelogram as shown. What is x in terms of a, b and c ?

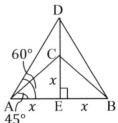

(A) $360 - a - b - c$

(B) $360 - a + b + c$

(C) $180 - a - b - c$

(D) $a + b + c - 180$

(E) $a + b + c$

> $\angle FDG = 180° - x°$
>
> $\angle GEF = a° \ (opposite \angle)$
>
> $EFDG$ is a quadrilateral:
>
> $a + b + c + (180 - x) = 360$
>
> $a + b + c + 180 - 360 = x$
>
> $x = a + b + c - 180$

5. In the figure on the right, ∠CAB = 45°, ∠DAB = 60°, DE bisects $\overline{AB}$, and $\overline{DE} \perp \overline{AB}$. If AB = 2x, what is DC in terms of x?

(A) $\sqrt{3}x - x$

(B) $\sqrt{3}x - \dfrac{x}{2}$

(C) $\sqrt{3}x - \sqrt{2}x$

(D) $\dfrac{\sqrt{3}}{2}x - x$

(E) $\dfrac{\sqrt{3}}{2}x - \dfrac{x}{2}$

> $AE = BE = x$
>
> $\angle CAE = 45°: \ CE = AE = x$
>
> $\angle DAE = 60°: \ \dfrac{DE}{AE} = \dfrac{\sqrt{3}}{1}$
>
> $\therefore DE = \sqrt{3}AE = \sqrt{3}x$
>
> $\therefore DC = DE - CE \ = \sqrt{3}x - x$

Note: Figure not drawn to scale.

5. Tangent to a Circle

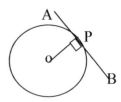

Tangent to a circle: A line that touches a circle at only one point.

    ex. $\overline{AB}$ is tangent to the circle with center O, and P is the point of tangency.

<u>Tangent property 1</u>: If P is the point of tangency, then

$$\boxed{\overline{OP} \perp \overline{AB} \quad \text{or} \quad \angle APO = 90° \quad \text{(OP is the radius)}}$$

    ex.1. In the figure below, $\overline{AB}$ is a tangent to the circle at M, and M bisects line segment $\overline{AB}$. If AB is $8x$, and the radius OM is $2x$, What is the length AO?

        a) $2\sqrt{5}x$ b) $3x$ c) $3\sqrt{5}x$ d) $4x$ e) $5x$

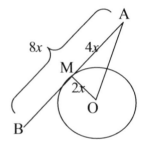

    Solution: since AB = $8x$,

        ∴   AM = $4x$, since M bisects $\overline{AB}$

            since AB is a tangent at M, and OM is a radius,

        ∴ $\overline{OM} \perp \overline{AB}$, ∴ $\angle AMO = 90°$

        ∴ $AO^2 = AM^2 + OM^2$ (by Pythagorean Theorem)

        ∴ $AO^2 = (4x)^2 + (2x)^2 = 20x^2$

        ∴ $\sqrt{AO^2} = \sqrt{20x^2}$, ∴ AO $= \sqrt{20x^2} = \sqrt{4*5}x = 2\sqrt{5}x$

    The correct answer is (a).

<u>Tangent property 2</u>:

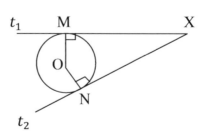

If t_1, t_2 are tangent lines to a circle from an external point X, and M, N are points of tangency, then

$$\boxed{XM = XN}$$

If O is the center, then $\angle OMX = \angle ONX = 90°$.

5.1 Practice and Solutions

1. In the figure on the right, A is the point of tangency to the circle with center O.
    AB = 8.8cm and OB = 10cm, what is the radius rounded to the nearest tenth?

    (A) 4.1
    (B) 4.7
    (C) 5.3
    (D) 6.9
    (E) 7.4

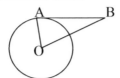

Note: Figure not drawn to scale.

2. The circle on the right has a center O with radius 5. $\overline{XY}$ is a tangent to the
    circle at P, and P bisects $\overline{XY}$. If OX is 13cm, what is the length XY?

    (A) 28.6
    (B) 24.0
    (C) 18.4
    (D) 16.0
    (E) 12.0

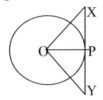

Note: Figure not drawn to scale.

3. In the figure on the right, A and B are points of tangency,
    what is the measure of ∠AOB ?

    (A) 168°
    (B) 150°
    (C) 142°
    (D) 138°
    (E) 122°

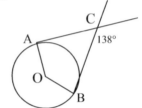

Note: Figure not drawn to scale.

4. In the figure on the right, , l_1 and l_2 are tangents of the circle with center O,
    what is m in terms of n ?

    (A) $90 - n$
    (B) $90 + n$
    (C) $180 - n$
    (D) $180 + n$
    (E) n

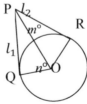

5. In the figure on the right, l_1 and l_2 are tangents of the circle with center O, and
    m_1 and m_2 are the radii. Which of the following is true?

    I. $m_1 = m_2$
    II. $l_1 = l_2$
    III. $x_1 = x_2$

    (A) I only
    (B) II only
    (C) III only
    (D) I and II only
    (E) I, II and III

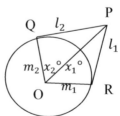

Note: Figure not drawn to scale.

Solutions to 5.1 practice: 1(B), 2(B), 3(D), 4(A), 5(E)

1. In the figure on the right, A is the point of tangency to the circle with center O.
   AB = 8.8cm and OB = 10cm, what is the radius rounded to the nearest tenth?

   (A) 4.1
   (B) 4.7
   (C) 5.3
   (D) 6.9
   (E) 7.4

   $\angle OAB = 90°, \ by \ Pythagorean:$
   $OB^2 = OA^2 + AB^2$
   $OA^2 = OB^2 - AB^2 = 10^2 - 8.8^2 = 22.56$
   $r = OA = \sqrt{22.56} = 4.7$

   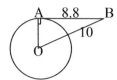
   Note: Figure not drawn to scale.

2. The circle on the right has a center O with radius 5. $\overline{XY}$ is a tangent to the
   circle at P, and P bisects $\overline{XY}$. If OX is 13cm, what is the length XY?

   (A) 28.6
   (B) 24.0
   (C) 18.4
   (D) 16.0
   (E) 12.0

   $\Delta OPX \ is \ a \ right \ \Delta:$
   $OX^2 = OP^2 + XP^2$
   $13^2 = 5^2 + XP^2$
   $XP = \sqrt{13^2 - 5^2} = \sqrt{144} = 12$
   $XY = 2XP = 2 * 12 = 24cm$

   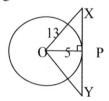
   Note: Figure not drawn to scale.

3. In the figure on the right, A and B are points of tangency,
   what is the measure of ∠AOB ?

   (A) 168°
   (B) 150°
   (C) 142°
   (D) 138°
   (E) 122°

   $\angle ACB = 180° - 138° = 42°$
   $\angle OAC = \angle OBC = 90°$
   $AOBC \ is \ a \ quadrilateral:$
   $42° + 90° + 90° + \angle AOB = 360°$
   $\angle AOB = 138°$

   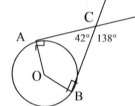
   Note: Figure not drawn to scale.

4. In the figure on the right, , l_1 and l_2 are tangents of the circle with center O,
   what is m in terms of n ?

   (A) 90 − n
   (B) 90 + n
   (C) 180 − n
   (D) 180 + n
   (E) n

   $By \ Tangent \ property \ 2 ; \ l_1 = l_2$
   $\Delta POQ \cong \Delta POR \ since \ corresponding$
   $sides \ are \ equal. \ Corresponding$
   $angles \ are \ equal: \ \angle QPO = m°$
   $\Delta PQO = righ\_ang \ \Delta: n + m + 90 = 180$
   $m = 90 - n$

   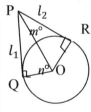

5. In the figure on the right, l_1 and l_2 are tangents of the circle with center O, and
   m_1 and m_2 are the radii. Which of the following is true?

   I. $m_1 = m_2$
   II. $l_1 = l_2$
   III. $x_1 = x_2$

   (A) I only
   (B) II only
   (C) III only
   (D) I and II only
   (E) I, II and III

   $m_1 = m_2 = radius$
   $l_1 = l_2 \ by \ Tangent \ poperty \ 2$
   $\Delta PQO \cong \Delta PRO \ since$
   $corresponding \ sides \ are \ equal.$
   $Corresponding \ angles \ are$
   $equal: x_1 = \ x_2$

   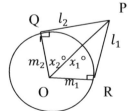
   Note: Figure not drawn to scale.

6. Perimeter, Area, Surface Area and Volume

Notation: s = side, l = length, w = width, b = base, h = height, r = radius
A = area, SA = surface area, P = perimeter, V = volume

6.1 Area and Perimeter

Square: $A = s*s$ $P = 4*s$

Rectangle: $A = l*w$ $P = 2l + 2w$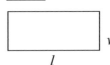

Parallelogram: $A = l*h$ $P = 2l + 2w$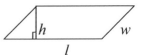

In a parallelogram, the top and bottom sides are equal in length and parallel, so is the pair of left and right sides. The height (h) is the perpendicular distance from any vertex to the side opposite to that vertex.

Triangle: $A = \frac{1}{2}(b*h)$ $P = a + b + c$

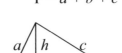

The height (h) of a triangle is a perpendicular distance from the base (b) to the vertex opposite to the base as shown above. A base can be any one side of the triangle.

Circle: $A = \pi r^2$ Circumference $= 2\pi r$

ex.1. In the figure below, what is the total area?

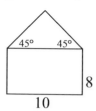

a) 25   b) 40   c) 65   d) 80   e) 105

Solution: The rectangle:
$$A = l*w = 10 * 8 = 80$$

The triangle:
Since the triangle has two equal
angles, 45°, it is an isosceles triangle.
The height, h, bisects the triangle into
two smaller triangles as shown on the right.

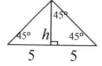

Half of the base = $10 \div 2 = 5$
Since the smaller triangle is also a 45°-45°-90° triangle,
∴ $5 : h = 1 : 1$ (See 4.3, 45°-45°-90° triangle)
∴ $h = 5$
$$A = \frac{1}{2}(b*h) = \frac{1}{2}(10 * 5) = 25$$
Total Area = Area of rectangle + Area of Triangle
$$= 80 + 25 = 105$$
The correct answer is (e).

ex.2 If the area of a circle is $9\pi(m + n)^2$, what is the circumference of the
circle in terms of m and n?

a) $3(m + n)$ b) $6\pi(m + n)$ c) $8\pi(m + n)$ d) $(m + n)^2$ e) $9\pi(m + n)^2$
Solution: since $A = \pi r^2$
∴ $\pi r^2 = 9\pi(m + n)^2$
∴ $r^2 = 9(m + n)^2$
∴ $r = \sqrt{9(m + n)^2}$
$$= 3(m + n)$$
since Circumference $= 2\pi r$
∴   Circumference $= 2\pi * 3(m + n)$
$$= 6\pi(m + n)$$
The correct answer is (b).

eg.3 In the figure below, ABCD is a parallelogram with a perimeter of 24.
If AB is twice AC, and ∠PAC measures 60°, what is the area of the
the parallelogram rounded to the nearest tenth?

Note: Figure not drawn to scale.

a) 4.0   b) 8.0   c) 24.0   d) 27.7   e) 29.3

Solution: let $x = AC$, $h =$ height, and $\overline{AM} \perp \overline{CD}$

given $AB = 2*AC$, $\therefore AB = 2x$

since Perimeter $= 24$

$\therefore$ $AB + CD + AC + BD = 24$

$2x + 2x + x + x = 24$

$\therefore$ $x = 4$

since $\overline{PB} \parallel \overline{CD}$, (See 2.4)

$\angle ACD = \angle PAC = 60°$

$\therefore$ $\triangle ACM$ is $30°$-$60°$-$90°$

$\therefore$ $x : h = 2 : \sqrt{3}$

since $x = 4$, $\therefore$ $\dfrac{4}{h} = \dfrac{2}{\sqrt{3}}$ (See section 4.3)

$\therefore$ by cross multiplication,

$2h = 4\sqrt{3}$ and $\therefore h = 2\sqrt{3}$,

and base $= CD = AB = 2x = 8$

$\therefore$ Area $=$ base $* h = 8 * 2\sqrt{3} = 27.7$

The correct answer is (d).

ex.4 In the figure on the right, if the area of the circle is $9\pi p^2$
what is the shaded area equal to in terms of p?

a) $9p(4 - \pi)$ b) $9p^2(4 - \pi)$ c) $12p^2(4 - \pi)$ d) $9p^2\pi$ e) $12p^2\pi$

Solution: since Area of circle $= \pi r^2 = 9\pi p^2$

$\therefore$ $r^2 = 9p^2$ and $r = 3p$

$\therefore$ let $s =$ length of the square

$\therefore$ $s = 2r = 6p$

$\therefore$ Area of square $= s^2 = (6p)^2 = 36p^2$

$\therefore$ Shaded Area $=$ Area of square $-$ Area of circle

$= 36p^2 - 9\pi p^2$

$= 9p^2(4 - \pi)$

The correct answer is (b).

6.2 Surface Area and Volume

Cube: $V = s*s*s = s^3$
$SA = 6(s*s) = 6s^2$

Rectangular Prism: $V = l*w*h = lwh$
$SA = 2(l*w)+2(w*h)+2(l*h)$
$= 2lw + 2wh + 2lh$

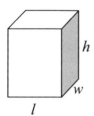

Cylinder(cone) : $V = \pi r^2 h$
$SA = 2\pi r^2 + 2\pi rh$

ex.1 If the volume of a cylinder is 72π and its height is 8, what is the diameter of the cylinder?

a) 3   b) 6   c) 7   d) 9   e) 12

Solution: since V of a cylinder $= \pi r^2 h$

∴ $72\pi = \pi r^2 h = \pi r^2 (8)$

∴ $72\pi = 8\pi r^2$

∴ $9 = r^2$ and $r = 3$

∴ diameter $= 2r = 2*3 = 6$

The correct answer is (b).

ex.2 If the volume of a cube is $512cm^3$, and 4 such cubes are stacked up together, what is the height of the stack?

a) 32cm   b) 38cm   c) 62cm   d) 75cm   e) 82cm

Solution: since V of cube $= s^3$ (s = side)

∴ $s^3 = 512$

∴ $s = \sqrt[3]{512} = 8$ (by calculator: $512 \wedge (1 \div 3) = 8$)

∴ the height of each cube $= 8$

∴ height of the stack $= 4 * 8 = 32cm$

The correct answer is (a).

Page 153

6.3   Practice and Solutions

1. What is the area of a triangle with a base of 12.5cm, and a height of 4.8cm?

2. If the circumference of a circle is 5π, what is the area of the circle?

3. If the area of a rectangle is $48cm^2$, and the length is 2cm longer than the width, what is the width?

4. If each side of a cube is double in length, how many times larger is the volume?

5. In the figure on the right, the larger circle has diameter of 16cm which passes through the centers of two smaller circles of equal size, what is the shaded area?

   (A) $16\pi\ cm^2$

   (B) $24\pi\ cm^2$

   (C) $32\pi\ cm^2$

   (D) $48\pi\ cm^2$

   (E) $64\pi\ cm^2$

6. In the figure on the right, RT = 21.7, ST = 12.3, TP = 8.8, what is the shaded area?

   (A) 34.38

   (B) 41.36

   (C) 54.12

   (D) 71.36

   (E) 95.48

   Note: Figure not drawn to scale.

7. In the figure on the right, what is the shaded area?

   (A) 4.4

   (B) 39.0

   (C) 46.40

   (D) 53.78

   (E) 58.65

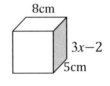

   Note: Figure not drawn to scale.

8. In the figure on the right, if the volume is $280cm^3$, what is the value of x?

   (A) 6

   (B) 5

   (C) 4

   (D) 3

   (E) 2

9. A glass tube has an outer radius of x, an inner radius of y, and a height of 2.
   If the volume of the material of the glass is 20 cubic unit, what is x in terms of y?

   (A) $10 - 6.28y$

   (B) $10 + 3.14y^2$

   (C) $3.18 + y^2$

   (D) $\sqrt{10 + 3.14y^2}$

   (E) $\sqrt{3.18 + y^2}$

Solutions to 6.3 Practice: 1 (30), 2 (6.25π), 3 (6), 4 (8), 5(C), 6(B), 7(C), 8(D), 9(E)

1. Area of a triangle $= \frac{1}{2}(bh) = (12.5 * 4.8) \div 2 = 30 cm^2$

2. $C = 2\pi r = 5\pi$, $r = 2.5$, $A = \pi r^2 = \pi(2.5)^2 = 6.25\pi$

3. Let x = width, $A = lw$, $(x + 2) * x = 48$,
   $x^2 + 2x - 48 = 0$; $(x + 8)(x - 6)$ $x = -8$ or $x = 6$; $\therefore x = 6$

4. If Let s = side, $V_1 = s^3$, double the side = $2s$, $V_2 = (2s)^3 = 8s^3 = 8V_1$

5. In the figure on the right, the larger circle has diameter of 16cm which passes
   through the centers of two smaller circles of equal size, what is the shaded area?

   (A) $16\pi \ cm^2$
   (B) $24\pi \ cm^2$
   (C) $32\pi \ cm^2$
   (D) $48\pi \ cm^2$
   (E) $64\pi \ cm^2$

   Area of the large circle $= \pi * 8^2 = 64\pi$
   Area of the small circle $= \pi * 4^2 = 16\pi$
   Area of the shaded region:
   $64\pi - 2 * 16\pi = 32\pi \ cm^2$

   $r_1 = 4$
   $r_2 = 8$

6. In the figure on the right, RT = 21.7, ST = 12.3, TP = 8.8, what is the shaded area?

   (A) 34.38
   (B) 41.36
   (C) 54.12
   (D) 71.36
   (E) 95.48

   Area of the shaded region:
   $A \ of \ \Delta RSP = \frac{1}{2}bh = \frac{1}{2}RS * TP$
   $= \frac{1}{2}(9.4)(8.8) = 41.36$

   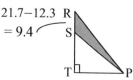
   21.7−12.3 R
   = 9.4   S
   T   P
   Note: Figure not drawn to scale.

7. In the figure on the right, what is the shaded area?

   (A) 24.4
   (B) 39.0
   (C) 46.40
   (D) 53.78
   (E) 58.65

   $A_1 = Area = \frac{1}{2}\pi * 2.5^2 = 9.81$
   $A_2 = Area = (7.8) * 5 - \frac{1}{2}(2.2)^2$
   $= 39 - 2.42 = 36.58$
   $A_1 + A_2 = 9.81 + 36.58 = 46.4$

   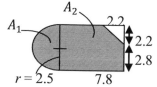
   A_2
   2.2
   A_1
   2.2
   2.8
   $r = 2.5$ 7.8
   Note: Figure not drawn to scale.

8. In the figure on the right, if the volume is $280 cm^3$, what is the value of x?

   (A) 6cm
   (B) 5cm
   (C) 4cm
   (D) 3cm
   (E) 2cm

   $Volume = length * width * height$
   $280 = 8 * 5 * (3x - 2)$
   $280 = 120x - 80$
   $360 = 120x$
   $x = 3$

   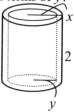
   8cm
   $3x-2$
   5cm

9. A glass tube has an outer radius of x, an inner radius of y, and a height of 2.
   If the volume of the material of the glass is 20 cubic unit, what is x in terms of y?

   (A) $10 + 6.28y$
   (B) $10 + 3.14y^2$
   (C) $3.18 + y^2$
   (D) $\sqrt{10 + 3.14y^2}$
   (E) $\sqrt{3.18 + y^2}$

   The volume of glass material
   $= \pi x^2 * 2 - \pi y^2 * 2 = 20$
   $\pi x^2 - \pi y^2 = 10$, $\pi x^2 = 10 + \pi y^2$
   $x^2 = \frac{10}{\pi} + y^2 = 3.18 + y^2$
   $x = \sqrt{3.18 + y^2}$

   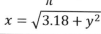
   x
   2
   y

7. Coordinate Geometry

7.1 Coordinate plane

A plane formed by the intersection of a horizontal number line, the **x-axis**, and a vertical number line, the **y-axis**. The point of intersection is called the **Origin.** The coordinates of each point, the (x, y), represent the signed distances along the x-axis and the y-axis respectively from the origin.

ex.1

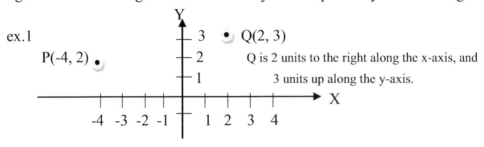

Q is 2 units to the right along the x-axis, and 3 units up along the y-axis.

ex.2 What is the area of the parallelogram ABCD ?

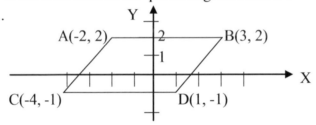

a) 15   b) 16   c) 18   d) 20   e) 24

Solution: Area of Parallelogram = base * height

base = CD = $x_D - x_C$ = 1−(−4) = 5   (5 units horizontally)

height = $y_B - y_D$ = 2 − (−1) = 3   (3 units vertically)

∴   Area = 5 * 3 = 15

The correct answer is (a).

ex.3 If point A is $(-2, 1)$, what is the distance from A to the origin?

a) 2.0   b) 2.24   c) 4.46   d) 5.0   e) 5.62

Solution:

let label the three sides

a, b, and c as shown on the right:

where $a = |-2| = 2$, $b = 1$, and

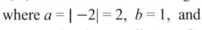

c = the shortest distance from A to O, the origin.

by Pythagorean Theorem:

$c^2 = a^2 + b^2 = 2^2 + 1^2 = 5$

$c = \sqrt{5} = 2.24$

The correct answer is (b).

7.2 Distance, Slope and Midpoint of a Line Segment

let $P_1(x_1, y_1)$, and $P_2(x_2, y_2)$ be two points of a line segment:

Distance (D) between two points $P_1(x_1, y_1)$ and $P_2(x_2, y_2)$:

$$D = \sqrt{(x_2 - x_1)^2 + (y_2 - y_1)^2}$$

Slope (m): $\quad m = \dfrac{y_2 - y_1}{x_2 - x_1}$, slope of the line segment joining

$$P_1(x_1, y_1) \text{ and } P_2(x_2, y_2), \text{ for } x_1 \neq x_2$$

Mid-point (x_m, y_m): the mid-point of the line segment joining
$$P_1(x_1, y_1) \text{ and } P_2(x_2, y_2):$$

$$x_m = \frac{x_1 + x_2}{2}, \qquad y_m = \frac{y_1 + y_2}{2}$$

ex.1   Given two points A $(3, -2)$ and B $(7, 4)$,
   Find a) the distance between the two points,
      b) the mid-point of the line segment $\overline{AB}$,
      c) the slope of the line segment $\overline{AB}$. ,

Solutions: Let A$(3, -2)$ be (x_1, y_1) and B$(7, 4)$ be (x_2, y_2):

a) $D = \sqrt{(3-7)^2 + (-2-4)^2} = \sqrt{16 + 36} = \sqrt{52} = 2\sqrt{13}$

b) $x_m = \dfrac{3+7}{2} = 5, \quad y_m = \dfrac{-2+4}{2} = 1 \quad \therefore$ mid-point: $(5, 1)$

c) $m = \dfrac{-2-4}{3-7} = \dfrac{-6}{-4} = \dfrac{3}{2}$

ex.2   Which of the following are the coordinates of the midpoint of a
   line segment with endpoints A$(3, -4)$ and B$(-2, 3)$?
   a) $(\frac{-1}{2}, \frac{-1}{2})$ b) $(\frac{1}{2}, \frac{-1}{2})$ c) $(\frac{-1}{2}, \frac{1}{2})$ d) $(\frac{1}{2}, \frac{1}{2})$ e) $(1, \frac{-1}{2})$

   Solution: $x_m = \dfrac{x_1 + x_2}{2} = \dfrac{3 + (-2)}{2} = \dfrac{1}{2}$

   $$y_m = \dfrac{y_1 + y_2}{2} = \dfrac{-4 + 3}{2} = \dfrac{-1}{2}$$

   $\therefore$ The midpoint of $\overline{AB}$ is $(\frac{1}{2}, \frac{-1}{2})$

   The correct answer is (b).

7.3 The Equation and Graph of a Straight Line

Equation of a straight line (the slope and y-intercept form):

$$\boxed{y = mx + b}$$

where m = slope

when $m > 0$: *an ascending line,* ╱

when $m < 0$: *a descendsing line,* ╲

when $m = 0$: a horizontal line parallel to x-axis ──

(The slope of a vertical line parallel to y-axis is undefined,

and its equation has the form x = constant.)

b = y-intercept (where the line cuts y-axis)

ex. $y = 2x + 1$ (slope =2 and y-intercept = 1)

Graph of a straight line:

To sketch the line, $y = 2x + 1$, find two points on the line:

- 1st point can be the y-intercept, since b = 1, ∴ (0, 1)
- 2nd point can be any point on the line,

say let $x = 1$, ∴ $y = 2(1) + 1 = 3$ ∴ (1, 3)

- draw a line through the two points (0, 1) and (1, 3).

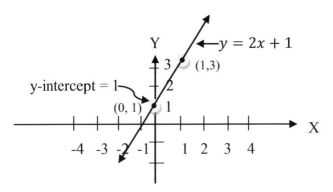

Equation of a straight line (the standard form):

$$\boxed{ax + by + c = 0}$$ ex. $4x + 2y - 6 = 0$

Converting from the slope and y-intercept form to the standard form:

from: $y = 2x + 1$ ⟵ $y = mx + b$ form

to: $2x - y + 1 = 0$ ⟵ standard form

Converting from the standard form to the slope and y-intercept form:

from: $3x - 5y + 7 = 0$ ⟵ standard form

to: $-5y = -3x - 7$ (dividing both side by -5)

$$y = \frac{3}{5}x + \frac{7}{5}$$ ⟵ $y = mx + b$ form

7.4 Parallel and Perpendicular lines

Let m_1 and m_2 be the slope of two lines.

When two lines are **parallel**, they have the same slope:

$$m_1 = m_2$$

When two lines are **perpendicular**:

$$m_1 = \frac{-1}{m_2} \quad \text{or} \quad m_1 * m_2 = -1$$

for $m_1, m_2 \neq 0$

Examples of perpendicular:

ex.1 $m_1 = 7$; $m_2 = -\frac{1}{7}$

ex.2 $m_1 = -\frac{2}{5}$; $m_2 = \frac{5}{2}$

ex.3 Which of the following two lines are parallel, and which two are perpendicular?

a) $y = 3x + 4$ b) $y = \frac{2}{3}x + \frac{5}{6}$ c) $y = \frac{-1}{3}x + 2$ d) $y = \frac{2}{3}x - 9$

Solution: (b) and (d) are parallel, since they have same slope $= \frac{2}{3}$

$$m_1 = m_2 = \frac{2}{3}$$

(a) and (c) are perpendicular,

since in (a), $m_1 = 3$ and in (c), $m_2 = \frac{-1}{3}$,

and $m_1 * m_2 = 3 * \frac{-1}{3} = -1$

ex.4 Which of the following is the equation of a line that is perpendicular to line $y = 3x + 2$, and has y-intercept -3?

a) $y = \frac{-1}{3}x + 3$ b) $y = \frac{-1}{3}x - 3$ c) $y = 3x - 3$ d) $y = 3x + 3$

Solution: since $y = 3x + 2$ has slope $m = 3$,

so the line perpendicular to it must has slope $= \frac{-1}{3}$

($m_1 = 3$, $\therefore m_2 = \frac{-1}{3}$ for perpendicular)

(a) and (b) are the possible answers,

since (b) has y-intercept $= -3$,

so $y = \frac{-1}{3}x - 3$ is the line.

The correct answer is (b).

ex.5 Which of the following is the equation of the line that is perpendicular to $y = -2x + 3$ and passes through the point $(4, -2)$?

a) $y = -2x + 4$ b) $y = -2x - 2$ c) $y = 2x + 3$

d) $y = \frac{1}{2}x - 4$ e) $y = -\frac{1}{2}x - 4$

Solution: let m_1 be the slope of $y = -2x + 3$, $\therefore \; m_1 = -2$,

let m_2 be the slope of the perpendicular line,

$$m_2 = \frac{-1}{m_1} \qquad \therefore \; m_2 = \frac{-1}{-2} = \frac{1}{2}$$

$\therefore$ the equation of the perpendicular line is:

$$y = \frac{1}{2}x + b$$

sub $(4, -2)$ to find b:

$$\therefore \quad -2 = \frac{1}{2}(4) + b = \frac{4}{2} + b, \quad -2 = 2 + b,$$

$$b = -4$$

$\therefore$ the equation of the perpendicular line is:

$$y = \frac{1}{2}x - 4$$

The correct answer is (d).

ex.4 Which of the following is the equation of the line which passes through points $A(3, \frac{2}{3})$ and $B(-1, -3)$?

a) $11x - 12y - 25 = 0$ b) $11x + 12y - 47 = 0$ c) $12x - 11y - 36 = 0$

Solution: first, find the slope of the AB:

$$m = \frac{y_2 - y_1}{x_2 - x_1} = \frac{-3 - \frac{2}{3}}{-1 - 3} \qquad \text{(see Geometr 7.2, for Slope)}$$

(see Basic Math 6.3, Fraction)

$$= \frac{\frac{-9}{3} - \frac{2}{3}}{-4} = \frac{\frac{-11}{3}}{-4} = \frac{11}{12}$$

second, find the equation using point $B(-1, -3)$

since $m = \frac{y_2 - y_1}{x_2 - x_1}$

$$\therefore \quad \frac{11}{12} = \frac{y - (-3)}{x - (-1)} = \frac{y + 3}{x + 1}$$

by cross multiplication:

$$11(x + 1) = 12(y + 3)$$

$$11x + 11 = 12y + 36$$

$$11x - 12y - 25 = 0$$

The correct answer is (a).

7.5 Practice and Solutions

1. What is the distance between the two points $(-2,\ 3)$ and $(1,\ -2)$?

2. What is the slope of the line that passes through the points $(5,\ -4)$ and $(6, 1)$?

3. What is the mid-point between the two points $(5,\ -4)$ and $(6, 1)$?

4. What is the equation of the line that passes through $(-3,\ 4)$ and $(1, 3)$?

5. In the figure on the right, what is the area of the triangle formed by the three points?

    (A) 3.0
    (B) 4.5
    (C) 5.2
    (D) 6.4
    (E) 9.0

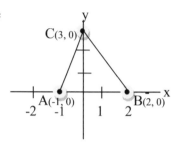

6. In the figure on the right, what is the perimeter of the triangle formed by the three points?

    (A) 4.7
    (B) 5.2
    (C) 5.8
    (D) 6.9
    (E) 7.6

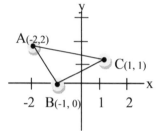

7. Which of the following equations represents the line on the right?

    (A) $y = -\frac{2}{3}x + 2$
    (B) $y = -\frac{3}{2}x + 2$
    (C) $y = -3x + 2$
    (D) $y = \frac{2}{3}x + 2$
    (E) $y = 3x + 2$

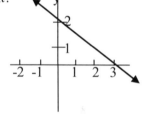

8. For what value of p will the lines $px + 2y - 3 = 0$, and $y = 3x + 2$ be parallel ?

    (A) -6
    (B) -3
    (C) 1.5
    (D) 4.5
    (E) 6

9. In the figure on the right, what is the equation of the line that passes through point A and is perpendicular to line l ?

    (A) $y = -\frac{2}{3}x + 3$
    (B) $y = -x + 3$
    (C) $y = -\frac{1}{2}x + 2$
    (D) $y = -x + 2$
    (E) $y = -2x + 2$

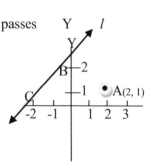

Solutions to 7.5 Practice: 1(5.8), 2(5), 3($\frac{11}{2}, -\frac{3}{2}$), 4($y = -\frac{1}{4}x + \frac{13}{4}$), 5(B),6(E),7(A),8(A),9(B)

1. $(-2, 3)$ and $(1, -2)$: $D = \sqrt{(-2-1)^2 + (3-(-2))^2} = 5.8$

2. $(5, -4)$ and $(6, 1)$: $m = \frac{1-(-4)}{6-5} = \frac{5}{1} = 5$

3. $(5, -4)$ and $(6, 1)$: $x_m = \frac{5+6}{2} = \frac{11}{2}$, $\quad y_m = \frac{-4+1}{2} = \frac{-3}{2}$

4. $(-3, 4)$ and $(1, 3)$: $m = \frac{4-3}{-3-1} = \frac{1}{-4}$, $\quad y = \frac{1}{-4}x + b$, $\quad 3 = \frac{1}{-4}(1) + b$, $\quad b = \frac{13}{4}$

5. In the figure on the right, what is the area of the triangle formed by the three points?

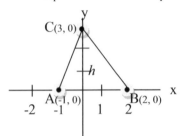

   (A) 3.0
   (B) 4.5
   (C) 5.2
   (D) 6.4
   (E) 9.0

   $AB = 3$, $\quad h = 3$

   $Area \ of \ \Delta ABC = \frac{1}{2} AB * h$

   $= \frac{1}{2} * 3 * 3 = 4.5$

6. In the figure on the right, what is the perimeter of the triangle formed by the three points?

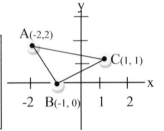

   (A) 4.7
   (B) 5.2
   (C) 5.8
   (D) 6.9
   (E) 7.6

   $AB = \sqrt{(-2-(-1))^2 + (2-0)^2} = \sqrt{1+4} = \sqrt{5}$

   $BC = \sqrt{(1-(-1))^2 + (1-0)^2} = \sqrt{4+1} = \sqrt{5}$

   $AC = \sqrt{(1-(-2))^2 + (1-2)^2} = \sqrt{9+1} = \sqrt{10}$

   $Perimeter = \sqrt{5} + \sqrt{5} + \sqrt{10} \approx 7.6$

7. Which of the following equations represents the line on the right?

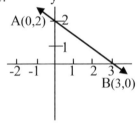

   (A) $y = -\frac{2}{3}x + 2$
   (B) $y = -\frac{3}{2}x + 2$
   (C) $y = -3x + 2$
   (D) $y = \frac{2}{3}x + 2$
   (E) $y = 3x + 2$

   $y = mx + b$, $\quad m = slope$
   $b = y - intercept.$
   $A = (0,2)$, $\quad B = (3,0)$
   $m = \frac{2-0}{0-3} = -\frac{2}{3}$, $\quad b = 2$
   $\therefore y = -\frac{2}{3}x + 2$

7. For what value of p will the lines $px + 2y - 3 = 0$, and $y = 3x + 2$ be parallel ?

   (A) -6
   (B) -3
   (C) 1.5
   (D) 4.5
   (E) 6

   $px + 2y - 3 = 0; \ 2y = -px + 3,$
   $y = -\frac{p}{2}x + \frac{3}{2}; \ slope = -\frac{p}{2}$
   $y = 3x + 2; \ slope = 3$
   $parallel \ lines \ have \ equal \ slopes: -\frac{p}{2} = 3, \quad p = -6$

8. In the figure on the right, what is the equation of the line that passes through point A and is perpendicular to line l ?

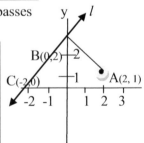

   (A) $y = -\frac{2}{3}x + 3$
   (B) $y = -x + 3$
   (C) $y = -\frac{1}{2}x + 2$
   (D) $y = -x + 2$
   (E) $y = -2x + 2$

   $C = (-2,0)$, $\quad B = (0,2)$
   $slope \ of \ line \ l \ (\overline{CB}) = \frac{2-0}{0-(-2)} = 1$
   $slope \ of \ line \perp l = -1$
   $y = mx + b; \ y = -x + b; \ sub(2,1)in:$
   $1 = -2 + b; \ b = 3, \quad y = -x + 3$

Scoring

To estimate your score for the following practice tests:

1. Add 1 for each multiple choice question you got right, and subtract 0.25 for each you got wrong.
2. Add 1 for each grid-in question you got right and no penalty for any wrong answer in the grid-in. (skip step 2 if there is no grind-in question)
3. Sum up the total from step 1 and 2, and divide this sum by the total number of questions in the test. The result will be the percentage. (e.g. 0.75 = 75%)
4. Multiply 800 by the result from step 3, since SAT full score in each section is 800. The result will be an estimated score of SAT equivalent.

Example: In Practice 2, there are 18 questions in total, 8 multiple-choice and 10 grid-in. You got 6 corrects and 2 wrongs in the multiple-choice, and 8 corrects in the grid-in, the SAT equivalent will be: $\dfrac{6-2(0.25)+8}{18} * 800 = 600$ (See References 2)

Practice Tests:

Use of a scientific or graphing calculator is allowed with SAT mathematics questions. (See References 3 for acceptable calculators)

The similar Reference Information as in the following will be provided for every SAT Math section Test.

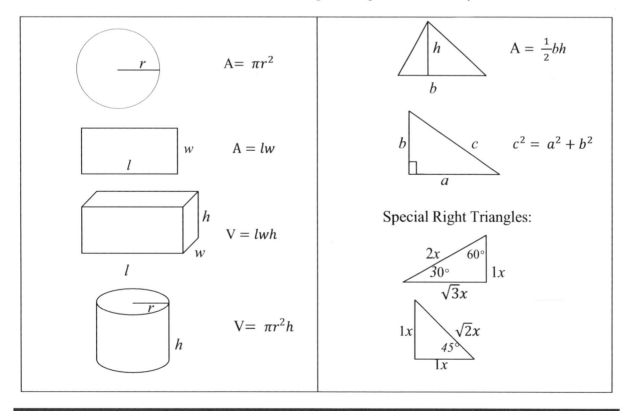

Practice Test 1
25 minutes, 20 questions

1. What percent of 85 is 17?

   (A) 30%
   (B) 25%
   (C) 20%
   (D) 18%
   (E) 15%

2. Two million, five hundred thousand, five hundred and eighty two is:

   (A) 2,500,582
   (B) 2,582,000
   (C) 20,500,582
   (D) 200,500,582
   (E) 256,825,820

3.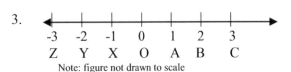

   Note: figure not drawn to scale

   On the number line above, the length AY is the same as the length

   (A) AC
   (B) BO
   (C) BX
   (D) CX
   (E) XZ

4. Four boxes are labeled as a, b, c and d, and the average weight of boxes a, b and c is 12kg. What is the average weight of all four boxes if d weights 16kg?

   (A) 15 kg
   (B) 13 kg
   (C) 12 kg
   (D) 10 kg
   (E) 9 kg

5. Two endpoints of a line segment are A (2, 3) and B (0, 9), what is the length AB?

   (A) 6.32
   (B) 7.90
   (C) 8.22
   (D) 8.40
   (E) 9.78

6. How many ways can Sarah choose her lunch including a fruit, a sandwich, a drink and a desert, if she has 4 kinds of fruits, 2 different kinds of sandwiches, 3 different types of drinks and 2 kinds of desserts to choose from?

   (A) 12
   (B) 20
   (C) 24
   (D) 30
   (E) 48

7. Given $f(x) = 2x^2 - 3$, determine the value of f(2).

   (A) 1
   (B) 2
   (C) 4
   (D) 5
   (E) 11

8. Mary is 20 years older than her son. In 10 years she will be twice as old as he will be. How old is her son now?

   (A) 5
   (B) 8
   (C) 10
   (D) 11
   (E) 12

9.

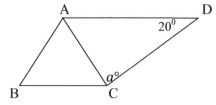

Note: figure not drawn to scale.

In the figure above, the three sides of $\triangle ABC$ are equal, and $AD \parallel BC$, what is the measure of a?

(A) 105
(B) 100
(C) 90
(D) 80
(E) 70

10. Which of the following lines is perpendicular to $y = -\frac{1}{3}x + 2$?

(A) $y = -\frac{1}{3}x - \frac{1}{2}$
(B) $y = -\frac{1}{3}x$
(C) $y = -3x + 2$
(D) $y = 3x + 2$
(E) $y = 2$

11. If $(2x - 4)^{\frac{3}{2}} = 64$, what is the value of $2x$?

(A) 20
(B) 16
(C) 10
(D) 8
(E) 6

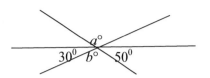

Note: Figure not to scale

12. In the figure above, what is the value of $a + b$?

(A) 80
(B) 100
(C) 160
(D) 200
(E) 220

13. If $5a + 2b = 14$ and $3a + 4b = 0$, what is $a - b$ equal to?

(A) -3
(B) 1
(C) 2
(D) 4
(E) 7

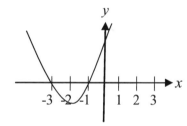

Note: figure not drawn to scale

14. Which of the following equations best represents the graph above?

(A) $y = x^2 + x - 1$
(B) $y = x^2 + 4x + 3$
(C) $y = -x^2 + x + 2$
(D) $y = -x^2 + 4x + 3$
(E) $y = x^2 - 1$

15. When x is divided by 9, it equals to y with a remainder 3. If $\frac{y}{3} - 2 = 4$, what is the value of x?

(A) 165
(B) 172
(C) 188
(D) 200
(E) 204

16. If $f(x) = -(x - 2)^2 + 3$, which of the following represent the range of $f(x)$?

(A) $y \le -2$
(B) $y \le 0$
(C) $0 \le y \le 3$
(D) $y \le 3$
(E) $y \ge 2$

17. In a jar there are 15 coins of quarters and dimes. If the number of dimes is 3 more than twice the number of quarters, how much money is in the jar?

(A) $2.10
(B) $2.50
(C) $2.85
(D) $3.00
(E) $4.50

18. Which of the following is the remainder of $(x^3 + 3x^2 - 2x - 3) \div (x - 2)$?

(A) 8
(B) 10
(C) 12
(D) 13
(E) 15

19.

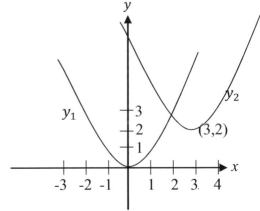

Note: figure not drawn to scale

From the graph above, if $y_1 = x^2$, what is the equation of y_2?

(A) $y_2 = (x - 3)^2$
(B) $y_2 = (x - 3)^2 + 2$
(C) $y_2 = (x + 3)^2 - 2$
(D) $y_2 = (x + 3)^2$
(E) $y_2 = (x + 3)^2 + 2$

20. Which of the following is equivalent to $\frac{x^2 - 4x - 12}{x + 2}$, for $x \ne -2$?

(A) $x + 2$
(B) $x - 4$
(C) $x + 4$
(D) $x - 6$
(E) $x + 6$

Practice Test 1 Solutions

1. **(C)**

   Solution 1: (See Basic Math 8, Percent)
   $$\frac{17}{85} * 100\% = 20\%$$
   The correct answer is (C).

2. **(A)**

   Solution 2: (See Basic Math 2, Place Value)

   ```
     2000000
      500000
         500
   +      62
   ─────────
     2500562
   ```

   The correct answer is (A).

3. **(C)**

   Solution 3: (See Basic Math 11, Number Lines)
   Length AY = 3
   AC = 2,
   BO = 2
   BX = 3
   CX = 4
   XZ = 2
   $\therefore$ BX = AY = 3

4. **(B)**

   Solution 4: (See Basic Math 7, Average)
   Total weight of boxes a, b and c :
   $a + b + c = 12 * 3 = 36$
   $\therefore$ Total weight of all 4 boxes:
   $36 + 16 = 52$
   $\therefore$ The Average weight of 4 boxes:
   $52 \div 4 = 13$

5. **(A)**

   Solution 5: (See Geometry 7.2, Distance)
   $$d = \sqrt{(x_2 - x_1)^2 + (y_2 - y_1)^2}$$
   $$= \sqrt{(2 - 0)^2 + (3 - 9)^2}$$
   $$= \sqrt{(2)^2 + (-6)^2}$$
   $$= \sqrt{4 + 36}$$
   $$= \sqrt{40} = 6.32$$

6. **(E)**

   Solution 6:
   (See Data Analysis 1, FCP)

   Use Fundamental Counting Principal:
   $4 * 2 * 3 * 2 = 48$

7. **(D)**

   Solution 7: (See Algebra 12, Composition of Functions)
   $$f(x) = 2x^2 - 3$$
   $$f(2) = 2 * (2)^2 - 3$$
   $$= 5$$

8. **(C)**

   Solution 8:
   (See Algebra 4. Word Problems)

   Let x = Her son's age now

	Son	Mary
Now	x	$x + 20$
+ 10 years	$x + 10$	$(x + 20) + 10$

   In 10 years:
   $$2(x + 10) = (x + 20) + 10$$
   $$2x + 20 = x + 30$$
   $$2x - x = 30 - 20$$
   $$\therefore \quad x = 10$$

9. (B)

Solution 9:
(See Geometry 2.4, Angles in Parallel lines and 4.1, Equilateral Triangles)

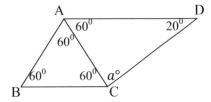

$\triangle ABC$ is equilateral, since all three sides are equal.

$\angle A = \angle B = \angle C = 60^0$

Given that AD ∥ BC ,

$\angle DAC$ and $\angle ACB$ are alternate angles.

∴ $\angle DAC = \angle ACB = 60^0$

$a = 180 - 20 - 60$

$= 100$

∴ $a = 100$

10. (D)

Solution 10: (See Geometry 7.3)

For two lines to be perpendicular, their slopes, m_1 and m_2 should satisfy

$m_1 * m_2 = -1$

Since $y_1 = -\frac{1}{3}x + 2$ has slope

$m_1 = -\frac{1}{3}$, m_2 must equals 3

to satisfy $m_1 * m_2 = -\frac{1}{3} * 3 = -1$

Since in (D), $y_2 = 3x + 2$

has slope $m_2 = 3$

∴ line y_2 in (D) is perpendicular to y_1.

11. (A)

Solution 11: (See Algebra 8)

$(2x - 4)^{\frac{3}{2}} = 64$

$(2x - 4) = (64)^{\frac{2}{3}}$

$2x - 4 = 16$

$2x = 16 + 4 = 20$

12. (D)

Solution 12: (See Geometry 2, Angles Relationships)

$b = 180 - (30 + 50)$

$= 100$

∴ $a = b = 100$ (opposite angles)

∴ $a + b = 200$

13. (E)

Solution 13: (See Algebra 3.2)

Equations:

$5a + 2b = 14$ (1)

$3a + 4b = 0$ (2)

Multiplied (1) by 2:

$10a + 4b = 28$ (3)

(3) – (2):

$10a + 4b = 28$

$- (3a + 4b = 0)$

$7a + 0 = 28$

$a = 4$

Now Substitute $a = 4$ into original equation (1):

$5(4) + 2b = 14$

$20 + 2b = 14$

$2b = 14 - 20; \quad b = -3$

Therefore, $a - b = 4 - (-3) = 7$

14. (B)

Solution 14: (See Algebra 2.2, ex.3)

Method 1:

Since the graph y has x-intercepts at -3 $and - 1$.

∴ $(x + 3)$ and $(x + 1)$ are factors of quadratic equation:

∴ $y = (x + 3) (x + 1)$

$= x^2 + x + 3x + 3$

$= x^2 + 4x + 3$

Method 2:

In quadratic equations,

$y = ax^2 + bx + c$,

c is the y-intercept; when $x = 0, y = c$.

(B), (C), (D) have positive y-intercepts, but (C) and (D) have negative a, indicating a parabola opening down. In the given graph, it is open up, so only (B) can represent the graph.

15. (A)
Solution 15:

Since $\frac{y}{3} - 2 = 4$

$\frac{y}{3} = 6$

$y = 6 * 3 = 18$

Since $\frac{x}{9} = 18$ with remainder 3.

∴ $x = 9 * 18 + 3 = 165$

16. (D)
Solution 16: (See Algebra 11.2)
The graph of $f(x) = -(x - 2)^2 + 3$
is a parabola with vertex (2, 3),
opening down

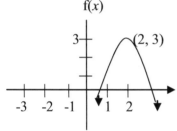

Note: figure not drawn to scale

∴ The values of $f(x)$ must be less than
or equal to 3,
∴ R = { $y \le 3$ }

17. (A)
solution 17: (See Algebra 4)
Let q = number of quarters
∴ d = number of dimes
$d = 2q + 3$
Since $d + q = 15$
∴ $(2q + 3) + q = 15$
$3q = 15 - 3$
$q = 4$
∴ Number of quarters is 4, and
Number of dimes is $15 - 4 = 11$
Since value of quarter = 25 cents, and
value of dime = 10 cents

∴ The amount of money in the jar:
$(4 * 25) + (11 * 10) = 210$ cents
$= \$2.10$

18. (D)
Solution 18: (See Algebra 13)
Set $f(x) = x^3 + 3x^2 - 2x - 3$
By Remainder theorem,
the remainder of
$f(x) \div (x - 2)$ is equal to $f(2)$.
∴ $f(2) = (2)^3 + 3 * (2)^2 - 2*(2) - 3$
$= 13$

19. (E)
(See Algebra 11.2)
Comparing y_2 with y_1:
The vertex of y_1 is (0, 0) and
the vertex of y_2 is (3, 2)
y_2 is 3 units right, and
2 units up from y_1,

$y_2 = (x - 3)^2 + 2$

(3 units right)   (2 units up)
The correct answer is (B).

20. (D)
Solution 20: (See Algebra 2.2)
$x^2 - 4x - 12$
$2 * -6 = -12$
$2 + -6 = -4$
∴ $x^2 - 4x - 12 = (x + 2)(x - 6)$

∴ $\frac{x^2 - 4x - 12}{x+2} = \frac{(x + 2)(x - 6)}{(x + 2)}$

$= x - 6$

Practice Test 2
Time --- 25 minutes
18 Questions

Reference Information:

1. Angles on one side of a straight line add to 180°.
2. There are 360° in a circle.

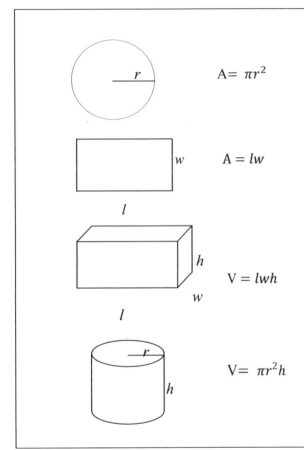

$A = \pi r^2$

$A = lw$

$V = lwh$

$V = \pi r^2 h$

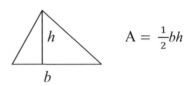

$A = \frac{1}{2}bh$

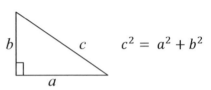

$c^2 = a^2 + b^2$

Special Right Triangles:

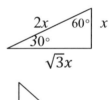

---

1. Which one of the following is the slope of the line $3x - y - 5 = 0$?
   (A) -5
   (B) -3
   (C) 3
   (D) 4
   (E) 5

2. If $\frac{2x+4}{3} = 6$, what is the value of $3x$?
   (A) -6
   (B) -3
   (C) 6
   (D) 15
   (E) 21

---

3. If the average cost of three books is $15.00, and the first two books cost $12.50 and $14.00, what is the cost of the third book?
    (A) $15.00
    (B) $16.50
    (C) $18.00
    (D) $18.50
    (E) $19.50

4.
    Note: figure not drawn to scale.
    In the triangle above, what is the area of $\triangle ABC$?
    (A) $6cm^2$
    (B) $9.5cm^2$
    (C) $12.4cm^2$
    (D) $15.0cm^2$
    (E) $16.0cm^2$

5. There are 108 apples and oranges in a basket. If the ratio of apple to orange is 7:5, how many oranges are in the basket?
    (A) 40
    (B) 45
    (C) 56
    (D) 63
    (E) 65

6.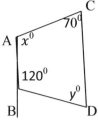
    Note: figure not drawn to scale.

    In the figure above, $\overline{AB} \parallel \overline{CD}$, What is the value of x?
    (A) 70
    (B) 90
    (C) 100
    (D) 110
    (E) 120

7. Mary left union station at 12pm and drove towards her university at 60 miles/hr, Cole left the station an hour later and drove on the same route at 70 miles/hr. At what time would Cole pass Mary?
    (A) 4:00pm
    (B) 5:30pm
    (C) 6:00pm
    (D) 6:30pm
    (E) 7:00pm

8. Two colors are chosen from red, blue, yellow, orange and white to print a team t-shirt. What is the probability that the red and white are chosen?
    (A) $\frac{1}{2}$
    (B) $\frac{2}{5}$
    (C) $\frac{1}{5}$
    (D) $\frac{1}{10}$
    (E) $\frac{1}{20}$

Grid-in Practice

9. If $x^2 + kx + 7 = 0$ has two distinct solutions, both negative integers, what is the possible value of k?

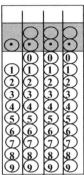

---

10. If $2a = 3$ and $3b = 1$, what is the value of $a + b$?

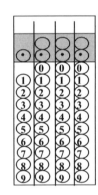

---

11. In a geometric sequence, 4, −8, 16, ..., what is the eleventh term?

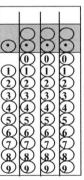

12. If $f(x) = x^2 + 2$, and $g(x) = -2x$, what is the value of $f(g(2))$?

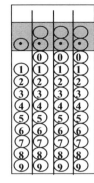

---

13. The length of a rectangle is 5cm more than twice the width. The total perimeter is 55 cm, what is the width?

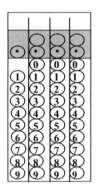

---

14. If $x^{\frac{3}{2}} = 7$, what is the value of x?

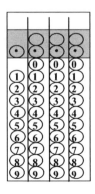

15.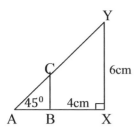

In the figure above, if XY = 6 cm and BX = 4 cm, and $\overline{BC} \parallel \overline{XY}$, what is the area of $\triangle ABC$?

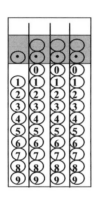

16. What is the smallest integer which is a multiple of 3, 4 and 5, and it produces a remainder of 5 when it is divided by 7?

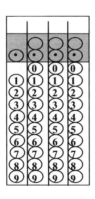

17. If $3y - x = 7$ and $\frac{23}{x+y} = 1$, what is the value of $x + 2y$?

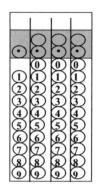

18. In the figure below, if $f(x) = \sqrt{x}$, and is transformed to $g(x)$, where $g(x) = a\sqrt{x - b} + c$, what is the value of abc?

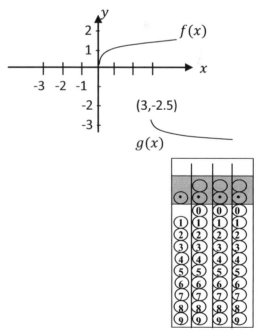

Practice Test 2 Solutions:

1. C
   (See Geometry 7.2)
   Change $3x - y - 5 = 0$ to the
   $y = mx + b$ form :
   $3x - y + 5 = 0$
   $-y = -3x - 5$ (divide both sides by -1)
   $y = 3x + 5$
   $\therefore$ slope: $m = 3$

2. E
   (See Algebra 3.1, Solving Linear Equations)
   $\frac{2x+4}{3} = 6$
   Multiplying both sides by 3:
   $2x + 4 = 3 * 6$
   $2x = 18 - 4$
   $x = 7$
   $\therefore 3x = 21$

3. D
   (See Basic Math 7, Average)

   Total cost of 3 books = $3 * 15.00 = 45.00$
   The cost the 3rd book $= 45.0 - 12.5 - 14.00$
   $= 18.50$

4. A
   (See Geometry 3 and 6)

   By Pythagorean theorem:
   $AB^2 = AC^2 + BC^2$
   $BC^2 = AB^2 - AC^2$
   $\therefore BC = \sqrt{(5^2 - 4^2)} = \sqrt{9} = 3$
   $\therefore$ Area of $\triangle ABC = \frac{1}{2} * b * h$
   $= \frac{1}{2} * 4 * 3 = 6\ cm^2$

5. B
   (See Basic Math 9, Ratio)

   Let $x = \#\ of\ oranges$
   $\therefore \#\ of\ apples = 108 - x$
   $\frac{Apple}{Orange} = \frac{7}{5} = \frac{108 - x}{x}$
   By cross multiplication:
   $5 (108 - x) = 7x$
   $540 - 5x = 7x$
   $540 = 12x$
   $45 = x$

6. D
   (See Geometry 2.4 and 2.6)

   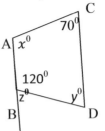

   Since $\overline{AB} \parallel \overline{CD}$
   $z = 180 - 120 = 60$
   $y = z = 60$ (Alternate angles)
   Sum of interiors angles of a quadrilateral, $n=4$:
   $180*(n - 2) = 180 * (4 - 2) = 360$
   $\therefore x = 360 - (120 + 70 + y)$
   $= 360 - (120 + 70 + 60)$
   $= 110$

7. E
   (See Basic Math 7.3)
   Distance (D) = Time (T) * Speed (S)

   Let $x = \#$ of hours taken by Cole before
   passing Mary

	S(mi/hr)	T(h)	D(mi)
Mary	60	x+1	60(x+1)
Cole	70	x	70x

   When Cole passed Mary, they covered the
   same distance:
   $\therefore 60 (x + 1) = 70x,\quad 60x + 60 = 70x$
   $60 = 70x - 60x$
   $\therefore x = 6$ hours
   Since Cole left at 1pm
   $\therefore$ Time when Cole passed Mary
   $= 1pm + 6h = 7pm$

8. D
   (see Data Analysis 3 and 4)

   Use nC_r to find the total # of ways choosing
   2 colors from 5, order is not important:
   $_5C_2 = \frac{5*4}{2*1} = 10$
   There is only 1 choice of red and white,
   $\therefore$ The probability $= \frac{1}{10}$

9. (See Algebra 2.2)
Since the only two factors
of 7 are 1 and 7,
so $x^2 + kx + 7$ can be
factored as:
$x^2 + kx + 7$
$\quad = (x + 1)(x + 7)$,
and $x = -1 \ and -7$ are
the two distinct negative
solutions.
and $(x + 1)(x + 7)$
$\quad = x^2 + 8x + 7$
$\therefore k = 8$

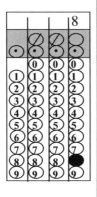

10. (See Basic Math 6.1)
Since $2a = 3$ and $3b = 1$,
$\therefore \ a = \frac{3}{2}$ and $b = \frac{1}{3}$
$\therefore \ a + b = \frac{3}{2} + \frac{1}{3}$
Common denominator = 6
$\therefore \ a + b = \frac{3*3}{2*3} + \frac{1*2}{3*2}$
$\quad = \frac{9}{6} + \frac{2}{6} = \frac{11}{6}$

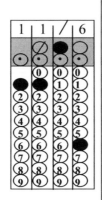

Note: Can be gridded in as: 11/6 or 1.83
Both will be accepted as correct answers.
Never grid in a mixed number fraction
as $1\frac{5}{6}$ for $\frac{11}{6}$. (see References 4)

11. (See Basic Math 13.2)
Formula for term n:
$t_n = ar^{n-1}$
where a = first term
$\qquad r$ = common ratio
Given:
$a = 4$ and $r = \frac{-8}{4} = -2$

$\therefore \ t_n = 4 * (-2)^{n-1}$
$\therefore \ t_{11} = 4(-2)^{11-1}$
$\quad = 4 * (-2)^{10}$
$\quad = 4096$

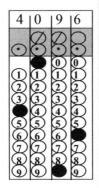

12. (See Algebra 12.3)
$f(x) = x^2 + 2$
$g(x) = -2x$
$f(g(x)) = (-2x)^2 + 2$
$\qquad\quad = 4x^2 + 2$
$\therefore f(g(2)) = 4 * 2^2 + 2$
$\qquad\qquad = 18$

Or alternatively:
$g(2) = -2(2) = -4$
$f\big(g(2)\big) = f(-4)$
$\qquad\quad = (-4)^2 + 2 = 18$

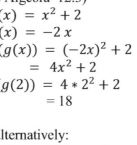
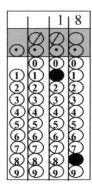

13. (See Algebra 4)
Let x = the width length

w	x
l	5 + 2x

Perimeter = $2w + 2l$
$55 = 2x + 2(5 + 2x)$
$55 = 2x + 10 + 4x$
$45 = 6x$
$x = \dfrac{45}{6} = 7.5$

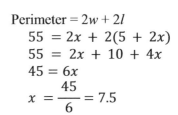

Note: can be gridded in as: 45/6 or 7.5
Both will be accepted as correct answers.

14. (See Algebra 8.2)
$(x^{\frac{3}{2}})^{\frac{2}{3}} = 7^{\frac{2}{3}}$
$x = 7^{\frac{2}{3}}$
$\quad = 3.6593057$
$\quad = 3.66$

(by calculator:
$7 \wedge (2 \div 3) = 3.6593057$)

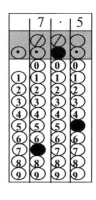
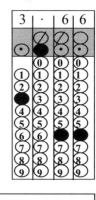

Note: Both 3.65 (truncated) and 3.66 (rounded)
will be accepted as correct answers,
but a less accurate answer such as 3.6
will be considered as incorrect.

15. (See Geometry 4.3
and 6.1)
Since $\triangle AXY$ is 45°-45°-90°
AX : XY = 1 : 1
∴ AX = YX = 6 cm
∴ AB = 6 − BX
$= 6 − 4 = 2$ cm
Since $\overline{BC} \parallel \overline{XY}$
∴ $\angle ABC = 90^0$
∴ AB : BC = 1 : 1
∴ BC = AB = 2 cm
∴ Area of $\triangle ABC$
$= ½ (b * h) = ½ (2 * 2)$
$= 2\ cm^2$

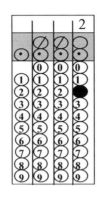

16. (See Basic Math 5)
The LCM of 3, 4, and 5 is:
$3*4*5 = 60$
The common multiples of
3, 4, and 5 are therefore:
60, 120, 180, 240, ...
Since 180 is the first
multiple that produces a
remainder of 5 when being
divided by 7,
∴ the answer is 180.

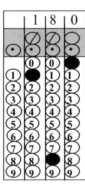

17. (See Algebra 3.2)
$3y − x = 7$ (1)
$\frac{23}{x+y} = 1$ (2)
From (2):
by cross multiplication,
$23 = x + y$
From (1): $x = 3y − 7$
∴ $23 = (3y − 7) + y$
$4y = 23 + 7 = 30$

$$y = \frac{30}{4} = 7.5$$

Sub into (1):
$3y − x = 7$
$3 * (7.5) − x = 7$
$x = 22.5 − 7 = 15.5$
$x + 2y = 15.5 + 2 * (7.5)$
$= 15.5 + 15 = 30.5$

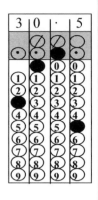

18. (See Algebra 11.4)

$g(x)$ can be obtained from
$f(x)$ by reflecting in the
x-axis:
∴ $a = −1$
$g(x) = − f(x − b) + c$

And then moving
3 units right, and
2.5 units down:
∴ $g(x) = −f(x − 3) − 2.5$
$g(x) = −1\sqrt{x − 3} − 2.5$
∴ $b = 3$
$c = −2.5$
∴ $a * b * c = (−1) * 3 * (−2.5)$
$= 7.5$

Practice Test 3
Time --- 25 minutes
20 Questions

Reference Information:

1. Angles on one side of a straight line add to 180°.
2. There are 360° in a circle.

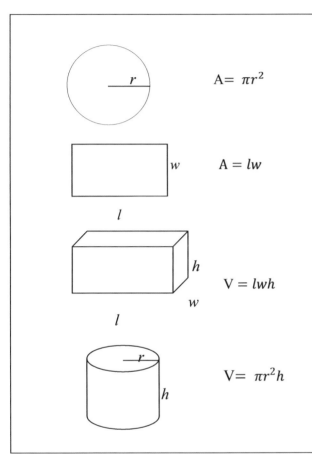

$A = \pi r^2$

$A = lw$

$V = lwh$

$V = \pi r^2 h$

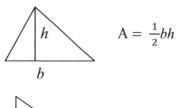

$A = \frac{1}{2}bh$

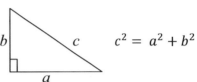

$c^2 = a^2 + b^2$

Special Right Triangles:

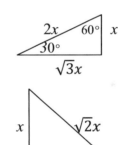

1. If the average weight of 8 balls is 7.5 kg, what is the total weight of 8 balls?
    (A) 7.5
    (B) 10
    (C) 56
    (D) 60
    (E) 75

2. If $3x - 4 = 8$, what is the value of $6x - 5$?
    (A) -2
    (B) 8
    (C) 19
    (D) 24
    (E) 41

3. What percent of a half-day is 144 minutes?

   (A) 10.8
   (B) 14.0
   (C) 15.5
   (D) 20.0
   (E) 32.8

---

4. In the figure below, what is the value of x?

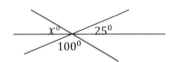

   Note: figure not drawn to scale.

   (A) 25
   (B) 55
   (C) 60
   (D) 110
   (E) 135

---

5. Jason bought a pack of 25 pencils at $6.00. He sold all the pencils at 50¢ each. How much profit did Jason make?
   (A) $4.00
   (B) $5.50
   (C) $6.50
   (D) $10.00
   (E) $12.50

6.

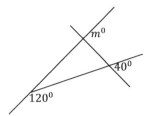

   Note: figure not drawn to scale

   In the figure above, what is the value of m?
   (A) 40
   (B) 60
   (C) 80
   (D) 90
   (E) 100

---

7. How many prime numbers are there between 47 and 57 inclusively?
   (A) 2
   (B) 3
   (C) 4
   (D) 5
   (E) 6

8.

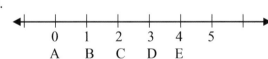

   Note: figure not drawn to scale.

   On the number line above, the length $(BE - CD)$ is equal to the length
   (A) AB
   (B) BD
   (C) CD
   (D) DE
   (E) AD

---

9. When $f(x) = \dfrac{x^2 + 2}{3}$, and $f(\sqrt{a}) = b$, what is a in terms of b?
   (A) $(3b - 6)^2$
   (B) $(b - 2)^2$
   (C) $3b - 2$
   (D) $\sqrt{3b - 2}$
   (E) $\sqrt{b - 3}$

10. How many four-letter codes can be arranged using the letters A, B, C and D with no repeating letters?
   (A) 36
   (B) 24
   (C) 20
   (D) 18
   (E) 12

11. If $3x = 2$, what is $x + \dfrac{1}{x}$ equal to?

   (A) $\dfrac{2}{3}$
   (B) $1\dfrac{1}{2}$
   (C) $1\dfrac{5}{6}$
   (D) $2\dfrac{1}{6}$
   (E) $3\dfrac{1}{2}$

12. If $2^{2x-2} = 8^2$, x must be:
   (A) 4
   (B) 5
   (C) 6
   (D) 8
   (E) 9

13. If $a = 2x$ and $a - b = 3y$, which of the following must be true?
   (A) $a - 4x = -b - 3y$
   (B) $a - 4x = b - 3y$
   (C) $a + 4x = b + 3y$
   (D) $a + 2x = b + 3y$
   (E) $a - 2x = -b - 3y$

14.

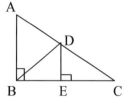

Note: figure not drawn to scale.

In the figure above, AB = 10cm, DE = 3cm and the area of $\triangle ABC$ is 30 cm^2. What is the area of $\triangle ABD$?
   (A) $9cm^2$
   (B) $20cm^2$
   (C) $21cm^2$
   (D) $30cm^2$
   (E) Not enough information

15. If $x \, \Omega \, y = \dfrac{(x+y)^2}{(x-y)}$, what is the value of $11 \, \Omega \, 6$?
   (A) 57.8
   (B) 62.3
   (C) 83.2
   (D) 86.0
   (E) 94.7

16. When $f(x) = x^2 - kx + 22$ is divided by $x + 4$, the remainder is 2. What is the remainder when $f(x)$ is divided by $x + 1$?
    (A) -12
    (B) -9
    (C) -1
    (D) 9
    (E) 14

17. In the square on the right, if AD is $\sqrt{8}\ cm$, what is the perimeter of the square?
    (A) $8cm$
    (B) $2\sqrt{8}\ cm$
    (C) $4\ cm$
    (D) $\sqrt{8}\ cm$
    (E) $2cm$

18. If $\sqrt{3x} - 4 = -1$, what is $\dfrac{27}{x}$?
    (A) 3
    (B) 4
    (C) 5
    (D) 6
    (E) 9

19. The perimeter of a square is 34cm. If the area of this square is half the area of a circle, what is the radius of the circle?
    (A) 4.25
    (B) 5.22
    (C) 6.78
    (D) 7.37
    (E) 8.50

20.

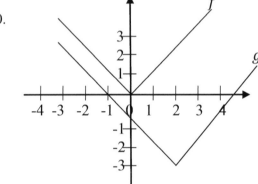

Note: figure not drawn to scale.

The graph of $f = |x|$ is shown, which equation represents g?
    (A) $g = |x - 3| - 2$
    (B) $g = |x - 2| - 3$
    (C) $g = |x - 2|$
    (D) $g = |x + 2| - 3$
    (E) $g = |x| + 3$

Practice Test 3 Solutions:

1. (D)

    (See Basic Math 7, Average)
    Average $= total \div 8 = 7.5$
    $\therefore$ Total weight $= 8 * 7.5$
    $\qquad\qquad\quad = 60\ kg$

2. (C)

    (See Algebra 3.1,
    $\qquad$ Solving Linear Equation)
    Since $3x - 4 = 8$
    $\therefore$ $3x = 12, \quad x = 4$
    $\therefore$ $6(4) - 5 = 24 - 5 = 19$

3. (D)

    (See Basic Math 8, Percent)
    A half-day has 12 hours,
    12 $* 60$ minutes $= 720$ minutes
    $\frac{144}{720} * 100\% = 0.2 * 100\% = 20\%$

4. (B)

    (See Geometry 2, Angle Relationship)

    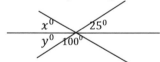

    Note: figure not drawn to scale.

    Let y be as indicated in the figure,
    $y = 25$ (opposite angles)
    $x = 180 - 100 - y$
    $\quad = 180 - 100 - 25 = 55$
    $\therefore$ $x = 55$

5. (C)

    $50\cent = \$0.50$
    Total earning: $25 * \$0.50 = \$12.50$
    Profit $= \$12.50 - \$6.00 = \$6.50$

6. (E)

    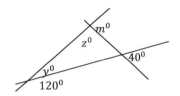

    (See Geometry 2, Angle Relationships)

    Let x, y and z be angles as indicated.
    $\therefore$ $x = 40$ (opposite angle)
    and $y = 180 - 120 = 60$
    and $z = 180 - x - y$
    $\qquad = 180 - 40 - 60 = 80$
    $\therefore$ $m = 180 - z = 180 - 80$
    $\qquad = 100$

7. (A)
    (See Basic Math 1, Numbers)
    Prime numbers are numbers that
    have no other factor besides 1 and
    themselves:
    3, 5, 7, 11, 13, ...

    $\therefore$ Prime numbers between 47 and 57 are:
    47, 53
    $\therefore$ 2 is correct.

8. (B)
    (See Basic Math 11, Number Lines)
    Length BE $= 3$, CD $= 1$
    $\therefore$ BE $-$ CD $= 3 - 1 = 2$
    Since:
    $\quad$ AB $= 1$
    $\quad$ BD $= 2$
    $\quad$ CD $= 1$
    $\quad$ DE $= 1$
    $\quad$ AD $= 3$
    $\therefore$ BD is correct.

9. (C)

(See Algebra 12, Composite Functions)

$$f(\sqrt{a}) = \frac{(\sqrt{a})^2 + 2}{3} = b$$

Multiplied both sides by 3:

$(\sqrt{a})^2 + 2 = 3b$

$a + 2 = 3b$

$a = 3b - 2$

10. (B)

(See Data Analysis 1,
      Fundamental Counting Principle)

___   ___   ___   ___

The four blanks above represent the
4 spaces for the 4 letters.
There are 4 choices to fill in the 1st blank,
            3 choices for the 2nd blank,
            2 choices for the 3rd blank,
    and 1 choice for the 4th blank.

$\therefore$ _4_   _3_   _2_   _1_

by FCP: # of ways = $\underline{4} * \underline{3} * \underline{2} * \underline{1} = 24$

11. (D)

(See Basic Math 6, Fraction and
 Algebra , Solving Linear Equations)
Since $3x = 2$

$\therefore \quad x = \frac{2}{3}$

$\therefore \quad x + \frac{1}{x} = \frac{2}{3} + \frac{1}{(\frac{2}{3})}$ (note: $\frac{1}{(\frac{2}{3})} = 1 * \frac{3}{2} = \frac{3}{2}$)

$\qquad = \frac{2}{3} + \frac{3}{2} = \frac{2*2}{3*2} + \frac{3*3}{2*3}$

$\qquad = \frac{4}{6} + \frac{9}{6} = \frac{13}{6} = 2\frac{1}{6}$

12. (A)

(See Algebra 8.2, Solving
        Equations Involving Exponents)
Since $8^2 = (2^3)^2 = 2^6$

$\therefore \quad 2^{2x-2} = 2^6$

$\quad 2x - 2 = 6$

$\quad 2x = 8$

$\quad x = 4$

13. (A)

Since $a = 2x$ and $a - b = 3y$

$\therefore \quad 2x - b = 3y$

$\therefore \quad b = 2x - 3y$

$a + b = 2x + (2x - 3y)$

$a + b = 4x - 3y$

$\therefore \quad a - 4x = -b - 3y$

14. (C)

(See Geometry 6.1, Area and Perimeter)

Area of triangle $= \frac{1}{2} * b * h$

Area of $\triangle ABC = \frac{1}{2} * AB * BC$

$\qquad\qquad 30 = \frac{1}{2} * 10 * BC$

$\therefore \quad BC = 6\ cm$

Area of $\triangle BDC = \frac{1}{2} * 3 * 6 = 9\ cm^2$

Area $\triangle ABD = $ Area $\triangle ABC - $ Area $\triangle BDC$

$\therefore$ Area of $\triangle ABD = 30 - 9 = 21\ cm^2$

15. (A)

(See Basic Math 14, Special Symbols)

$11\ \Omega\ 6 = \frac{(11+6)^2}{(11-6)} = \frac{(17)^2}{5} = \frac{289}{5} = 57.8$

16. (E)

(See Algebra 13,
    Remainder Theorem)
Use the Remainder Theorem:
Since $x + 4$ is $x - (-4)$,
to find the remainder is to evaluate $f(-4)$:
$f(-4) = (-4)^2 - k(-4) + 22$
Since the remainder is 2:
$\therefore \quad 16 + 4k + 22 = 2 \quad \therefore \quad k = -9$
$\therefore \quad f(x) = x^2 + 9x + 22$
To find the remainder of $f(x)$ divided
by $x + 1$:
$f(-1) = (-1)^2 + 9(-1) + 22 = 14$

17. (A)

(See Geometry 3 and 6.1)
By Pythagorean theorem:
$AD^2 = AC^2 + CD^2$
Since $AC = CD$
$AD^2 = AC^2 + AC^2 = 2\ AC^2$
$\therefore \quad (\sqrt{8})^2 = 2\ AC^2$
$\qquad 8 = 2\ AC^2$
$\qquad 4 = AC^2$
$\therefore \ AC = 2\ cm$
$\therefore \quad$ Perimeter $= 4 * AC = 4 * 2 = 8cm$

18. (E)

(See Algebra 7,
    Solving Radical Equations)
$\sqrt{3x} = -1 + 4$
$\sqrt{3x} = 3$
$\left(\sqrt{3x}\right)^2 = 3^2$
$3x = 9$
$\therefore \ x = 3$
$\dfrac{27}{x} = \dfrac{27}{3} = 9$

19. (C)

(See Geometry 6, Perimeter,
        Area, Surface Area and Volume)

Perimeter of the square = 34 cm
$\therefore$ Each size of the square $= \dfrac{34}{4} = 8.5$ cm
Area of square $= s * s$
$\qquad\qquad = 8.5 * 8.5 = 72.25\ cm^2$
$\therefore$ Area of the circle $= 2 * 72.25$
$\qquad\qquad\qquad = 144.50\ cm^2$
Area of circle $= \pi r^2$
$\qquad \pi r^2 = 144.50 \quad (\pi = 3.14)$
$\therefore \quad r = \sqrt{\dfrac{144.50}{3.14}} = 6.78$ cm

20. (B)

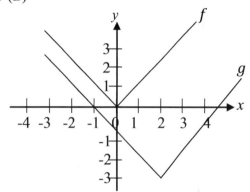

(See Algebra 11, Functions and
        Their Graphs, Domain and Range)
Comparing f and g, f has moved
    2 unit right and
    3 unit down to transform into g.

$\therefore \quad g = |x - 2| - 3$

Practice Test 4
Time --- 25 minutes
18 Questions

Reference Information:

1. Angles on one side of a straight line add to 180°.
2. There are 360° in a circle.

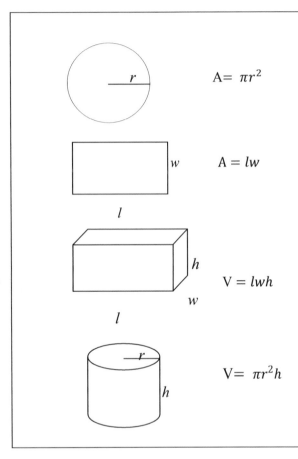

$A = \pi r^2$

$A = lw$

$V = lwh$

$V = \pi r^2 h$

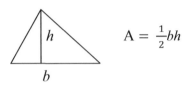

$A = \frac{1}{2}bh$

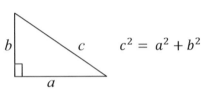

$c^2 = a^2 + b^2$

Special Right Triangles:

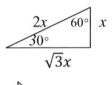

---

1. What is the value of
   $(4 * 10^5) + (3 * 10)^4 + (2 * 10^2)$?

   (A) 121200
   (B) 403,200
   (C) 850,200
   (D) 1,210,200
   (E) 4,030,200

2. If $\frac{2x}{3} = x + 3$, what is the value of $3x + 2$?

   (A) -25
   (B) -13
   (C) -9
   (D) 17
   (E) 23

3. If l_1 and l_2 are parallel, what is the value of x?

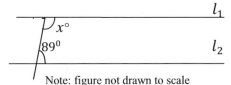

Note: figure not drawn to scale

(A) 85
(B) 89
(C) 90
(D) 91
(E) Not enough information

4. There are 15 baskets of apples, each contains 8 apples. If these apples are packed into boxes, with 30 apples in each box, how many boxes are needed?

(A) 3
(B) 4
(C) 8
(D) 10
(E) 12

5. If the ratio of boys to girls is 4:5, and a class has 54 students, how many boys are there?

(A) 18
(B) 22
(C) 24
(D) 25
(E) 30

6.

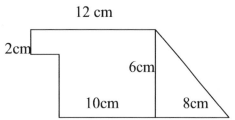

Note: figure not drawn to scale.

What is the total area of the figure above?

(A) $88cm^2$
(B) $90cm^2$
(C) $98cm^2$
(D) $100cm^2$
(E) $120cm^2$

7. If $\frac{\sqrt{2a}}{2} + 11 = b$, what is a in terms of b?

(A) $4(b-11)^2$
(B) $2(b-11)^2$
(C) $(b-11)^2$
(D) $2(b-11)$
(E) $b-11$

8. A computer initially costs \$2800, and each year, the value drops to 35% of the previous year. What will it be worth 9 years later?

(A) \$280
(B) \$28
(C) \$9.8
(D) \$0.63
(E) \$0.22

Grid in Practice:

9. If $4^x = 16\sqrt{4}$, what is the value of $\frac{2x}{3}$?

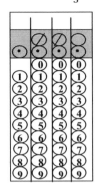

10. When $f(x) = 2x^3 - 3x^2 + x - 2$ is divided by $x - 3$, the remainder is equal to?

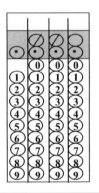

11. If $a \nabla b = \frac{\sqrt{a+b}}{a^2}$, what is the value of $7 \nabla 9$?

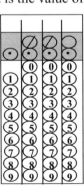

12.

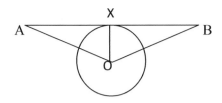

In the figure above, AB is tangent to the circle at point X, and O is the center of the circle. If AB = 9cm, and the circumference of the circle is 12.5π cm, what is the area of $\triangle$AOB?

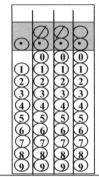

13. One side of a square has two endpoints A (2, 0) and B (1, 3), what is the perimeter of the square?

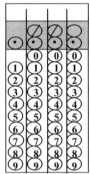

14. There were 450kg apples in a famer's stall, $\frac{1}{9}$ of them went bad and the farmer sold 80% of the good ones at \$1.99/kg. How much did the farmer make from the sale?

15.

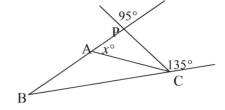

Note: figure not drawn to scale.

In the figure above, if $\overline{AB} = \overline{AC}$, what is the value of x?

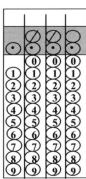

16. The order of skating performance of 8 finalists in an Olympic game is randomly drawn. If there are three U.S. skaters, what is the probability that the first three performers are U.S. skaters?

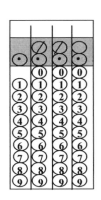

17. Lisa has 15 quarters and dimes, with a total value of $3.15. How many quarters does Lisa have?

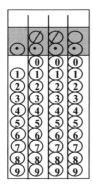

18.

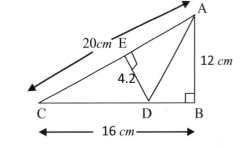

In the figure above, AB = 12, BC = 16, AC = 20, and DE = 4.2, what is AD?

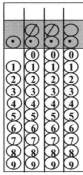

Practice Test 4 Solutions:

1. **D**

   (See Basic Math 2, Place Values)

   $$4 * 10^5 \quad = \quad\quad 400,000$$
   $$+ (3 * 10)^4 = + \ 810,000$$
   $$+ 2 * 10^2 \quad = + \quad\quad\quad 200$$
   $$\overline{\quad\quad\quad\quad\quad\quad\quad 1,210,200}$$

2. **A**

   (See Algebra 3.1, Solving Linear Equations)

   $\frac{2x}{3} = x + 3$

   Multiplied both sides by 3:

   $2x = 3x + 9$

   $-x = 9$

   $x = -9$

   $\therefore \quad 3x + 2 = 3 * (-9) + 2 = -27 + 2$

   $\quad\quad\quad = -25$

3. **D**

   (See Geometry 2.4, Angles in Parallel lines)

   Since $l_1 \parallel l_2$

   $\therefore \ \angle x = \angle y$

   $\angle y = 180^0 - 89^0 = 91^0$

   $\therefore \ \angle x = 91^0$

4. **B**

   Total number of apples $= 8 * 15 = 120$

   Boxes needed $= 120 \div 30 = 4$

5. **C**

   (See Basic Math 9, Ratio)

   Let $x = $ # of boys

   $\frac{b}{g} = \frac{4}{5}$

   $\frac{x}{54 - x} = \frac{4}{5}$

   $5x = 4 * (54 - x)$

   $5x = 216 - 4x$

   $9x = 216$

   $x = \frac{216}{9} = 24$

6. **A**

   (See Geometry 6, Area and Perimeter)

   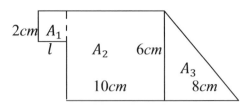

   $l = 12 - 10 = 2 \ cm$

   $A_1 = 2 * 2 = 4 \ cm^2$

   $A_2 = 6 * 10 = 60 \ cm^2$

   $A_3 = \frac{1}{2}(6 * 8) = 24 \ cm^2$

   Total Area $= A_1 + A_2 + A_3$

   $\quad\quad\quad\quad = (4 + 60 + 24) \ cm^2 = 88 \ cm^2$

7. **B**

   (See Algebra 7, Solving Radical Equations)

   $\frac{\sqrt{2a}}{2} + 11 = b, \quad\quad \frac{\sqrt{2a}}{2} = b - 11$

   Multiplied both sides by 2:

   $\quad \sqrt{2a} = 2(b - 11)$

   Square both sides:

   $\quad \left(\sqrt{2a}\right)^2 = 4(b - 11)^2$

   $\quad\quad 2a = 4(b - 11)^2,$

   Divide both sides by 2:

   $\quad a = 2(b - 11)^2$

8. **E**

   (see Basic Math, 13.2 Geometric Sequence)

   This is a geometric sequence with

   $\quad a = 2800,$

   $\quad r = 35\% = 0.35.$

   $2800, 2800*.35, 2800*.35^2, 2800*.35^3,...$

   $\quad\quad$ after 1 year $\quad$ 2 years $\quad$ 3 years

   $t_n = ar^{n-1}$

   After 9 years would be the 10th term,

   $\therefore \quad n = 10, \quad t_n = ar^{(n-1)}$

   $t_{10} = ar^9$

   $\quad\quad = \$2800 \ (0.35)^9$

   $\therefore \quad t_{10} = \$0.22$

9. (See Algebra 8.2)

$4^x = 16\sqrt{4}$

$= 4^2 * 4^{\frac{1}{2}}$

$= 4^{2+\frac{1}{2}}$

$= 4^{\frac{1}{2}+\frac{4}{2}}$

$= 4^{\frac{5}{2}}$

$\therefore x = \frac{5}{2}$

$\frac{2x}{3} = \frac{\cancel{2}}{3} * \frac{5}{\cancel{2}} = \frac{5}{3}$

(Grid: 5 / 3)

10. (See Algebra 13)
   By Remainder Theorem:

$f(x) \div (x - 3)$,
remainder is f(3).

$f(x) = 2x^3 - 3x^2 + x - 2$
$f(3) = 2(3)^3 - 3(3)^2 + 3 - 2$
$\quad\quad = 28$

(Grid: 2 8)

11. (See Basic Math 14,
       Special Symbols)

Since $a \nabla b = \frac{\sqrt{a+b}}{a^2}$,

$\therefore 7 \nabla 9 = \frac{\sqrt{7+9}}{7^2}$

$= \frac{\sqrt{16}}{7^2}$

$= \frac{4}{49}$

(Grid: 4 / 4 9)

12. (See Geometry 6)
   Circumference of a circle
      $= 2\pi r$
   $12.5\cancel{\pi} = 2\cancel{\pi} r$
   $\frac{12.5}{2} = r$
   $r = 6.25 \ cm$
   $\therefore \ XO = 6.25 \ cm$
   AB is a tangent at X.
   $\angle AXO = 90^0$,
   XO is the height(h) of $\triangle AOB$

   Area of triangle $= \frac{1}{2} * b * h$
   Area of $\triangle AOB$
   $= \frac{1}{2} * 9 * 6.25$
   $= 28.125$
   $\cong 28.1 \ cm^2$

(Grid: 2 8 . 1)

13. (See Geometry 6.1, Perimeter
      and 7.2, Distance)
   Distance between two points:
   $= \sqrt{(x_2 - x_1)^2 + (y_2 - y_1)^2}$
   length AB
   $= \sqrt{(2-1)^2 + (0-3)^2}$
   $= \sqrt{1+9}$
   $= \sqrt{10} = 3.16$
   Perimeter of a square
   $= 4*AB = 4 * 3.16$
   $= 12.64$

(Grid: 1 2 . 6)

14. (See Basic Math, 8. Percent)
   Total $= 450kg$
   Bad ones $= \frac{1}{9} * 450 = 50kg$
   Good ones $= 450 - 50$
   $\quad\quad\quad\quad = 400kg$
   Sold $= 0.8 * 400 = 320kg$
   Income $= 320 * \$1.99$
   $\quad\quad\quad = \$636.8$
   $\quad\quad\quad \cong \$637.$

(Grid: 6 3 7 .)

Note: can be gridded in either as
(636.) (truncated) or (637.) (rounded)
Both are accepted as correct answers.

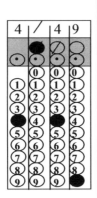
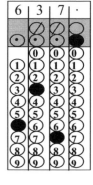

15. (See Geometry 2 and 4.2)

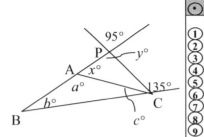

In ΔPBC:

$y = 95$, (opposite angles)

∠BPC = 95°,

∠BCP = 180° − 135° = 45°

∠B = 180 − ∠BPC − ∠BCP

= 180° − 95° − 45°

= 40°   (or $b = 40$)

In ΔABC:

Since AB = AC,

∴ ΔABC is isosceles, $b = c = 40$

$a = 180 − b − c$

= 180 − 40 − 40 = 100

$x = 180 − a = 180 − 100 = 80$

16. (See Data Analysis,
3. Combination and
4. Probability)

To find the number of ways
of taking 3 out of 8 without
considering the order, use

$n\mathbf{C}r$

(combination formula)

$$_8\mathbf{C}_3 = \frac{8 * 7 * 6}{3 * 2 * 1} = 56$$

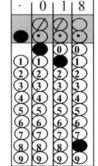

Out of these 56 triples,
only 1 triple is of three US skaters.

∴ P (first 3 are US skaters) $= \frac{1}{56} = 0.0179$

= 0.018

Note: can be gridded in either as
(1/56) or (.017) (truncated) or (.018) (rounded)

17. (See Algebra 4.Word
Problems)

The value of a
Quarter = 25¢
Dime = 10¢

Total value = \$3.15 = 315¢
Let x = # of quarters

	Q	D	Total
#	x	$15 - x$	15
Value	$25x$	$10(15 - x)$	$25x + 10(15 - x)$

Total:

$25x + 10(15 − x)= 315$

$15x = 315 − 150$

$15x = 165$

$x = 165/15$

∴ $x = 11$

18. (See Geometry, 3. and 6.1)

Area of triangle $= \frac{1}{2} * b * h$

Area of ΔABC

$= \frac{1}{2} * 16 * 12 = 96 \ cm^2$

Area of ΔACD

$= \frac{1}{2} * 20 * 4.2 = 42 \ cm^2$

Area of ΔABD

$= 96 – 42 = 54 \ cm^2$

Area of ΔABD

$= \frac{1}{2} * BD * 12$

$54 = BD * 6$

$BD = \frac{54}{6} = 9 \ cm$

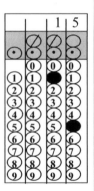

By Pythagorean theorem:

$AD^2 = AB^2 + BD^2$

$= 9^2 + 12^2 = 225$

$AD = \sqrt{225} = 15 \ cm$

Practice Test 5
Time --- 25 minutes
20 Questions

Reference Information:

1. Angles on one side of a straight line add to 180°.
2. There are 360° in a circle.

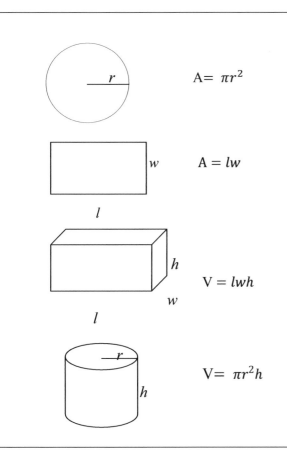

$A = \pi r^2$

$A = lw$

$V = lwh$

$V = \pi r^2 h$

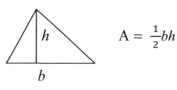

$A = \frac{1}{2}bh$

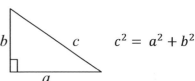

$c^2 = a^2 + b^2$

Special Right Triangles:

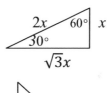

1. Jason and his younger brother made $160 one day by mowing lawn, and he gave his brother 40% of that. How much was left for Jason?

   (A) $64
   (B) $72
   (C) $88
   (D) $96
   (E) $100

2. If $5x - 3 = 3x + 11$, what is the value of $7x$?

   (A) 63
   (B) 49
   (C) 28
   (D) 21
   (E) 7

3.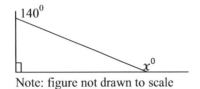

Note: figure not drawn to scale

In the figure above, what is the value of x?

(A) 40
(B) 50
(C) 110
(D) 130
(E) 140

4. If $f(x) = \sqrt{x} - 1$, what is the value of $f(16) - f(9)$?

(A) -3
(B) -1
(C) 1
(D) 4
(E) 12

5. If $(k + 2)$ is the largest common factor of 16, 36 and 52, what is the value of k?

(A) 2
(B) 4
(C) 6
(D) 9
(E) 10

6. What is the range of $y = (x + 3)^2 - 2$?

(A) $y \geq -3$
(B) $y \geq -2$
(C) $y \geq 0$
(D) $y \geq 2$
(E) All real numbers

7. 660 pencils are packed into two types of boxes, A and B. Each box A holds 15 pencils and each box B holds 24. If number of type A used is 5 more than type B, how many boxes of type B are used?

(A) 8
(B) 12
(C) 15
(D) 20
(E) 23

8. The ratio of x to y is 2 to 3. If y is 48, what is x?

(A) 18
(B) 28
(C) 32
(D) 38
(E) 40

9. If $(m - n)$ is odd for $m > n$ and both m and n are positive integer, which of the following must be true?
    I. m is odd
    II. $(m + n)$ is odd
    III. $m^2 - n^2$ is odd
    (A) I only
    (B) II only
    (C) III only
    (D) II and III only
    (E) I, II, and III only

10. In the figure below, BX = 12, what is the length CX?

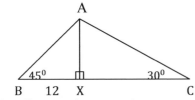

    B   12   X   C
    Note: figure not drawn to scale.

    (A) 12
    (B) $12\sqrt{2}$
    (C) $12\sqrt{3}$
    (D) 24
    (E) $24\sqrt{2}$

11. If $5a = 6b$ and $3a - 2b = 8$, what is $a + b$ equal to?

    (A) 5
    (B) 6
    (C) 8
    (D) 10
    (E) 11

12. Set A contains all even integers from 50 to 90 inclusive, set B are all integers divisible by 5, and set C are all integers divisible by 6. How many integers are in the intersection of sets A, B and C?

    (A) 1
    (B) 2
    (C) 6
    (D) 7
    (E) 8

13. In the figure below, $\overline{XY} \parallel \overline{BN}$, $\overline{XC} \parallel \overline{MN}$ and AB = AC, what is the value of m?

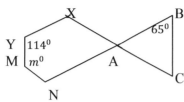

Note: figure not drawn to scale.

(A)   50
(B)   116
(C)   126
(D)   130
(E)   136

14. The sum of three consecutive integers is 14 more than twice of the smallest integer. What is the smallest integer?

(A)   6
(B)   7
(C)   9
(D)   10
(E)   11

15. If A (6, 1) and B (-2, 7) are the endpoints of a diameter of a circle, what is the area of the circle?

(A) 25π
(B) 16π
(C) 9π
(D) 4π
(E) π

16. If $4^{a+5b} = (64)^{b-1}$, what is a in terms of b?

(A) $-2b - 3$
(B) $-2b - 1$
(C) $4b + 3$
(D) $8b - 3$
(E) $8b + 1$

17. Which of the following is equivalent to $\frac{x^2-4x-5}{1-x^2}$, for $1 - x^2 \neq 0$?

(A) $\frac{(x-5)}{(1-x)}$
(B) $\frac{(x-5)}{(1+x)}$
(C) $\frac{(x-4)}{(x-1)}$
(D) $\frac{(x+4)}{(x-1)}$
(E) $\frac{(x-5)(x-4)}{(1-x)}$

18. In the figure below, which of the following is always true?

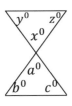

(A) $a + c = x + z$
(B) $a - b = x - y$
(C) $b + y = c + z$
(D) $b + z = c + y$
(E) $b - z = y - c$

19. In the figure below, the radius equals 5, and XP equals 2. What is the area of the shaded region?

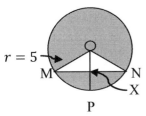

$r = 5$

M   N
        X
   P

(A) $(9\pi - 6)cm^2$
(B) $(16\pi - 12)cm^2$
(C) $(20\pi - 6)cm^2$
(D) $(25\pi - 12)cm^2$
(E) $(25\pi - 6)cm^2$

20.

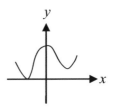

If the figure above represents $y = f(x)$, which of the following could be a graph of $y = f(x - a) + b$, for $a > 0$ and $b > 0$?

(A)
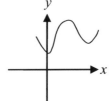

(B)
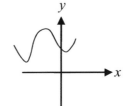

(C)
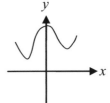

(D)
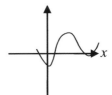

(E)
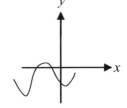

Practice Test 5 Solutions:

1. (D)
   (See Basic Math 8, Percent)
   Jason's brother got 40%,
   so Jason had 60%.
   $\frac{60}{100} * \$160 = 0.6 * \$160$
   $\qquad = \$96$

2. (B)
   (See Algebra 2.1)
   $5x - 3 = 3x + 11$
   $5x - 3x = 11 + 3$
   $2x = 14, \quad x = 7$
   $7x = 49$

3. (D)
   (See Geometry 2, Angle Relationships)

   Note: figure not drawn to scale

   $a = 180 - 140 = 40$
   $b = 180 - 40 - 90 = 50$, or $(90 - 40 = 50)$
   $\therefore \; x = 180 - 50 = 130$

4. (C)
   (See Algebra 12)
   $f(x) = \sqrt{x} - 1$
   $f(16) = \sqrt{16} - 1$
   $\qquad = 4 - 1 = 3$
   $f(9) = \sqrt{9} - 1$
   $\qquad = 3 - 1 = 2$
   $\therefore f(16) - f(9) = 3 - 2 = 1$

5. (A)
   (See Basic Math 4, Factors and
   Multiples)
   Factors of 16 are $1, 2, \mathbf{4}, 8, 16$
   Factors of 36 are $1, 2, 3, \mathbf{4}, 6, 9, 12, 18, 36$
   Factors of 52 are $1, 2, \mathbf{4}, 13, 26, 52$
   $\therefore$ The LCF is 4.
   $(k + 2) = 4$
   $k = 4 - 2$
   $\qquad = 2$

6. (B)
   (See Algebra 11.2, Quadratic Functions…)
   The graph of $y = (x + 3)^2 - 2$ is:

   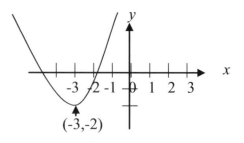

   Note: figure not drawn to scale

   $\therefore$ The range is $y \geq -2$.

7. (C)
   (See Algebra, 4. Word Problems)
   Let x = number of type B boxes

	A	B
# of boxes	$x + 5$	x
# of pencils	$15 * (x + 5)$	$24 * x$

   Total number of pencils = 660
   $660 = 15(x + 5) + 24x$
   $\qquad = 15x + 75 + 24x$
   $\qquad = 39x + 75$
   $585 = 39x$
   $\quad x = 585 \div 39 = 15$
   $\therefore$ 15 boxes of type B are used.

8. (C)
   (See Basic Math, 9. Ratio)
   $\frac{x}{y} = \frac{2}{3}$

   By cross multiplication:
   $3 * x = 2 * 48$
   $x = \frac{96}{3} = 32$

---

9. (D)

(See Basic Math, 1. Numbers)

If $(m - n)$ is odd, there are two possible cases:

    m is even and n is odd   or

    m is odd and n is even.

Try: $m = 4$, $n = 3$ so $4 - 3 = 1$ (odd)

       $m = 3$, $n = 2$ so $3 - 2 = 1$ (odd)

(I.) is not always true since m can be even.

(II) is true since $m + n$ is the sum of one odd

    and one even number and hence it is odd.

(III) is also true since one of m^2, n^2 is even

    and the other is odd number so the

    different is odd.

10. (C)

(See Geometry 4.3, Special Right-Angled

           Triangles)

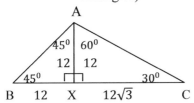

ΔABX is 45-45-90 triangle,

$\therefore$ BX:AX = 1:1, BX = AX =12

   AX = 12

ΔACX is a 30-60-90 triangle,

$\therefore$ AX:XC = 1: $\sqrt{3}$,

  $\frac{AX}{XC} = \frac{1}{\sqrt{3}} = \frac{12}{XC}$,

By cross multiplication:

  XC = $12\sqrt{3}$

11. (E)

(See Algebra 2.2, Systems of Linear

              Equations)

$5a = 6b$ …(1)

$3a - 2b = 8$ …(2)

$3 * (2)$:

$9a - 6b = 24$

Sub (1) into above:

$9a - 5a = 24$

$4a = 24$, $\boxed{a = 6}$

Sub into (1):

$5*(6) = 6b$, $30 = 6b$

$\boxed{b = 5}$

$a + b = 6 + 5 = 11$

12. (B)

(See Basic Math 12, Sets)

A: all even integers from 50 to 90 inclusive:

A = {50, 52, 54, …, 86, 88, 90}

B: all integers divisible by 5:

A∩B = {50, 60, 70, 80, 90}

C: all integers divisible by 6:

From the set of A∩B, only 60 and 90 are

divisible by 6:

$\therefore$ (A∩B) ∩ C ={ 60, 90}

Answer: 2

13. (B)

(See Geometry 2, Angle Relationships)

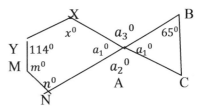

Note: figure not drawn to scale.

Let each angle be labeled as shown above,

Since AB = AC, ΔABC is isosceles,

$\angle B = \angle C = 65^0$,

$a_1 = 180 - 65 - 65 = 50$

$a_2 = 180 - a_1 = 180 - 50 = 130$

$a_3 = a_2 = 130$ (opposite angles)

Since $\overline{XY} \parallel \overline{BN}$ (Geometry.2.4 Angles

                     in Parallel lines)

$x = a_2 = 130$

Since $\overline{MN} \parallel \overline{XC}$ (Geometry.2.4 Angles

                     in Parallel lines)

$n = a_3 = 130$

The sum of all interior angles of a

pentagon = 540^0 (Geometry, 2.6)

$m + n + a_1 + x + 114 = 540$

$m = 540 - n - a_1 - x - 124$

   $= 540 - 130 - 50 - 130 - 114$

   $= 116$

14. (E)

(See Algebra 4, Word Problems)
Let x = smallest integer
$\therefore$ The 3 integers are x, $x + 1$, $x + 2$.
The sum $= x + (x + 1) + (x + 2)$
$\qquad = 3x + 3$
The sum is 14 more than twice of x:
The sum $= 2x + 14$
$\therefore \quad 3x + 3 = 2x + 14$
$\qquad 3x - 2x = 14 - 3$
$\therefore \quad x = 11$.

15. (A)

(See Geometry 6.1 and 7.2)
A (6, 1), B (-2, 7)
$$d = \sqrt{(x_2 - x_1)^2 + (y_2 - y_1)^2}$$

$\therefore$ AB $= \sqrt{(6 - (-2))^2 + (1 - 7)^2}$
$\qquad = \sqrt{64 + 36} = 10$
r (radius) $= 10 \div 2 = 5$
$\therefore$ A $= \pi r^2$
$\qquad = \pi * 5^2 = 25\pi$

16. (A)

(See Algebra 8.2, Solving Equations
$\qquad\qquad$ Involving Exponents)
$4^{a+5b} = (64)^{b-1}$
$4^{a+5b} = (4^3)^{b-1}$
$\qquad = 4^{3b-3}$
$a + 5b = 3b - 3$
$a = -5b + 3b - 3$
$\qquad = -2b - 3$

17. (A)

(See Algebra 3, Factoring)
$\dfrac{x^2 - 4x - 5}{1 - x^2} = \dfrac{(x-5)(x+1)}{(1-x)(1+x)}$

$\qquad = \dfrac{(x-5)}{(1-x)}$

18. (E)

(See Geometry 2, Angle Relationships)

$a = x$, (opposite angles)
$a = 180 - b - c$
$x = 180 - y - z$, Since $a = x$,
$\therefore \quad 180 - b - c = 180 - y - z$
$\qquad b + c = y + z$
$\therefore \quad b - z = y - c$

19. (D)

(See Geometry 6.1, Area and Perimeter)

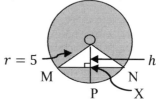

OP $= r = 5$
Let h be the height of the triangle,
$\therefore \quad h = $ OP $-$ XP $= 5 - 2 = 3$
In $\triangle$OMP, by Pythagorean's Theorem:
$r^2 = h^2 + $ MX^2 $\quad$ | Geometry 3, Typical
$5^2 = 3^2 + $ MX^2 $\quad$ | angles ratio: 5: 4: 3
MX $= \sqrt{25 - 9} = 4$
MN $= 2 * $ MX $= 2 * 4 = 8$

A of the $\triangle$OMN
$\qquad = \dfrac{1}{2}$(MN)$h = \dfrac{1}{2} * 8 * 3 = 12 cm^2$
A of the circle $= \pi r^2 = \pi * 5^2 = 25\pi cm^2$
A of the shaded $= (25\pi - 12) cm^2$

20. (A)

(See Algebra 11, Functions and Graphs)
For $y = f(x - a) + b$
b represents vertical translation,
$\quad$ since $b > 0$, the graph moves up,
$\quad$ and graphs (A), (B), (C) are possible.
a represents horizontal translation,
$\quad$ since $a > 0$, the graph moves right.
since only graph (A) moves right,
(A) is the correct answer.

References

1. About SAT test: http://sat.collegeboard.com/about-tests/sat/faq

2. SAT Scoring: http://sat.collegeboard.com/about-tests/sat/faq

3. Calculator: http://sat.collegeboard.com/register/sat-test-day-checklist

4. Grid-In Directions: http://sat.collegeboard.com/practice/sat-practice-questions-math-student-produced- response?practiceTestSectionIDKey=QuestionType.
    STUDENT_PRODUCED_RESPONSE

"If any of you lacks wisdom,
he should ask God,
who gives generously to
to all without finding fault,
and it will be given to him."

James1:5

Made in the USA
Charleston, SC
31 May 2011